Noël Coward
Collected Revue Sketches

"The best since W. S. Gilbert" Terence Rattigan

"The art of Revue writing is acknowledged by those unfortunates who have had anything to do with it as being a very tricky and technical business. Everything has to be condensed to appalling brevity. The biggest laugh must be on the last line before the black out. No scene or number should play for more than a few minutes at most, and, above all, the Audience must never be kept waiting. The moment their last splendid laugh at the end of a sketch has subsided into a general chuckle, their attention must immediately be distracted by a line of vivacious chorus girls (preferably with bare legs) or a treble-jointed acrobatic dancer with no bones at all ... If, upon reading the notices in the newspapers after the first night, it is found that different critics take exception to different scenes, you can safely predict a successful run." Noël Coward

In the 1920s and 30s Noël Coward mastered and defined the art of the revue – short and often topical or satirical sketches, many of which were a lead-in to song. He wrote sketches for such famous revues as *London Calling!* (1923), produced by André Charlot, and *On With the Dance* (1925), *This Year of Grace!* (1928), and *Cochran's Revue of 1931*, all produced by the celebrated showman Charles B. Cochran. This volume collects Coward's best and most witty pieces, including "*Rain Before Seven–*" (1922), the only sketch he performed with Gertrude Lawrence and one which pre-figures the characters they were to play in *Private Lives*, and its hilarious parody, *Some Other Private Lives*, in which Coward burlesques the second act of his famous play. Also included are some short one-act plays never before published.

Collected Revue Sketches and Parodies is edited and annotated by Barry Day whose introduction sets Coward's revues in their theatrical context. Sheridan Morley's preface adds to our understanding of Coward the playwright.

also by Noël Coward

Coward
Collected Plays: One
(Hay Fever, The Vortex, Fallen Angels, Easy Virtue)

Collected Plays: Two
(Private Lives, Bitter-Sweet, The Marquise, Post-Mortem)

Collected Plays: Three
(Design for Living, Cavalcade, Conversation Piece,
and Hands Across the Sea, Still Life, Fumed Oak
from Tonight at 8.30)

Collected Plays: Four
(Blithe Spirit, Present Laughter, This Happy Breed,
and Ways and Means, The Astonished Heart, "Red Peppers"
from Tonight at 8.30)

Collected Plays: Five
(Relative Values, Look After Lulu!
Waiting in the Wings, Suite in Three Keys)

Collected Plays: Six
(Semi-Monde, Point Valaine, South Sea Bubble,
Nude With Violin)

Collected Plays: Seven
(Quadrille, "Peace in Our Time",
and We Were Dancing, Shadow Play, Family Album, Star Chamber
from Tonight at 8.30)

The Complete Lyrics of Noël Coward

Collected Verse

Collected Short Stories

Pomp and Circumstance
A Novel

Autobiography

NOËL COWARD

Collected Revue Sketches and Parodies

Edited and introduced by Barry Day

With a preface by Sheridan Morley

Methuen Drama

METHUEN DRAMA

1 3 5 7 9 10 8 6 4 2

This collection first published in Great Britain in 1999
by Methuen Publishing Ltd
215 Vauxhall Bridge Road, London SW1V 1EJ

Peribo Pty Ltd, 58 Beaumont Road, Mount Kuring-Gai,
NSW 2080, Australia, ACN 002 273 761
(for Australia and New Zealand)

What Next? and *Woman And Whiskey* copyright © The Estates of
Esmé Wynne-Tyson and Noël Coward
Copyright in all other sketches, plays and lyrics © The Estate of Noël Coward

Preface copyright © 1999 by Sheridan Morley
Introduction and notes copyright © 1999 by Barry Day
Chronology copyright © 1987, 1999 by Jacqui Russell

The right of the authors to be identified as the authors of this work has
been asserted by them in accordance with the Copyright, Designs and
Patents Act, 1988

ISBN 0 413 73390 4

Methuen Publishing Limited Reg. No. 3543167

A CIP catalogue record for this book
is available from the British Library

What Next? and *Woman and Whiskey* included by kind permission of
Mr Jon Wynne-Tyson
All lyrics are included by kind permission of Overlook Press
from *The Complete Lyrics of Noël Coward* published in the UK by
Methuen and in the USA by Overlook Press

Typeset by Deltatype Ltd, Birkenhead, Merseyside
Printed and bound in Great Britain by
Cox & Wyman Ltd, Reading, Berkshire

Contents

Preface

Barry Day's fascinating anthology of long-lost Coward revue material from the 1920s (and other pieces still more mislaid than that) comes as a sharp reminder of the importance of the genre in Noël's life. It was in revue, notably *London Calling!* (1923), as Day recalls, that Noël first began to make his name as a songwriter and his early career, coinciding as it did with those of Jack Buchanan, Gertrude Lawrence and Beatrice Lillie, meant that he came to fame as a performer when the revues of Cochran and Charlot were at the height of their brief supremacy.

Noël always admitted, however, that anything he could do Buchanan could do better as a song-and-dance man; although he described himself "singing and dancing and acting throughout with unbridled vivacity" in *London Calling!*, critics were less than impressed. "Mr Coward," said the *Sunday Express*, "should sing only for the amazement of his friends." The number that provoked this comment was one called "Sentiment" which had in fact been staged for Noël by Fred Astaire, then dancing with his sister Adèle in the West End in *Stop Flirting*. "I bounded on," recalled Noël, "at the opening performance fully confident that I was going to bring the house down. It certainly wasn't from want of trying that I didn't. I was immaculately dressed, in tails with a silk hat and cane. I sang every couplet with perfect diction and a wealth of implication, which sent them winging out into the dark auditorium where they fell wetly, like pennies into mud."

Several months later, in New York, Coward was to watch Buchanan bring the house down nightly with precisely the same number. At first he told himself it was because Buchanan appeared so effortless, while he had patently been trying as hard as he could; ultimately, though, he admitted, if a little reluctantly, that Buchanan's whole revue technique was vastly superior to his own.

Though Coward was largely inexperienced at revue when *London Calling!* first opened, he had managed to see off most of the other writers and was horrified to find that Charlot only proposed to pay him fifteen pounds a week, half what he had been making as an actor in his own *The Young Idea* a year earlier. Coward held out for rather more on the dubious grounds that he was risking his prestige as a straight actor, then in those pre-*Vortex* days not so very great, by even deigning to write a revue, let alone appear in one. Charlot threatened to find a replacement, but had overlooked a clause in Noël's writing contract which gave him a veto over all major casting. For several weeks Noël then objected regularly to the suggestion of any other juvenile lead in the business, until Charlot was reluctantly forced to offer him forty pounds a week, an offer Noël was graciously pleased to accept with the demand only that he be given the right to escape back into the straight theatre after six months.

London Calling! also saw the beginning of a long alliance between Noël and Elsie April, a small, bird-like woman given to wearing remarkable hats who, while refusing ever to compose anything herself, would solemnly transcribe every note that Noël ever sang at her from now until well into World War Two. In that she transcribed and arranged all his songs in these twenty years, it is fair to assume that hers was the major influence on Coward harmonies and compositions.

Two papers did manage to offer him personal tributes for *London Calling!*; one noted that he was "the most promising amateur in the West End" and the other that he was "unmistakably talented, though not yet another Jack Hulbert". Nevertheless the show was a considerable hit, and the row with the Sitwell family over "Swiss Family Whittlebot", detailed by Barry Day here, did at least keep his name in the gossip columns for several months.

The triumph of *The Vortex* followed a few months later, and it was still running when Noël's next revue, *On With the Dance*, opened in Manchester; in order that he could attend, his role in the play was taken over for two nights by a young understudy, John Gielgud. The dress-rehearsal of the revue ran all of thirty-six hours, during which Noël was watched by a young actor later to present him in cabaret at the Café de Paris in the early fifties, Donald Neville-Willing:

> Noël at the time of *On With the Dance* was very cryptic; he would look at us through those half-closed eyes, and one never quite knew what he was thinking, though I suspected it was nothing very favourable where most of us young actors were concerned ... One realised, even then, there was something very different about Noël. He knew precisely what he wanted, and was ruthless about getting it where the show was concerned. He was also a tremendous leader, in that we all tried to follow the way he dressed and talked, because we knew it was very fashionable. He was also a very old young man; important and powerful, but fantastically kind in private. In the show one always worked for him, not the audience; his approval was all that mattered. Though he was only our age, he already knew it all; he was the first of the Bright Young Things.

Already the theatrical name of the season, Coward was now fêted accordingly; to say that all this success did not change him would be the oldest cliché in theatrical journalism, and it was at least partly untrue. If ever a man was ready and waiting for success, it was Noël; so far from it catching him unawares, he had been conscious of his own talent since his earliest professional days as a child actor, and in his view it had only ever been a question of time before critics and audiences alike endorsed that view, which now they vehemently did. Noël had now become a celebrity, and what he enjoyed most about that was the way it brought him into contact with other celebrities; his new membership of the Pen Club brought him into contact with Galsworthy, H.G.Wells and Arnold Bennett, and suddenly Coward was to be found with them at literary gatherings, which were in those days as much a feature of Bloomsbury as of Hampstead. Arriving at one of these in a suit, and straight from the theatre, he discovered everyone else present in full evening dress. "Now," he announced magnanimously, "I don't want anyone to feel embarrassed."

But because of a penetrating though never cocky self-appraisal, success did not change Noël beyond recognition. It merely confirmed in him what had been tentative, allowed him more freedom in what he said and where he went, and above all released him and his family from the need ever again to wonder where the money was coming from next. The self-confidence remained unchanged, but now there were hit plays and revues to justify it. "Success," said Noël in these late 1920s, "took me to her bosom like a maternal boa constrictor."

Despite that rocky dress-rehearsal in Manchester, *On With the Dance* was to run for two hundred and thirty performances at the London Pavilion on Piccadilly Circus; for the first night, stalls were boosted to an unthinkable twenty-seven shillings each, and the queue for standing room started at five in the morning. Another revue writer of the period, Herbert Farjeon, who doubled as drama critic of the *Sphere*, began to worry about Noël:

When you consider his present output compared with the output of other writers for the theatre, and when you consider that he is also acting six nights a week and two matinees in *The Vortex*, and when you consider moreover that he has his own public life to live, well, then you begin to realise that something is apt to get a little skimped now and then. It must be hard work throwing off a couple of lyrics before breakfast, setting them to music by eleven o'clock, finishing the big scene in Act II before dashing off to the Ivy Restaurant, appearing at a matinee, talking business with his agent between Acts I and II and letting off gas to a press interviewer between Acts II and III, sketching a new revue and practising the latest dance step before the evening performance, gathering copy and declaring that everything is just too marvellous or too shattering at the Midnight Follies or the Gargoyle; as I say, it must be hard work, and I do hope that Mr Coward will not suffer from a nervous breakdown as a result of it all.

Farjeon was alarmingly prescient; Noël suffered the first and worst of his nervous breakdowns just fifteen months later.

He was however sufficiently recovered to make 1928 *This Year of Grace!*; the revue ("a form of entertainment," wrote another practitioner, Ronald Jeans, "so designed that it doesn't matter how late you get there") was in the best Coward/Cochran/Charlot tradition of no-expense-spared entertainment, and critics went overboard in listing its merits. Virginia Woolf was also a keen if surprising fan of this revue: "Your numbers," she wrote to Noël, "struck me on the forehead like a bullet, and what's more I remember them all, and see them enveloped in atmosphere, works of art in short. I think you ought to bring off something that will put these cautious, creeping novels that one has to read silently in an armchair deep, deep into the shade."

Coward's next revue, *Words and Music*, came in 1932, by which time he had scored the treble of *Private Lives*, *Cavalcade* and *Bitter-Sweet* in less than three years. The new show starred John Mills, Ivy St. Helier, Joyce Barbour, Romney Brent and a young South African singer and dancer called Graham Payn who was to become Noël's constant companion in the years after the war. For a long time the show lacked a title, though Coward's old friend and America's most famous critic and broadcaster, Alexander Woollcott, had solemnly suggested "Here's to Mr Woollcott, May God Bless Him". Eventually they settled on *Words and Music*, and the revue opened as usual at the Opera House in Manchester before moving to the Adelphi; reviews were generally ecstatic, especially because Noël had tried to impose an altogether new and more coherent, intimate identity, though Brian Howard noted in his diary that "it could have been written by some immensely shrewd bird".

The public, surprisingly, did not take to it; expecting the usual lavish glitz of a Cochran big-band show, they resented the intimacy and apparently low budget, and this was the first

Coward revue not to make its money back. It closed after barely twenty weeks, and though much of its best material was to resurface in Broadway in 1939 as *Set To Music* (where the show had the additional advantage of Beatrice Lillie), Noël did not return to the revue form until 1945, when *Sigh No More* opened at the Piccadilly.

Coward had thought that, in the immediate aftermath of the war, an elegant return to 1930s revue might be a clever idea. Perhaps it was, though in rehearsal he had to remonstrate with the director Wendy Toye over a young dancer who had forgotten his codpiece. "For God's sake," he whispered, "have that boy take that Rockingham tea service out of his tights." However, critics in post-war vein did not take kindly to Noël's nostalgia, and despite a strong cast led by Cyril Ritchard, Joyce Grenfell and Graham Payn, the show barely survived six months. Though he was to contribute trium-phantly to the long-running *Lyric* and *Globe Revues* of the early 1950s, Coward was never again to write a complete revue, and within another decade, as Barry Day notes, the genre had effectively disappeared from West End sight.

But there is no doubt that Noël's early training in revue, his love of the brisk playlet-sketch and the haunting love song, stood him in admirable stead for his major work in musicals, operettas and, indeed, straight plays. When he eventually conquered America on television in the late 1950s with Mary Martin, it was in a classic live broadcast called *Together With Music* (the first ever to go out in colour), which effectively was just another revue, this one, of course, a two-hander. What follows is the first-ever anthology of a whole area of Noël's writing which threatened to disappear for ever, but which remains central to his development as the Jack of all theatrical trades and Master of most.

Sheridan Morley
1999

Introduction

A sketch for a revue must be quick, sharp,
funny (or sentimental) and to the point, with
a good, really good black-out line. Whether
the performers are naked or wearing crino-
lines is quite beside the point; the same rule
applies.

Noël Coward

The revue sketch, as we came to know it, had a relatively
short shelf-life – roughly from the beginning of the century
until television killed off the parent form in the mid-1950s.
The fact that such a hybrid form evolved at all owed more to
happenstance than artistic design.

Derived, as the name suggests, from the French, the
"revue" was extremely popular in Paris in the second half of
the nineteenth century. Trying to come to grips with this
exotic form of entertainment, a contemporary English definition described it as "a term of French origin, used to describe
a survey, mainly satiric, of contemporary events, with songs,
sketches, burlesques, monologues and so on. No satisfactory
English term has ever been found for this mixture, and the
French continues in use."

It was hardly surprising that the English stage should cast
an envious eye across the Channel. Satire and burlesque –
both social and political – had long been threads in our
theatrical tradition. A largely illiterate Elizabethan audience
had come to rely on the players and their playwrights to
provide them, however incidental to the plot proper, with
comment on the events of the day. By the middle of the
nineteenth century that comment had become so sharp-edged
that it led to the introduction of stage censorship in 1737.

This, naturally, did nothing but whet the public appetite for entertainers who could walk up to the accepted boundaries and give them a nudge. Apart from contemporary politicians – who have always been fair and easy game – the parodying of fellow actors seems to have been a favourite and increasingly incestuous sport and one that time has only hallowed into a tradition.

In England the sketch form evolved more or less accidentally as part of the *pot pourri* an evening at the theatre became in the wake of the Restoration. Only two theatres – the Theatre Royal, Drury Lane and Covent Garden – were granted royal licences to perform what we would now call "straight plays". Every other hall was forced to piece together a selection of opera, ballet, burlesque or whatever short forms of entertainment seemed likely to draw an audience. Naturally, there were sustained efforts on the part of managements to elongate the prose pieces until they were virtually short plays – and a series of running battles with the authorities were the result.

America had no such legal problems to contend with but nor, apparently, did it have any taste for "revue" on the few mid-Victorian occasions when the format was tried there. *Opéra bouffe* – with its exotic Continental associations – and homegrown burlesque would do very well to be going on with. In fact, the sketch evolved there in the degraded form of burlesque that became popular after the turn of the century, where it acted as a form of low comedy theatrical punctuation to allow the showgirls time to get ready for their next number.

In England the lack of thematic content had led to an emphasis on visual extravagance in the look of entertainments but, as the century ended, this emphasis on appearance was beginning to pall. It was his sense of this *ennui* that caused Seymour Hicks to try something new for domestic audiences. He decided to "write a musical play . . . on the lines of a Paris *revue*, but instead of satirizing general topics of interest make the travesty nearly wholly theatrical." The result – *Under the Clock* (1893) – is generally considered the first English revue.

Even then old traditions died hard. The revue formed only a third of a triple bill, which also included a one-act play and a comic opera. Interestingly, the critics didn't know how to categorise it, one of them referring to "this burlesque, *revue*, extravaganza, or what not". Whatever they called it, the format caught the public imagination, once the century had turned and Edwardian society developed a more liberal ambience. The Victorian music halls turned into Edwardian variety halls, seeking to attract wider family audiences.

It was at this point that a long-running argument came to the boil.

Since the passing of the Stage Play Act in 1843 all legitimate theatres had to be licensed by the Lord Chamberlain and all material played in them was "censored" by his office. Earlier legislation, however, had put music halls outside his jurisdiction and they had increasingly been using this freedom to build up the "dramatic" element of their programmes. As long as the sketch or sketches did not form the principal part of the entertainment, they remained within the letter if not the spirit of the new law.

With typical British stubbornness the two groups debated the definition of what constituted a "reasonable length" for a music hall sketch, until in 1912 the inevitable happened – and the music halls also found themselves in the Lord Chamberlain's bureaucratic embrace. The result was to restrict the early revues to a menu of mainly song, dance and mime.

Incidentally, there was to be one significant, if accidental, long-term benefit from the Lord Chamberlain's involvement in the music halls. Whereas, the least deserving play was likely to survive at least in manuscript and might well be subsequently published, the topicality of the average sketch tended to consign it to the theatrical scrap heap along with a show's discarded scenery, as far as the producers of the show were concerned. The Lord Chamberlain's Office, however, filed a copy of everything it received as a matter of course, thus providing future scholars with a source of material that would otherwise have vanished without trace.

Ironically, revue was just getting into its stride as the

shadows of war began to lengthen and perhaps the deter-
minedly light-hearted fare was something of an antidote – or
at least a placebo – for the darkening public mood.

The upbeat of ragtime, as interpreted by the likes of Irving
Berlin and imported by several London managements, kicked
off a new wave of interest and the emergence of several
powerful and competing impresarios did the rest. Seen in
retrospect, they resemble nothing more than the managers of
modern day football teams. There was Albert de Courville at
the London Hippodrome, Alfred Butt at the Empire, Oswald
Stoll at the Coliseum and a new name, André Charlot, across
the way from the Empire at the Alhambra. It was Charlot
who introduced a wholly new element into the mix, when
faced with the general reaction of the critics to revue British-
style, of which this 1913 quotation was typical:

> The humour of our *Revues* is characteristically obvious,
> and those finer shafts of satire which should give them their
> most appetising value, would, in all probability, fly high
> above the heads of those who laugh with their eyes, rather
> than with their minds.

The critic in question was referring to the predominance of
"spectacular" revues in the variety halls – shows built around
star singers, often using imported American material, and
large troupes of bespangled dancing girls. The shows were
modelled as closely as possible on the matrix created by
Broadway producer, Florenz Ziegfeld, who had first begun to
"glorify the American girl" back in 1907. They were undeni-
ably feasts for the eye but had all the lasting satisfaction of
Chinese food for the mind.

It was Charlot's insight – further developed by his soon-to-
be arch rival, Charles B. Cochran – to try and imitate more
closely the true nature of the original French *revue* format in
what came to be known as "intimate revue". Let the variety
halls entertain the general public with their spectacles; they
themselves would appeal to the mainstream theatre-going
audience with something altogether more sophisticated. And
to show how firmly their personal flags were nailed to the

mast, they would "sign" their shows. A Charlot or a Cochran Revue would not only be a guarantee of quality; it would signify a guiding vision co-ordinating a diverse range of talents.

As the "war to end wars" ended, the theatrical War of the West End was well under way with Charlot at the Vaudeville and Cochran at the London Pavilion. It was time to move the game on. Even Cochran in his early efforts had shown some uncertainty as to what revue was really about. Productions of the period were apt to refer to themselves as a "musical comedy revue", "one of those musical things" or something such. A new definition was needed and new kinds of talent to provide that definition.

Which is where the name Noël Coward first came into the credits as one of the new generation of more sophisticated writers and composers recruited to revitalise the generally lacklustre "books" that had typified the early revues.

It must have seemed ironic to Noël that his initial "sponsor" should turn out to be André Charlot, for it was Charlot who had rejected him summarily as a very young man, telling Beatrice Lillie (who had made the introduction) never to waste his time with such untalented people again!

Luckily the Charlot memory was conveniently short and it was in one of his shows – *Tails Up!* (1918) – that the first published Coward song, "Peter Pan", appeared and in his 1923 revue, *London Calling!* – ominously named after the call sign of the medium that was to become a major competitor to any form of variety theatre – that Noël was to be given his first significant assignment.

London Calling! was to be a collaboration with the more established writer, Ronald Jeans. Even then the idea of sharing the billing was not one that appealed to the precocious Coward. His bargaining power was not strong enough for him to insist. Instead he developed a lateral and creative solution to the impresario-as-God problem.

The 1920s was the theatrical Age of Interpolation. Emerging songwriters, such as Kern and Berlin, who were waiting for a show of their own – and often between shows – would be asked for a number that could be interpolated in someone else's show on the whim of the producer. The hope being that your single song might turn out to be the all-important hit. It was a frustrating experience for all concerned and the sole power of artistic life or death was wielded by the man whose name was at the top of the marquee.

Noël's fear was that somewhere in the middle of his carefully-crafted sketch Charlot (or his equivalent) might decide to slap a totally irrelevant song. (The average musical comedy of the period was not exactly known for its integration of book and score!) To prevent this possibility he developed a form of sketch in which – should it lead to a song ending – the characterisation and dialogue dictated the song. And since he just happened to have written the song, too, it would give Charlot (and subsequently, Cochran) more trouble than it was worth to prise them apart.

"Customs House, Dover" (1923) is a good example of the hybrid form of "musical sketch", as what apparently begins as a classic comedy interchange evolves into a sweetly nostalgic duet. In later revues he would become more ambitious still. "The Lido Beach/English Lido" sequence in *This Year Of Grace!* (1928) can be seen as either extended sketches or short-form comic opera in which the dialogue is used to link several numbers. It also illustrates a favourite Coward theme, which he used both in revues and plays such as *Cavalcade*, *This Happy Breed* and *Relative Values* among others. Class. The same events would be depicted from the points of view of both aristocratic and working man. Not even *Private Lives* was sacred. In the very year of production (1930) he was writing his "Parody" of the second act in which Fred and Floss push Elyot and Amanda into the wings . . .

London Calling! was Noël's only original Charlot revue, although much of his material was recycled by the impresario for his ground-breaking Broadway compilations in the mid-20s.

It was Charlot's great rival, Charles Cochran (known as "Cockie" to friend and theatrical foe alike) who was to stage three out of the remaining four Coward revues.

The first was *On With the Dance* (1925) and Noël found himself faced with the same problem he had encountered with Charlot. Cochran wanted him "only to write the book of the revue, and I wished to compose the entire score as well ... Finally his [Cochran's] armour of evasive politeness cracked, and he was forced to say that he was very sorry, but he frankly did not consider my music good enough to carry a whole show ... That settled it for the time being, and I retired, vanquished to concentrate on ideas for sketches and burlesques. The ideas came swiftly and, oddly enough, nearly every idea carried with it its accompanying song."

In this wide-eyed recollection Noël is exercising the expected licence of the autobiographer, since he was describing a practice at which he was already an adept! "... When the revue was complete it was discovered, to the embarrassment of everyone but me, that with the exception of three numbers by Philip Braham for which I had written the lyrics ... and one interpolated song for Delysia [the star], the whole score, book and lyrics were mine." Noël was all for renegotiating his fee but money being the *real* business of show business, on that point Cochran was not to be moved and, when it came down to it, the real and lasting satisfaction for the now Jack-of-all-trades was to see his name up in lights for the first time of many.

Revue was to provide him with a safe haven later in the decade after the very public failure of his 1927 play, *Sirocco*, had seriously undermined his confidence. He offered to release Cochran from his agreement to stage the forthcoming *This Year of Grace!* but Cochran would not hear of it, insisting that the two of them were about to have "the biggest success of our lives".

Nor was he far off the mark and Noël was to say late in life that he regarded it as the very best of his revues. This time there were no disputes over turf. Cochran remained the *deus ex machina* but every item in the show was signed – Noël Coward.

He and Cochran were to collaborate on one more revue – *Words and Music* (1932) – and learn one of the fundamental lessons of the form . . . that it is a collaboration.

His confidence restored by *Private Lives* (1930) and *Cavalcade* (1931), Noël came to Cochran with a revue worked out in absolute detail, down to and including the black-and-white "look" of the show his designer Gladys Calthrop had come up with. Despite the success of *This Year of Grace!*, Cochran was sceptical. The essence of revue, he'd always instinctively believed, lay in "variety, rapidity, change of mood and contrast of line and colour". What Noël was proposing was the antithesis of that. Just as importantly, perhaps, it was implicitly removing the contribution another mind – in this case, his own – can make to shaping the final form of the show.

Noël prevailed but the impresario was right. For all its many virtues, *Words and Music* (1932) did not turn out to be the "Cochran revue" the customers had paid to see and was only a modest success. Homogeneity – as Cochran had seen so often in the work of others – had led to monotony. Noël, however, didn't see things in that light and it was only when he had repeated the experience with similar effect in the post-war *Sigh No More* (1945) that he was obliged to acknowledge the fundamental truth of the observation. But by that time the fact was becoming academic. Revue – like variety – was feeling the chill wind of change in show business.

Radio had sustained a nation through the war and within a decade television would rationalise the entertainment-at-home habit still further. And once radio-with-pictures found its own style, the game was over for revue. Who needed to pay theatre prices to see less than top talent when a weekly TV show like *That Was the Week That Was* could pin down people and events in a way the Lord Chamberlain would never permit?

The form struggled through the fifties – and indeed, had something of a late flowering (again, somewhat reminiscent of the Elizabethan theatre) in the hands of the university "wits", before they turned their attention to the more lucrative new medium with its enormous and immediate audience. Ironically, it was the pick of that particular crop – *Beyond the Fringe* – that helped to put things in perspective for Noël himself, as far as the merits of collaboration were concerned. "Those four unprofessional, professional young men," he wrote – perhaps thinking of himself at their age – "are brilliant and *not* circumscribed by old formulas and little gossipy jokes." And that, it seemed, was that.

It's only now, when all playing fields are level and TV as a medium is so environmental as to be invisible, that intimate revue – with what we would now call its one-on-one quality – seems to have the opportunity to find a new audience, if only it can first find its Charlots and Cochrans with the faith to try again ...

What lessons did Noël learn from his own experience in revue? How he saw it in the retrospect of a long and varied career is not on record but when he made a personal selection in 1931 for *Collected Sketches and Lyrics* he had this to say:

> Everything has to be condensed to appalling brevity. The biggest laugh must be on the last line before the black out. No scene or number should play for more than a few minutes at most, and, above all, the Audience must never be kept waiting. The moment their last splendid laugh at the end of a sketch has subsided into a general chuckle, their attention must immediately be distracted by a line of vivacious chorus girls (preferably with bare legs) or a treble-jointed acrobatic dancer with no bones at all; in fact, anything arrestingly visual that will relax their strained minds and lull them into a gentle apathy while the next onslaught upon their risibilities is being prepared behind the scenes ...
>
> If some of the sketches [in the collection] seem to finish rather abruptly, please remember that that is the moment

when the reader is expected to rock with laughter. A fuller effect might be obtained by reading the sketches aloud with one hand on the electric switch and on the last line plunging the room in darkness, thereby achieving as near as possible a "Black Out".

What Noël so admired about the *Beyond the Fringe* team was that, not *knowing* the rules of revue, they had cheerfully broken them – something that he, as a card-carrying theatrical, had never quite dared to do. In the light of the prevailing management circumstances, it was hardly likely that he ever really could.

What he did achieve, working within the existing form, was to bring literacy and wit to the revue sketch where before there had been broad comedy and – as he reflected – far too many "gossipy jokes". In many cases the playwright in him – for he had written several plays, published and unpublished, before he came to write for revue – was instinctively trying to create mini-plays with genuine structure and characterisation.

Because of that much of his material manages to avoid the retrospective charge levelled by *New York Times* critic, Ben Brantley, that "topical satire, especially the kind found in musical revues, tends to age about as well as sushi". While poking his share of fun at current pretensions and preoccupations of the day, Noël was always more interested in the fundamental comedy of human behaviour going on behind the cocktails and laughter, bobbed hair and garden fêtes.

In selecting the material I have eliminated items of such extreme topicality that the footnotes would be longer than the sketch. I have also had to wrestle with the question: When is a sketch *not* a sketch? Since Noël himself was inclined to blur the lines, I have taken a broad-church approach and included three items that are described as "one-act plays" but which *read* like sketches. I hope the reader will feel that it was a permissible stretch.

For the Coward *aficionado*, it's interesting to read the sketches bearing in mind what he was writing for the theatre at the same time. It will be surprising if you don't find a hint of one familiar character here, an outline of another there. The almost-married couple in "Rain Before Seven–" (1923), for instance, behave very much as Elyot and Amanda will a few years later ... and the observations on "Class" (1924) will be expanded into *Cavalcade* (1931).

If you're that fortunate person who's coming to Coward for the first time, it will be even more surprising if you put this volume down without saying – "Let me see ... what *else* did he write?"

BARRY DAY
1999

Chronology

Paris). Jack Morrison in *The Happy Family*, Prince of Wales.

1917   "Boy pushing barrow" in D.W. Griffith's film *Hearts of the World*. Co-author with Esmé Wynne of one-acter *Ida Collaborates*, Theatre Royal, Aldershot. Ripley Guildford in *The Saving Grace*, with Charles Hawtrey, "who . . . taught me many points of comedy acting", Garrick. Family moved to Pimlico and re-opened boarding house.

1918   Called-up for army. Medical discharge after nine months. Wrote unpublished novels *Cats and Dogs* (loosely based on Shaw's *You Never Can Tell*) and the unfinished *Cherry Pan* ("dealing in a whimsical vein with the adventures of a daughter of Pan"), and lyrics for Darewski and Joel, including "When You Come Home on Leave" and "Peter Pan". Also composed "Tamarisk Town". Sold short stories to magazines. Wrote plays *The Rat Trap*, *The Last Trick* (unproduced) and *The Impossible Wife* (unproduced). Courtenay Borner in *Scandal*, Strand. *Woman and Whiskey* (co-author Esmé Wynne) produced at Wimbledon Theatre.

1919   Ralph in *The Knight of the Burning Pestle*, Birmingham Repertory, played with "a stubborn Mayfair distinction" demonstrating a "total lack of understanding of the play". Collaborated on *Crissa*, an opera, with Esmé Wynne and Max Darewski (unproduced). Wrote *I'll Leave It to You*.

1920   Bobbie Dermott in *I'll Leave It to You*, New Theatre. Wrote play *Barriers Down* (unproduced). *I'll Leave It to You* published, London.

1921   On holiday in Alassio, met Gladys Calthrop for the first time. Clay Collins in American farce *Polly with a Past*: during the run "songs, sketches, and plays were bursting out of me". Wrote *The Young Idea*, *Sirocco*, and *The Better Half*. First visit to New York, and sold parts of *A Withered Nosegay* to *Vanity Fair* and short-story adaptation of *I'll Leave It to You* to *Metropolitan*. House-guest of Laurette Taylor and Hartley Manners, whose family rows inspired the Bliss household in *Hay Fever*.

1922 *Bottles and Bones* (sketch) produced in benefit for Newspaper Press Fund, Drury Lane. *The Better Half* produced in "grand guignol" season, Little Theatre. Started work on songs and sketches for *London Calling!* Adapted Louise Verneuil's *Pour avoir Adrienne* (unproduced). Wrote *The Queen Was in the Parlour* and *Mild Oats*.

1923 Sholto Brent in *The Young Idea*, Savoy. Juvenile lead in *London Calling!* Wrote *Weatherwise*, *Fallen Angels*, and *The Vortex*.

1924 Wrote *Hay Fever* (which Marie Tempest at first refused to do, feeling it was "too light and plotless and generally lacking in action") and *Easy Virtue*. Nicky Lancaster in *The Vortex*, produced at Everyman by Norman MacDermott.

1925 Established as a social and theatrical celebrity. Wrote *On With the Dance*, with London opening in spring followed by *Fallen Angels* and *Hay Fever*. *Hay Fever* and *Easy Virtue* produced, New York. Wrote silent screen titles for Gainsborough Films.

1926 Toured USA in *The Vortex*. Wrote *This Was a Man*, refused a licence by Lord Chamberlain but produced in New York (1926), Berlin (1927), and Paris (1928). *Easy Virtue*, *The Queen Was in the Parlour*, and *The Rat Trap* produced, London. Played Lewis Dodd in *The Constant Nymph*, directed by Basil Dean. Wrote *Semi-Monde* and *The Marquise*. Bought Goldenhurst Farm, Kent, as country home. Sailed for Hong Kong on holiday but trip broken in Honolulu by nervous breakdown.

1927 *The Marquise* opened in London while Coward was still in Hawaii, and *The Marquise* and *Fallen Angels* produced, New York. Finished writing *Home Chat*.

Sirocco revised after discussions with Basil Dean and produced, London.

1928   Clark Storey in Behrman's *The Second Man*, directed by Dean. Gainsborough Films productions of *The Queen Was in the Parlour*, *The Vortex* (starring Ivor Novello), and *Easy Virtue* (directed by Alfred Hitchcock) released – but only the latter, freely adapted, a success. *This Year of Grace!* produced, London, and, with Coward directing and in cast, New York. Made first recording, featuring numbers from this show. Wrote *Concerto* for Gainsborough Films, intended for Ivor Novello, but never produced. Started writing *Bitter-Sweet*.

1929   Played in *This Year of Grace!* (USA) until spring. Directed *Bitter-Sweet*, London and New York. Set off on travelling holiday in Far East.

1930   On travels wrote *Private Lives* (1929) and song "Mad Dogs and Englishmen", the latter on the road from Hanoi to Saigon. In Singapore joined the Quaints, company of strolling English players, as Stanhope for three performances of *Journey's End*. On voyage home wrote *Post-Mortem*, which was "similar to my performance as Stanhope: confused, under-rehearsed and hysterical". Directed and played Elyot Chase in *Private Lives*, London, and Fred in *Some Other Private Lives*. Started writing *Cavalcade* and unfinished novel *Julian Kane*.

1931   Elyot Chase in New York production of *Private Lives*. Directed *Cavalcade*, London. Film of *Private Lives* produced by MGM. Set off on trip to South America.

1932   On travels wrote *Design for Living* (hearing that Alfred Lunt and Lynn Fontanne finally free to work with him) and material for new revue including songs "Mad about the Boy", "Children of the Ritz" and "The Party's Over Now". Produced in London as *Words and Music*, with book, music, and lyrics exclusively by Coward and directed by him. The short-lived Noël Coward Company, independent company which enjoyed his support, toured UK with *Private Lives*, *Hay Fever*, *Fallen Angels*, and *The Vortex*.

1933   Directed *Design for Living*, New York, and played Leo. Films of *Cavalcade*, *To-Night Is Ours* (remake of *The Queen Was in the Parlour*), and *Bitter-Sweet* released. Directed London revival of *Hay Fever*. Wrote *Conversation Piece* as vehicle for Yvonne Printemps, and hit song "Mrs. Worthington".

1934   Directed *Conversation Piece* in London and played Paul. Cut links with C. B. Cochran and formed own management in partnership with John C. Wilson. Appointed President of the Actors' Orphanage, in which he invested great personal commitment until resignation in 1956. Directed Kaufman and Ferber's *Theatre Royal*, Lyric, and Behrman's *Biography*, Globe. Film of *Design for Living* released, London. *Conversation Piece* opened, New York. Started writing autobiography, *Present Indicative*. Wrote *Point Valaine*.

1935   Directed *Point Valaine*, New York. Played lead in film *The Scoundrel* (Astoria Studios, New York). Wrote *To-Night at 8.30*.

1936   Directed and played in *To-Night at 8.30*, London and New York. Directed *Mademoiselle* by Jacques Deval, Wyndham's.

1937   Played in *To-Night at 8.30*, New York, until second breakdown in health in March. Directed (and subsequently disowned) Gerald Savory's *George and Margaret*, New York. Wrote *Operette*, with hit song "The Stately Homes of England". *Present Indicative* published, London and New York.

1938   Directed *Operette*, London. *Words and Music* revised for American production as *Set to Music*. Appointed adviser to newly-formed Royal Naval Film Corporation.

1939   Directed New York production of *Set to Music*. Visited Soviet Union and Scandinavia. Wrote *Present*

Laughter and *This Happy Breed*: rehearsals stopped by declaration of war. Wrote for revue *All Clear*, London. Appointed to head Bureau of Propaganda in Paris to liaise with French Ministry of Information, headed by Jean Giraudoux and André Maurois. This posting prompted speculative attacks in the press, prevented by wartime secrecy from getting a clear statement of the exact nature of his work (in fact unexceptional and routine). Troop concert in Arras with Maurice Chevalier. *To Step Aside* (short story collection) published.

1940 Increasingly "oppressed and irritated by the Paris routine". Visits USA to report on American isolationism and attitudes to war in Europe. Return to Paris prevented by German invasion. Returned to USA to do propaganda work for Ministry of Information. Propaganda tour of Australia and New Zealand, and fund-raising for war charities. Wrote play *Time Remembered* (unproduced).

1941 Mounting press attacks in England because of time spent allegedly avoiding danger and discomfort of Home Front. Wrote *Blithe Spirit*, produced in London (with Coward directing) and New York. MGM film of *Bitter-Sweet* (which Coward found "vulgar" and "lacking in taste") released, London. Wrote screenplay for *In Which We Serve*, based on the sinking of HMS Kelly. Wrote songs including "London Pride", "Could You Please Oblige Us with a Bren Gun?", and "Imagine the Duchess's Feelings".

1942 Produced and co-directed (with David Lean) *In Which We Serve*, and appeared as Captain Kinross (Coward considered the film "an accurate and sincere tribute to the Royal Navy"). Played in countrywide tour of *Blithe Spirit*, *Present Laughter*, and *This Happy Breed*, and gave hospital and factory concerts. MGM film of *We Were Dancing* released.

1943 Played Garry Essendine in London production of *Present Laughter* and Frank Gibbons in *This Happy Breed*. Produced *This Happy Breed* for Two Cities

Films. Wrote "Don't Let's Be Beastly to the Germans", first sung on BBC Radio (then banned on grounds of lines "that Goebbels might twist"). Four-month tour of Middle East to entertain troops.

1944 February–September, toured South Africa, Burma, India, and Ceylon. Troop concerts in France and "Stage Door Canteen Concert" in London. Screenplay of *Still Life*, as *Brief Encounter*. *Middle East Diary*, an account of his 1943 tour, published, London and New York – where a reference to "mournful little boys from Brooklyn" inspired formation of a lobby for the "Prevention of Noël Coward Re-entering America".

1945 *Sigh No More*, with hit song "Matelot", completed and produced, London. Started work on *Pacific 1860*. Film of *Brief Encounter* released.

1946 Started writing "Peace in Our Time". Directed *Pacific 1860*, London.

1947 Garry Essendine in London revival of *Present Laughter*. Supervised production of "Peace in Our Time". *Point Valaine* produced, London. Directed American revival of *To-Night at 8.30*. Wrote *Long Island Sound* (unproduced).

1948 Replaced Graham Payn briefly in American tour of *To-Night at 8.30*, his last stage appearance with Gertrude Lawrence. Wrote screenplay for Gainsborough film of *The Astonished Heart*. Max Aramont in *Joyeux Chagrins* (French production of *Present Laughter*). Built house at Blue Harbour, Jamaica.

1949 Christian Faber in film of *The Astonished Heart*. Wrote *Ace of Clubs* and *Home and Colonial* (produced as *Island Fling* in USA and *South Sea Bubble* in UK).

1950 Directed *Ace of Clubs*, London. Wrote *Star Quality* (short stories) and *Relative Values*.

1951 Deaths of Ivor Novello and C. B. Cochran. Paintings included in charity exhibition in London. Wrote *Quadrille*. One-night concert at Theatre Royal, Brighton, followed by season at Café de Paris, London, and beginning of new career as leading cabaret entertainer.

Directed *Relative Values*, London, which restored his reputation as a playwright after run of post-war flops. *Island Fling* produced, USA.

1952 Charity cabaret with Mary Martin at Café de Paris for Actors' Orphanage. June cabaret season at Café de Paris. Directed *Quadrille*, London. *"Red Peppers"*, *Fumed Oak*, and *Ways and Means* (from *To-Night at 8.30*) filmed as *Meet Me To-Night*. September, death of Gertrude Lawrence: "no one I have ever known, however brilliant ... has contributed quite what she contributed to my work".

1953 Completed second volume of autobiography, *Future Indefinite*. King Magnus in Shaw's *The Apple Cart*. Cabaret at Café de Paris, again "a triumphant success". Wrote *After the Ball*.

1954 *After the Ball* produced, UK. July, mother died. September, cabaret season at Café de Paris. November, Royal Command Performance, London Palladium. Wrote *Nude With Violin*.

1955 June, opened in cabaret for season at Desert Inn, Las Vegas, and enjoyed "one of the most sensational successes of my career". Played Hesketh-Baggott in film of *Around the World in Eighty Days*, for which he wrote own dialogue. October, directed and appeared with Mary Martin in TV spectacular *Together with Music* for CBS, New York. Revised *South Sea Bubble*.

1956 Charles Condomine in television production of *Blithe Spirit*, for CBS, Hollywood. For tax reasons took up Bermuda residency. Resigned from presidency of the Actors' Orphanage. *South Sea Bubble* produced, London. Directed and played part of Frank Gibbons in television production of *This Happy Breed* for CBS, New York. Co-directed *Nude With Violin* with John Gielgud (Eire and UK), opening to press attacks on Coward's decision to live abroad. Wrote play *Volcano* (unproduced).

1957 Directed and played Sebastien in *Nude With Violin*, New York. *Nude With Violin* published, London.

1958　Played Garry Essendine in *Present Laughter* alternating with *Nude With Violin* on US West Coast tour. Wrote ballet *London Morning* for London Festival Ballet. Wrote *Look After Lulu!*

1959　*Look After Lulu!* produced, New York, and by English Stage Company at Royal Court, London. Film roles of Hawthorne in *Our Man in Havana* and ex-King of Anatolia in *Surprise Package*. *London Morning* produced by London Festival Ballet. Sold home in Bermuda and took up Swiss residency. Wrote *Waiting in the Wings*.

1960　*Waiting in the Wings* produced, Eire and UK. *Pomp and Circumstance* (novel) published, London and New York.

1961　Alec Harvey in television production of *Brief Encounter* for NBC, USA. Directed American production of *Sail Away*. *Waiting in the Wings* published, New York.

1962　Wrote music and lyrics for *The Girl Who Came to Supper* (adaptation of Rattigan's *The Sleeping Prince*, previously filmed as *The Prince and the Showgirl*). *Sail Away* produced, UK.

1963　*The Girl Who Came to Supper* produced, USA. Revival of *Private Lives* at Hampstead signals renewal of interest in his work.

1964　"Supervised" production of *High Spirits*, musical adaptation of *Blithe Spirit*, Savoy. Introduced Granada TV's "A Choice of Coward" series, which included *Present Laughter*, *Blithe Spirit*, *The Vortex*, and *Design for Living*. Directed *Hay Fever* for National Theatre, first living playwright to direct his own work there. *Pretty Polly Barlow* (short story collection) published.

1965　Played the landlord in film, *Bunny Lake is Missing*. Wrote *Suite in Three Keys*. Badly weakened by attack of amoebic dysentery contracted in Seychelles.

1966　Played in *Suite in Three Keys*, London, which taxed his health further. Started adapting his short story *Star Quality* for the stage.

1967　Caesar in TV musical version of *Androcles and the*

Lion (score by Richard Rodgers), New York. Witch of Capri in film *Boom*, adaptation of Tennessee Williams's play *The Milk Train Doesn't Stop Here Any More*. Lorn Loraine, Coward's manager, and friend for many years, died, London. Worked on new volume of autobiography, *Past Conditional*. *Bon Voyage* (short story collection) published.

1968 Played Mr. Bridger, the criminal mastermind, in *The Italian Job*.

1970 Awarded knighthood in New Year's Honours List.

1971 Tony Award, USA, for Distinguished Achievement in the Theatre.

1973 26 March, died peacefully at his home in Blue Harbour, Jamaica. Buried on Firefly Hill.

Abbreviations

P.S.: prompt side
O.P.: opposite prompt
1E.R./2E.R./top E.R.: first/second/top exit right
1E.L./2E.L./top E.L.: first/second/top exit left
D.R.C.: downstage right centre
Tabs 1: curtain near front of stage

LONDON CALLING!

Presented by André Charlot at the Duke of York's Theatre, London, on 4 September 1923 (316 performances)

Book by Ronald Jeans and Noël Coward
Lyrics and music by Noël Coward

Noël's relationship with Charlot – one of the leading impresarios of his day – did not begin auspiciously. Introduced by Beatrice Lillie, who was currently appearing in a Charlot production, he was allowed to audition briefly under the producer's brooding gaze, before being hustled out with scant politeness. "Never," Charlot warned his star, "ever bother me again with that young composer who played the piano badly and sang worse."

Conveniently, Charlot soon forgot the incident – or, more probably, his appetite for material took priority. By 1918 Noël was contributing a song that gave him his first London theatre programme credit to the revue *Tails Up!*. The song was "The Story of Peter Pan", written in collaboration with Doris Joel. The first-night programme, unaware of the responsibility it owed to history, credited "Noel Farque". It was rapidly amended!

By 1923 Charlot had signed him up for a major revue, teaming him with the experienced Ronald Jeans as co-writer. None the less, with one exception, the "words and music" were by Noël Coward and already he was working on ways to ensure that in future productions he would colonise the sketch form.

"RAIN BEFORE SEVEN—"
or LOVE MATCHES

written 1922

Mention of "Noël and Gertie" conjures up an image of an impossibly elegant couple side by side on a Riviera balcony, facing a suddenly uncertain future, while that off-stage orchestra with its "remarkably small repertoire" plays "I'll See You Again".

In fact, they had performed together several times in the past before *Private Lives* froze the image for ever. As child actors they had played angels and at one memorable performance an excess of peppermints had resulted in an impromptu addition to their normal act. Gertie recalled that "Presently the audience was permitted an unexpected vision of Heaven in which two small angels were being violently sick."

Fortunately, the experience was not to be repeated in *London Calling!*, the one and only revue in which they were to appear. "Rain Before Seven—" prefigures the characters of Elyot and Amanda by some seven years and establishes the parameters of a relationship in which love and even passion is indissolubly bound up with bickering. Elyot and Amanda would kill – or at least maim – with greater kindness and wit but Tom and Mary were to provide the first draft. The sketch was considered effective although the critic of *The Times* considered that "its undoubted cleverness does not redeem it from being rather unpleasant".

CAST

TOM	Noël Coward
MARY	Gertrude Lawrence

The scene is a private sitting-room in an extremely luxurious hotel in Venice. There is an open window at the back looking on to the Grand Canal, from which comes the occasional hooting of steam-launches and the intermittent sound of someone singing to a guitar across the water. The sun streams in, illuminating an attractively prepared breakfast table, placed exactly in front of the window. There are two doors, one on each side of the room.

Tom enters from the left, attired in a dressing-gown and pyjamas. He goes across to the opposite door and knocks upon it.

TOM: Hurry up.

MARY (*inside*): Coming.

Tom goes rather moodily to the window and stares out. Enter MARY in an enchanting negligée; she goes up to Tom and shakes hands.

MARY: Good morning, Tom dear; are there any letters?

TOM: I forgot to look.

MARY: You always do. (*She sits down at table.*) Here they are—two for me.

TOM (*also sitting down*): Do pour out the coffee before you open them; I'm dying of thirst.

MARY (*pleasantly*): A little crotchety this morning. (*She begins to pour out coffee.*)

TOM: Not at all, but as breakfast's already been waiting a half an hour——

MARY: *How* you exaggerate!—Here you are—(*She hands him coffee and then opens a letter.*) This is from Freda Mainwaring.

TOM: What fun.

MARY: You used to like her.

TOM: I never said I didn't.

MARY: Have some grapefruit, dear—it's cooling.

3

There is silence for a moment.

She says she envies us terribly, spending our honeymoon in Venice, in the middle of such beauty, and romance, and everything——

Tom: If she only knew.

Mary: If she only knew what?

Tom: How different we're being.

Mary: She'd envy us more than ever, because she'd realise that we have the best thing of all—real companionship.

Tom: Yes, real companionship without sex. It's a marvellous achievement; I can't imagine why no one ever thought of it before, it's so sound—through and through——!

Mary: So many marriages have been ruined by people not being careful enough of their happiness.

Tom: Passion is such a terribly destroying thing. Once you let go it burns and burns until everything is consumed utterly, and then you have to grope among the dead ashes to find a little affection and comradeship, and it's generally too late.

Mary: I can't help feeling awfully proud of the way we're managing *our* lives—here we are in Venice together and it's perfect—much more perfect without ragged edges and cheap sentiment—we've got peace, and above everything else— freedom.

Tom: And all because we're exercising a little control and mental balance—I should like some toast, please.

Mary: Here you are—it's quite brittle, like china.

Tom (*taking toast*): Thanks—And it's so lovely to think that later on, when we know one another thoroughly and have grown to understand one another's every mood— then——

Mary: Then our real honeymoon—(*She sighs.*) Ah!

Tom (*also sighing*): Ah!—Pass the marmalade.

Mary: Did you sleep well?

Tom: Beautifully. Did you?

Mary: Yes. I read for a couple of hours before I dropped off.

TOM: So did I.

MARY: There was someone singing across the canal.

TOM (*gloomily*): There always is.

MARY: I'm beginning to know you awfully well already.

TOM (*with his mouth full*): Good.

MARY: Yes, the real you, not the bridegroom you.

TOM: I'm beginning to appreciate you, too, much more than at first.

MARY (*demurely*): Perhaps at the end of six months we shall be so sure of each other that it won't be necessary to wait the whole year until we——

TOM (*dreamily*): Until we—More coffee, please.

MARY: Do you remember that couple drifting along in the gondola last night?

TOM: Damned fools!

MARY: Stupid sentimentalists.

TOM: Still, they did look happy.

MARY: They looked very silly.

TOM: Where shall we lunch?

MARY: The Lido; then we can bathe.

TOM: I don't like bathing in front of all those people.

MARY: I'm sure they'd look away if you asked them nicely.

TOM: Don't be sarcastic.

MARY: I'm not; only everything I suggest you find fault with.

TOM: You're always so petulant in the early morning—I detest petulance.

MARY (*bitterly*): If you confined *your* unpleasant habits to the early morning I could bear them better——

TOM: This was how the row started yesterday.

MARY (*vehemently*): *And* the day before, *and* the day before that! We've been married exactly a week and we've had a sordid squabble every day.

TOM: On Tuesday we had two.

MARY: Well, it's nothing to boast of.

TOM (*with fearful calmness*): Mary *dear*, you won't be

irritating any more, will you, because I don't think I can cope with it.

MARY: Me irritating! I like that, I *must* say. You've been surly and disagreeable ever since breakfast.

TOM: I haven't been anything of the sort.

MARY: Must you go on drumming your spoon against your saucer? It isn't exactly an *aid* to conversation.

TOM (*gently and furiously*): Damn, damn, damn! (*He bangs his saucer with the spoon and breaks it.*)

MARY (*triumphantly*): There now.

TOM: If you racked your brains for hours you couldn't find a more utterly pointless remark than "There now".

MARY (*bitingly*): I find it exceedingly difficult to keep up to the level of your brilliant intelligence.

TOM: Obviously.

MARY (*rising, furiously*): Oh! (*She catches her sleeve in the milk jug and upsets it.*)

TOM: There now.

MARY (*with ominous calm*): Tom, there are moments when I find you quite insufferable.

TOM: Thank you. That was one of your grand remarks. You are exceedingly funny when you're grand.

MARY: Funny, am I? Huh!

TOM: Yes, extremely—Ha! ha! ha! (*He drums his spoon against his cup.*)

MARY: You're drumming again.

TOM: I'll drum as much as ever I like. (*He breaks cup.*)

BOTH: There now.

MARY: Control yourself.

TOM: Control! I defy the Archangel Gabriel to control himself on a honeymoon with you.

MARY: As there is not the least likelihood of my spending a honeymoon with the Archangel Gabriel it seems useless to pursue the subject.

TOM: You're trying to be clever and it's obviously a bitter strain.

MARY: All I can say is—thank God I was clever enough to persuade you to carry out our experiment——

TOM (*losing all control*): *You* clever enough! The idea was *entirely* mine.

MARY (*bursting into tears*): I didn't realise I was marrying a liar as well as a brute——

TOM: Now cry—go on—cry.

MARY: I am crying.

TOM: Well, stop then.

MARY: Thank heaven we're not really married.

TOM: We are.

MARY: I mean properly.

TOM: Don't be disgusting.

MARY: Oh, I hate you—I hate you! And I could go on my knees in thankfulness that I've found you out before it was too late——

TOM: Why must we go on quarrelling like this—why, why, why?

MARY: If you expect to find a solution by shouting you'll be disappointed.

TOM: Experiment! A damn successful experiment this has been. I'm as thankful as you are that we're only tied legally, not morally—at least there *is* a way out.

MARY (*sobbing*): Divorce, as soon as possible.

TOM: If you don't stop crying it will be murder.

MARY (*screaming*): Oh, you beast—you beast! ...

They both rush into their separate rooms and bang the doors—there is a silence for a moment—the voice of a singing GONDOLIER *draws near and passes the window— a sugar-sweet love song.* MARY *comes quietly out of her room sniffing a little. She goes across to* TOM's *door and is about to knock when a thought strikes her. She takes the box of cigarettes from the table and empties them all into a vase, then she bangs on his door.*

TOM: What is it?

7

MARY (*in a stifled voice*): There aren't any cigarettes—I want some.

TOM *after a moment gives her a handful of cigarettes round the door and then shuts it again firmly. She lifts her hand to knock again, then looks down at the cigarettes she is holding, then with a little cry of rage she throws them out of the window and stamps back into her room. There is a moment's pause, then* TOM *comes out of his room—he has an unlighted cigarette in his mouth—he goes to the table, picks up a match-box, strikes a match; as he is about to light his cigarette he pauses, thinking, until the match burns his finger. Then he puts the match-box into the vase and starts as his fingers encounter the cigarettes. He brings out a handful and stares at them thoughtfully for a moment, then looks towards her door. A slow smile dawns over his face, he puts the cigarettes back into the vase. The clock strikes ten—with a look of determination he whips a silk handkerchief out of his pocket and drapes it over the face of the clock, then walks quietly but firmly into* MARY'S *room, closing the door after him and turning the key in the lock.*

BLACKOUT

EARLY MOURNING
or "Sorry You've Been Troubled"

written 1923

As *The Times* critic concluded: "... Practically a monologue, giving Miss Gertrude Lawrence an opportunity of distinguishing herself."

Cast

Poppy Baker   Gertrude Lawrence
Her Maid   April Harmon

When curtain rises POPPY *is discovered asleep in bed. A breakfast tray is on a small table on her left, and a telephone on her right. Sunlight is streaming across the bed—the telephone rings violently.* POPPY *slowly wakes up.*

POPPY (*sleepily*): Oh damn! (*She takes off receiver and speaks with a pronounced Cockney accent.*) 'Allo! 'Allo! Who is it, please? Mr. Pringle—— No, sir—I'm afraid Miss Baker isn't awake yet—— Oh no, sir—I daren't, sir—she'd sack me on the spot, sir—yes, sir—— Good-bye, sir. (*She slams down receiver crossly.*) Old fool, waking me up!

She takes the breakfast tray from side table and rests it on her knees. She proceeds to pour out coffee, she sips some of it and then begins to eat a little toast. The telephone rings again. She takes off receiver and speaks with her mouth full.

'Allo, 'allo—who is it speaking? (*Abruptly changing her voice.*) Maggie darling, is it you?—— Yes, I thought it was old Potty Pringle—twice this morning, dear, really it is the limit, he ought to be at home dandling his grandchildren—— Oh yes, dear, orchids as usual—very mouldy looking with rude speckles all over them, but still they *are* expensive—what! *No!*—— You haven't got your Decree Nasty or whatever it is?—— Darling, I'm frightfully glad—— Well, if dragging you to *The Beggar's Opera* fourteen times isn't cruelty, I don't know what is—— You'll have to be awfully careful now for six months, won't you?—— Well, you'd better leave Claridge's and go to the Regent Palace, you'll be safer there —— Do you mean to say the Judge actually said that to you in Court?—— What a dreadful old man—but they're all the same, dear, no respect for one's finer feelings—— Fanny? Oh no, it was quite different with her, she won her case on points like a boxer—— No, nothing was ever proved because though she started for Brighton four times with the worst possible intentions, she never got further than Haywards Heath—— Well, dear, I really am most awfully glad—— I suppose they'll give you custody of the Daimler—— What? Oh no, darling, no such luck, I heard from him yesterday—he won't let me divorce him—— Beast!—— It isn't as if we were fond of one another, I haven't set eyes on him for five years—— Yes, he's with Freda Halifax now, she got him away from Vera—I believe she's driving him mad—serve him right—what I think of husbands!—— Oh no, Bobbie's different—besides, he isn't yet, I don't suppose he ever will be. (*She sniffs.*) You know, I love him terribly—— Don't go on giggling—— All right, Ciro's at one o'clock.

> *She puts receiver on and resumes her breakfast. Her expression is rather pensive and she occasionally sniffs pathetically. The telephone rings again, she answers it.*

Hallo—— Hallo—— Yes, who is it?—— What?—— I can't hear. What? Oh the line's buzzing—— Yes, yes, speaking—— Police Station! Why—what's happened?—— Yes—— Last night—— Oh, my God!—this is terrible—— Yes, at twelve o'clock—— I say—listen—— Oh, they've cut me off!

> *She puts the receiver on again and sits in stricken silence for a moment. She bites her lip and dabs her eyes with her handkerchief—then a thought strikes her—she grabs the telephone.*

Hallo—— Exchange—get me Mayfair 7160 at once—— Yes—— Claridges?—— Put me through to Mrs. Fanshaw, please—— Oh, quick, quick, it's urgent—— Hallo—— Maggie—— Maggie, is that you?—— Oh, my dear, listen, the most awful thing—the police have just rung me up—— Jim jumped over Waterloo Bridge last night—— No, darling, I don't know what time—— Yes, I knew you'd be sympathetic—— That's a little callous of you, dear; remember he *was* my husband after all—— I'm wretched—utterly wretched—— Yes, naturally they communicated with me first, how were they to know we hadn't seen each other for years?—— Oh, it's awful—awful! Yes, Ciro's one o'clock. (*She hangs up receiver for a moment, then bangs lever violently.*) Hallo—— Hallo—— Kensington 8712—yes, quickly. Hallo, is that you, Flossie? Poppy speaking—— My dear, Jim's dead! (*She sniffs.*) Thank you, darling, I knew you'd be a comfort—— No, dear, he jumped off Waterloo Bridge—— Yes, the one next to Charing Cross—— No, no, no, *that's* Blackfriars. Don't be so silly, Flossie, you know perfectly well Westminster comes first, then Charing Cross— the one with trains on it, *then* Waterloo—— Oh, how *can* you—you do say the most dreadful things, you'll only make me break down again in a minute—I'm having such a struggle—such a bitter, bitter struggle—— (*She sobs.*) Anyhow, I'm quite successful enough without that kind of advertisement—— Look here, lunch with Maggie and me at Ciro's one o'clock—— All right—*thank you*, darling. (*She hangs up receiver again. Then after a moment's pause she calls up.*) Hallo, hallo, Regent 2047, please—yes—I want to speak to Miss Hancox, please—— Yes, it's important—— Hallo, is that you, Violet? Poppy speaking. You know when you told my cards the other day you told me something dreadful was going to happen? Well, it has!—— Oh, no, darling, not *that*, anyhow I haven't seen him since Tuesday—no, no, much worse—— Jim's dead. Yes, dead—— I know, dear, I try to look at it in that light, but it's very very hard—you see, after all he was my husband—— I know three months wasn't long, but still—— You do say divine things—it wasn't very kind of him, was it?—— Well, dear, Maggie and Flossie and I are lunching at Ciro's at one—come too, and we'll talk it all over then. Good-bye.

She hangs up receiver and then rings up again.
Hallo, hallo, Exchange—— Mayfair 6773, please—yes—— Hallo, is that the Guards' Club?—yes, put me through to Lieutenant Godalming, please—yes, please—— (*She puts receiver down for a moment while she takes puff from under her pillow and powders her nose—then she speaks again.*)

Hallo, is that you, darling?—— Oh, I'm sorry, Higgins, I thought it was Lieutenant Godalming—in his bath?—— Please, please get him out of it, Higgins, it's frightfully important—— Yes, I'll hold on—— (*There is a pause.*) Darling—something too fearful has happened—yes, absolutely appalling—Jim's dead. What—who's Jim? He's my husband, of course—yes, he jumped off Waterloo Bridge last night—— *He jumped off Waterloo Bridge last night. No! Waterloo Bridge!* Your ears must be full of soap—— Isn't it dreadful?—— Now, Bobbie, dear, you mustn't be naughty —— No, darling, I won't listen to you—I'm very, very miserable—it's been a terrible shock—— Very well, I'll forgive you—— Kiss me, then. (*She responds to his kisses over the telephone.*) Yes, to-night—somewhere quiet—really quiet—I shan't have any appetite—— No, that would be too heartless—— No, that would be too dull—— Say the Embassy—— All right, good-bye, darling—Bobbly wobbly——

> *She hangs up receiver and rings up again.*

Hallo—— Brixton 8146, please—— Hallo, is that you, Mr. Isaacstein? It's Miss Baker speaking—will you fetch my mother down, please—— Yes, it's important. (*A slight pause.*) Is that you, Mum?—— What do you think, Jim's been and drowned himself—— I don't know—I expect Freda drove him to it—— No, Mother, I won't have you saying things like that—besides, he's too young to marry yet—— Look here, Flossie, Violet, Maggie and I are lunching at Ciro's—— One o'clock—come along too and we'll talk it all over—— You can wear that old one of mine—— All right.

> *She rings off and screams for her* MAID.

Lily—Lilee—come here——

> *She pushes breakfast tray to the end of the bed and is just about to spring out when her* MAID *enters, sobbing bitterly.*

What is it?—What's the matter with you?

LILY: It's dreadful, dreadful——

POPPY: What's dreadful?

LILY: That poor dear upstairs——

POPPY: Mrs. Straker?

LILY: Yes, Mrs. Straker—she's just heard that her husband jumped off Waterloo Bridge last night.

POPPY: What!

The telephone rings violently. POPPY *snatches up the receiver, listens for a moment, then hurls the instrument to the floor.*

(*Through clenched teeth.*) Sorry you've been troubled!

BLACKOUT

THE SWISS FAMILY WHITTLEBOT
In a short exposition of Modern Art

written 1923

The Times: "... a broad and amusing satire on very modern poetry."

Being both a traditionalist and an out-and-out romantic, Noël was understandably somewhat sceptical about some of what passed in the immediate post-war period for "modern poetry". In 1922 he tried his hand at a collection of "cod pieces" by a series of fictitious poets under the heading of *A Withered Nosegay*. Encouraged by its modest success, he decided on a more public reprise the following year in a revue sketch.

For some reason Edith Sitwell was by this time a particular *bête noire*. Whether it was her impenetrable literary style or her *outré* dress sense that irritated him more, she inspired him in the early 1920s to write a series of pseudo-Sitwell verses under the pen name of Hernia Whittlebot, some of which were eventually published in *Chelsea Buns* (1925).

Meanwhile, he gave the lady centre stage – along with her brothers, Osbert and Sacheverell – in the thin guise of Hernia, Gob and Sago, the Swiss Family Whittlebot.

To Noël's apparent surprise, the Sitwells were distinctly not amused. "I received ... a cross letter from Osbert Sitwell; in fact, so angry was it, that I first of all imagined it to be a joke. However, it was far from being a joke, and shortly afterwards another letter arrived, even crosser than the first. To this day [1937] I am still a little puzzled as to why that light-hearted burlesque should have aroused him, his brother and sister to such paroxysms of fury. But the fact remains that it did ..."

It did and it went on doing so for forty years until peace was declared over tea at the Sitwell flat. Noël reflected: "How strange that a forty-year feud should finish so gracefully and so suddenly." The feud may have finished but nothing altered his view of the Sitwell *œuvre*. "I really think that three-quarters of it is gibberish. However, I must crush down these thoughts, otherwise the dove of peace will shit on me."

CAST

STAGE MANAGER	Tubby Edlin
GOB	Leonard Childs
SAGO	William Childs
HERNIA WHITTLEBOT	Maisie Gay

Miss Hernia Whittlebot *should be effectively and charmingly dressed in undraped dyed sacking, a cross between blue and green, with a necklet of uncut amber beads in unconventional shapes. She must wear a gold band rather high up on her forehead from which hang a little clump of Bacchanalian fruit below each ear. Her face is white and weary, with a long chin and nose, and bags under the eyes. Her brothers* Gob *and* Sago Whittlebot *are dressed with self-conscious nonchalance in unusual clothes.* Gob *wears cycling breeches and a bottle-green velvet coat with a big floppy bow, cloth-topped boots and a tweed shooting hat.* Sago *is faultlessly dressed in a slightly Victorian morning suit. His shirt and boots are not quite right and his silk hat is upside down by his side. Their musical instruments are rather queer in shape.*

Miss Hernia Whittlebot *speaks.*

It is difficult for me to explain to you in words that which I have to say regarding Life, and Art, and Rhythm. Words are inadequate at the best of times. To me life is essentially a curve, and Art an oblong within that curve. Rhythm is fundamental in everything. My brothers and I have been brought up on Rhythm as other children are brought up on Glaxo. Always we have tried to create Sound and Reality and Colour. My brothers, on their various instruments (and they have many), and myself, with all the strength and courage I can summon up, will endeavour to prove to you the inevitable Truth in Rhythmic Colour Poetry. People have jeered at us, often when walking in the street they have thrown fruit and vegetables at us, but it is all colour and humour. We see humour in everything, especially the primitive. My first Poem is an early Peruvian Love Song.

Accompanied in fitful gusts by Gob *and* Sago *she recites.*

17

Beloved, it is Dawn, I rise
   To smell the roses sweet,
Emphatic are my hips and thighs,
   Phlegmatic are my feet.
Ten thousand roses have I got
   Within a garden small,
God give me strength to sniff the lot,
   Oh, let me sniff them all.

Beloved, it is Dawn, I rise
   To smell the roses sweet,
Emphatic are my hips and thighs,
   Phlegmatic are my feet.

The next poem strikes an exultantly gay note—the colours are vivid and ruthless because they are Life.

Rain, Rain, Pebbles and Pain,
   Trickle and truckle and do it again,
Houpla, Houpla, Dickery Dee,
   Trolderol trolderol, fancy me.
(*Musical interlude.*)
   Fancy me!

I will now recite my tone poem "Passion" to which special music has been set by my brother Gob on the Cophutican.

Passion's dregs are the salt of life
   Spirits trodden beneath the heel of Ingratitude.
   Drains and Sewers support the quest
Of eternal indulgence.
   Thank God for the Coldstream Guards.

I will now give you a very long and intensely primitive poem entitled "The Lower Classes". I have endeavoured to portray the bottomless hostility of the Labour Party towards themselves and everybody else—I wrote most of the first part in a Lighthouse.

At this moment sounds become audible from the

prompt corner. The STAGE MANAGER *is making signs to them that their time is up.*

War and life and the Albert Bridge
Fade into the mists of Salacious obscurity
Street hawkers cry apathetically
Mothers and children rolling and slapping
Wet on the grass—I wonder why.
Guts and Dahlias and billiard balls
Swirling along with spurious velocity
Ending what and where and when
In the hearts of little birds
But never Tom Tits.
Freedom from all this shrieking vortex
Chimneys and tramcars and the blackened branches
Of superfluous antagonism
Oxford and Cambridge count for naught
Life is ephemeral before the majesty
Of Local Apophlegmatism
Melody semi-spheroidal
In all its innate rotundity
Rhubarb for purposes unknown, etc. etc.

The STAGE MANAGER *having despaired of making her hear, has signed to the Orchestra to strike up the next number. Unmoved by this* MISS WHITTLEBOT *produces a megaphone—at last in desperation the* STAGE MANAGER *begins to set the next scene and the* WHITTLEBOT FAMILY *are eventually pushed off the stage still playing and reciting.*

ON WITH THE DANCE

Presented by Charles B. Cochran at the London Pavilion on 30 April 1925 (229 performances)

Book and lyrics by Noël Coward
Music by Philip Braham and Noël Coward

On With the Dance was Noël's first revue collaboration with impresario Charles B. Cochran. In the mid-1920s the rivalry between Cochran and Charlot was fierce but Cochran steadily prevailed by displaying broader theatrical vision. Charlot, it was said, made stars but it was Cochran who turned them into galaxies. Certainly the ten-year professional relationship between Cochran and Coward profited both men.

By 1925 Noël was determined to turn the toehold he had gained with *London Calling!* into an outright occupation. This he certainly achieved, only to encounter the alternative ego of Cochran who insisted on billing it as "Charles B. Cochran's Revue". Noël lamented: "Since I had done three-quarters of the score, all the lyrics, all the book, and directed all the dialogue, scenes and several of the numbers, [this] seemed to be a slight overstatement." It was one that was not to be repeated . . .

THE CAFÉ DE LA PAIX
or FIN DE SIÈCLE

written 1925

CAST

GUIDE	Ernest Thesiger
1ST ENGLISHMAN	Richard Dolman
2ND ENGLISHMAN	Nigel Bruce
1ST ENGLISH GIRL	Greta Fayne
2ND ENGLISH GIRL	Jessie Taylor
FRENCH WOMAN	Violet Gould
FRENCH MAN	Ernest Lindsay
MR. HAMMAKER	Harry Baker
MRS. HAMMAKER	Betty Shale
HARRY	Emmott Baker
IRMA	Joan Nurick
A FLOWER-SELLER	Hermione Baddeley
MRS. HUBBARD	Douglas Byng
AMY	Dolly Nepean
VIOLET	Helen Gardom
REGGIE	Richard Dolman
FREDA	Dorothea Varda
JAMES	Nigel Bruce
A WOULD-BE SUICIDE	Lance Lister
A COMMISSIONAIRE	Fred Winn
A COSMOPOLITAN LADY	Alice Delysia
HER ADMIRER	Ernest Thesiger

THE PUPILS: Greta Beronius, Nora Lorrimore, Decilia Mobray, Vera Bryer, Terri Storri, Rita Robinson, Hettie Steer, Florence Desmond, Thalia Barberova, Nancy Barnett, Averil Haley, Peggy Heather

VISITORS, WAITERS, STREET-HAWKERS, THE KEEPER *etc.*

It is about 11.30 p.m. outside the Café de la Paix. Only two
windows of the café can be seen and a revolving glass
door in the centre. Silhouettes of people supping are
thrown against the windows. Outside there are three
rows of tables and chairs, allowing enough space for the
passing up and down of people who are constantly
promenading. The footlights should represent the kerb.
There is a newspaper kiosk on the left of the stage.

When the curtain rises, there should be a babel of noise;
everybody talking at once, people walking up and down;
a small newsboy shouting and the constant peek-peek of
motor-cars. All the tables are filled with various types of
people, drinking coffee and syrups, and there are three or
four WAITERS, *one with large pots of coffee and hot milk.*
Two young ENGLISHMEN *in dinner jackets and silk hats*
stroll languidly on.

1ST ENGLISHMAN: God, what a row these foreigners kick
up.

2ND ENGLISHMAN: I wish we were in Piccadilly.

A typical Parisian GUIDE *with a long black moustache*
approaches them.

GUIDE: You wish to see something very very curious?

1ST ENGLISHMAN: What?

GUIDE: You come with me, *hein*?

2ND ENGLISHMAN: Where to?

GUIDE: Not far, we take taxi or walk—as you wish.

1ST ENGLISHMAN: I don't want to do either.

GUIDE: I show you lovely girls; they do plastic poses, very
amusing.

2ND ENGLISHMAN: God forbid.

GUIDE: You have not seen *Le Tango d'Amour*?

1ST ENGLISHMAN: No, and we don't want to, thanks. Come
on, Freddie.

They stroll off.

The GUIDE *spits and wanders away. Two vivacious* ENGLISH GIRLS *walk along, chatting. They are in day clothes and hats.*

1ST GIRL: And, my dear, I looked him full in the face and said, "Just because you're in France, don't imagine you can take liberties."

2ND GIRL: My dear, you didn't.

1ST GIRL: My dear, I did.

2ND GIRL: What did he do?

1ST GIRL: He took hold of both my hands suddenly and kissed me.

2ND GIRL: My dear, he didn't.

1ST GIRL: My dear, he did.

They go off.

Two very excited people nearly bump into them—a MAN *and* WOMAN. *They walk rapidly across, arguing violently.*

WOMAN: Tais toi, tais toi. En tous cas tu m'as donné rien encore.

MAN (*protestingly*): Mais, chérie, chérie, je vous assure——

WOMAN: Mais voyons, je ne suis pas une femme comme ça, d'ailleurs il n'y a pas le temps——

They go off, still arguing.

An American family stroll on. They are peculiarly but appropriately dressed. They consist of MRS. HAMMAKER, MR. HAMMAKER, *their eldest son,* HARRY, *their daughter* IRMA. *A party of people vacate one of the front tables, and so they seat themselves.*

MRS. HAMMAKER: Are we in Paris or Brussels, Harry?

HARRY: What day of the week is it?

IRMA: Thursday.

HARRY: We are in Paris.

MRS. HAMMAKER: Call the garçon, Earl.

MR. HAMMAKER (*weakly*): Hi, waiter!

IRMA: Isn't it all too darling heavenly? Look at that cute man selling carpets, Papa.

HARRY (*grandly*): He's always here.

MRS. HAMMAKER: Harry knows his Paris.

MR. HAMMAKER: What the hell's he selling carpets for at this time of night?

HARRY: He's got to make a living somehow.

IRMA: I think he's divine.

    A drab WOMAN *approaches them, selling violets. She is singing gustily.*

> Nous avons fait un beau voyage,
> Nous avons fait un beau voyage,
> Nous arrêtant à tous les pas,
> Nous arrêtant à tous les pas,
> Buvant du cidre à chaque village,
> Cueillant dans les clos des lilas,
> Cueillant dans les clos des lilas.

IRMA: Papa, give her fifty cents.

MR. HAMMAKER: Hi, you!

    WOMAN *approaching.*

WOMAN: Les belles violettes toutes fraîches, toutes fraîches.

    She attempts to force a large bunch of violets on to IRMA's *chest;* IRMA *screams.*

HARRY: Hi! Allons, allons, vite. Partez.

WOMAN: Ah, monsieur, ayez pitié de moi. J'attends un petit, peut-être deux si le bon Dieu l'ordonne.

MRS. HAMMAKER: What does she say?

HARRY: Something about having a little something.

MR. HAMMAKER (*giving her money*): Here you are; go away.

WOMAN (*moving on*): Merci, que Dieu vous bénisse.

> Nous avons fait un beau voyage...

MRS. HUBBARD *enters with her daughter* AMY; *they are*

in typical dressy blouses, cloaks and no hats, they have been to the Opera.

MRS. HUBBARD: Let's sit down here, Amy.

AMY: Look at all the people, Mother.

MRS. HUBBARD: It's always the same in Paris, dear. I remember just before your father had his operation——

AMY: Oh! Mother, look at that young man.

MRS. HUBBARD: Don't stare, dear, he might accost us.

AMY: What would happen if he did?

MRS. HUBBARD: Sh! Amy, here comes the waiter. Oh—er—garçon, deux cafay o lay.

WAITER: Complet, madame.

MRS. HUBBARD: Deux cafay o lay.

WAITER: Brioches, madame?

MRS. HUBBARD (*offended*): Certainly not. Non. Pas de toot.

AMY: What did he say, Mother?

MRS. HUBBARD: Nothing for your ears to hear, dear. Oh, I wish we had a man with us.

AMY: What language are those people speaking at the next table?

MRS. HUBBARD: Spanish, I think, dear; or is it American?

The two ENGLISHMEN *have again strolled on. The* GUIDE *again approaches them. The ensuing scene takes place exactly opposite* MRS. HUBBARD's *table.*

GUIDE: You wish to buy a postcard?

1ST ENGLISHMAN: Oh, go away.

GUIDE (*showing card under his coat*): Look, very amusing.

2ND ENGLISHMAN: Look here, if you don't leave us alone, I'll call a gendarme.

1ST ENGLISHMAN (*knocking postcards out of* GUIDE's *hand*): Come on, let's go and have a drink.

GUIDE (*picking cards up and swearing*): Sacré nom du chien sale tipe. (*He wanders away, having retrieved his postcards; one has fallen beneath* AMY's *chair. She picks it up.*)

AMY: Oh! Mother, *look!*

MRS. HUBBARD: Where are my glasses? (*She finds them and looks at it.*) Oh! (*She falls back clutching her heart.*)

AMY: What's the matter?

MRS. HUBBARD: Oh! what a turn that gave me—it's the living image of your Auntie Clara.

AMY: Aren't these foreigners awful?

MRS. HUBBARD: Never mind, dear, we're all made the same, though some more than others.

A party of ENGLISH PEOPLE *come on in evening dress. They slowly saunter across the stage.*

VIOLET: Reggie, darling, it's much too early to go to Mitchell's.

REGGIE: What about Zellie's?

FREDA: No, it's always so packed; you can't call even your corns your own.

JAMES: What about the Jardin?

VIOLET: I daren't go there, I'm so terrified of being caricatured by Sem. He did poor Lady Trimble as an otter.

FREDA (*languidly*): Why an otter?

VIOLET: I suppose because she makes such peculiar noises when drinking.

REGGIE: Let's get a taxi and tell him to take us where he likes.

FREDA (*wearily*): The Paris taxi men only know the Moulin Rouge.

VIOLET: I think I shall go to bed.

JAMES: Why did anyone ever call Paris "the gay city"?

FREDA: God knows, dear; only in comparison to New York and London, I expect.

They wander off.

MRS. HUBBARD: Do you know who that was, Amy?

AMY: No, Mother.

MRS. HUBBARD: Lady Violet Edgware; she's been divorced three times.

AMY: Who was the dark one?

MRS. HUBBARD: Lady Freda Mannering. They say her

husband beats her dreadfully. I read her life story in the *Girl's Companion.*

AMY: Oh! do look at that man with the beard, isn't he like Uncle Bob?

MRS. HUBBARD: Certainly not, Amy. Whatever your Uncle Bob's failings were, he never tucked his serviette into his dickey.

> *Their conversation is interrupted by the sudden ejection of a young man from the restaurant. He is in rather shabby clothes. He tears himself free from the* COMMISSIONAIRE, *and producing a revolver, shoots it twice into the air. At once there is an uproar. Everyone rises and talks at once. The* YOUNG MAN *falls down in a picturesque attitude. In the middle of the turmoil the* COSMOPOLITAN LADY *comes out of the restaurant escorted by several immaculate* YOUNG MEN.

COMMISSIONAIRE: Ah! Madame, madame, il meurt, il meurt.

COSMOPOLITAN LADY: No, that is the usual thing; he always does it. He's crazy about me; take him away.

YOUNG MAN: I say, aren't you rather heartless?

COSMOPOLITAN LADY: Tais-toi, mon petit. Tu ne comprends pas l'amour française. There are more fireworks than in England, but fewer people get burned.

YOUNG MAN: But he shot himself.

COSMOPOLITAN LADY: No, no, he's not hurt at all. Look!

> *She goes over to the young man and kisses him. He immediately jumps up and clasps her in his arms, muttering violent endearments. She disentangles herself from his embrace and signs to the* COMMISSIONAIRE, *who drags him away dithering ecstatically.*

COSMOPOLITAN LADY: Call me a taxi.

> *Three of her escort rush down to the floats and proceed to shout for taxis. They run along, pushing one another out of the way. The* COSMOPOLITAN LADY *is accosted by the flower-seller. She gives her some notes. Then she buys*

two rugs from the rug-seller. The YOUNG MEN *take charge of them. Suddenly* TWELVE GIRLS *march on, all dressed demurely alike, with an elderly man in attendance. They all salute the* COSMOPOLITAN LADY *and form a polite semicircle round her.*

YOUNG MAN: What on earth is all this?

COSMOPOLITAN LADY: It's a little school I started after seeing L'École des Cocottes. They all come to watch me leave the restaurant after dining. Such an education for them. (*To the* KEEPER.) Why are you late?

KEEPER: We were delayed, watching Cécile Sorel getting out of her car at the Comédie Française.

COSMOPOLITAN LADY: That's not an education, it's a warning.

KEEPER: Three of the elder girls insisted. They said it was most interesting to compare the old-world methods with the new.

COSMOPOLITAN LADY: That's a breach of discipline; I must give them an imposition. Ring up the Guaranty Trust and ask for two Chicago Millionaires and a Pittsburgh Senator.

1ST GIRL (*rushing forward*): Let us off this time, madame, please.

COSMOPOLITAN LADY: No, it will be good for you. If you wish to be a successful Cosmopolitan, you must learn to take the rough with the smooth.

2ND GIRL: Have a little pity.

COSMOPOLITAN LADY: No one ever had any pity on me!

"COSMOPOLITAN LADY"

Verse

When I was quite a little mite of seven,
I secretly decided on my course;
Though maybe I'm not heading straight for heaven,
I have never put the cart before the horse.

Chorus

She wouldn't do that of course!

Verse

It's seldom that my "joie de vivre" forsakes me,
I frequently succeed where others fail,
And when the day of judgment overtakes me,
I shall make a very firm appeal for bail!

Chorus

She seems successfully to dominate
And utterly control her fate,
We'll try to follow firmly on her trail!

Refrain

I'm a cosmopolitan lady,
With a cosmopolitan soul,
Every dashing blonde
Of the demi-monde
Starts to quake when I take a stroll,
As my past's incredibly shady,
And my future grows more doubtful every day,
Though determined to be pleasant,
I shall utilise the present
In a cosmopolitan way.

Verse

The world to me will always be a gamble,
I don't care if I win or if I lose;
The straight and narrow path is such a scramble,
And is such an unattractive life to choose.

Chorus

We'd like to be in your shoes!

Verse

I much prefer a flutter at the tables,
I treat my whole existence as a game,
And if I end in sackcloth or in sables
I shall not have lived for nothing, all the same!

Chorus

Were really quite impatient to begin
A life of unassuming sin,
And try to reach your pinnacle of fame!

Refrain

I'm a cosmopolitan lady,
With a cosmopolitan heart,
And I've lived so long
Between right and wrong,
That I can't tell the two apart,
Though my past's incredibly shady,
And my future grows more doubtful every day;
Though my methods may be breezy,
I find virtue very easy,
In the cosmopolitan way.

ORANGES AND LEMONS

written 1925

Morning Post: "One was astonished to find oneself laughing at the sight of Mr. Ernest Thesiger and Mr. Douglas Byng, dressed as middle-aged women, disrobing in a bedroom."

There was one further recorded performance. On 17 June 1934 at the Theatrical Garden Party in aid of the Actors' Orphanage – of which Noël was President from 1934 to 1956 – the sketch was performed in the "Theatre Royal" with David Hutchinson (Grace), Reginald Purdell (Violet), Jack Hobbs (Charlie) and Jerry Verno (Stephen).

When the sketch was revived in *Non-Stop Revels*, a variety programme at the Leicester Square Theatre in 1936, Noël was granted a Court injunction to prevent the performance of a sketch in a form other than that in which it was written. It was alleged that the script had been amended and some unsavoury words had been added, such as to damage the author's reputation.

CAST

GRACE HUBBARD	Douglas Byng
VIOLET BANKS	Ernest Thesiger
STEPHEN HARRIS	Nigel Bruce
CHARLIE FRENCH	Lance Lister

The scene is a bedroom in a Bloomsbury boarding house. There are two single beds facing each other. A window at back of stage and a dressing-table, complete with duchess set, including hair-tidy, pin-cushions, etc. There is also a washstand with a rose-bespattered toilet set. One incandescent gas-burner with crinkly pink glass shade. A small table beside each bed with candle and matches, etc., on each. There are some Pears' Annual *pictures, the frames of which have been decorated with some depressed sprigs of holly. There are also two dusty-coloured paper chains stretched across the room, and in the grate a large pink paper fire-screen ornament. It is New Year's Eve.*

GRACE HUBBARD and VIOLET BANKS enter. GRACE is somewhere between forty-five and fifty and rather set for maturity. She is wearing what may technically be described as a "dressy blouse" with lots of beads on it and a plain black skirt, rather up in front and down at the back. Her shoes and open-work stockings are very festive. VIOLET, on the other hand—though more or less the same age—is distinctly more "skittish". She is angular and fair, dressed in a tea-gown of voluptuous design; flowers (artificial) on one shoulder. She wears gold-rimmed pince-nez on a chain. Both the ladies are wearing coloured paper caps. GRACE turns up the gas which had been turned low.

GRACE (*enters door right. Crosses to fireplace, turns up light*): I do think Mrs. Rogers might have given us a fire.

VIOLET (*sits chair centre*): No idea of comfort; the English are always like that.

GRACE: You're English yourself, aren't you? (*Crosses to bed right.*)

VIOLET (*tittering*): Well, I'm not altogether; my grandmother was Spanish, and I was nearly always abroad until I married.

GRACE: Is your husband dead?

VIOLET: Oh, yes, quite; he behaved very badly to me.

GRACE: They're all the same. Do you mind very much if I take this bed? I always sleep on my right side, and I don't like facing the window.

VIOLET: Certainly. I always sleep curled up. My husband nicknamed me "Pixie", you know.

GRACE: Did he?

VIOLET: Yes; he was whimsical, I will say that for him.

GRACE (*sits on bed*): It is funny. Do you know I haven't shared a room with anyone since my eldest sister's funeral?

VIOLET (*rises, crosses to right of chair centre*): Well, I don't mind confessing, just between our two little selves, that I was very upset when Mrs. Rogers asked me to have another bed put in here. But after all, I said to myself, one mustn't be disagreeable in the middle of so much jollity.

GRACE: Quite, quite. (*Takes hair down.*) Will you wash first, or shall I?

VIOLET (*beginning to undo her dress*): I'll rinse my hands later. I never touch my face with water. (*Up to dressing-table.*) I shall massage it gently with this delicious cream. Smell . . . (*She proffers a pot of cream.*)

GRACE (*sourly*): Very nice; I like Oatine better.

VIOLET: Well, Gladys Cooper uses this, and look at her skin!

GRACE (*unpinning her paper cap*): She married Arthur Bourchier, didn't she? (*Takes belt off.*)

VIOLET: No, you're thinking of Fay Compton.

GRACE: I'm very tired, you know; it was that last game we played, so energetic.

VIOLET (*crosses to chair left*): Would you think it frightfully naughty of me if I smoke a cigarette?

GRACE: Not at all. (*Begins to undress.*)

VIOLET: I do so love a little puff before going to bye-byes.

GRACE (*takes off blouse, and then skirt. Sits on bed and*

takes off her shoes): It's been a very successful evening, hasn't it?

VIOLET: Scrumptious.

GRACE: I do wish my daughter Amy had been here. She does make a party go so.

VIOLET: Fancy you having a grown-up daughter ... (*Sits chair centre.*) Just think now!

GRACE: Everybody says that. She's a bundle of talent, Amy!

VIOLET: I'm sure she is. Quite a bundle!

GRACE: She says the most killing things. Only the other day at tea a young man said to her, "A penny for your thoughts", and what do you think she said?

VIOLET (*taking her hair down*): I can't think. (*Crosses to left.*)

GRACE: She turned round quick as lightning and said, "They're worth more than that." (*She laughs immoderately.*)

VIOLET: Very quick, very quick indeed. (*Starts to undo dress.*)

GRACE: Whenever she goes out anywhere, she keeps the table in fits with her hospital stories. She was a V.A.D., you know, and really, the things she had to do to those poor soldiers, you'd die laughing.

VIOLET: I wonder if you would unhook me. (*Crosses to centre.*)

GRACE: Certainly. (*She proceeds to do so.*)

VIOLET: One does feel so lost without a maid, doesn't one? Thank you so much. (*In execrable French ... Pause.*) Oh! mon Dieu, com say frwor! (*Crosses right.*)

GRACE (*crosses up centre to washstand*): I beg your pardon?

VIOLET: I'm so sorry. When one's used to speaking French, one simply can't find the English words sometimes. (*She giggles affectedly.*)

GRACE (*going to washstand*): Amy's just the same; such a gift for languages. (*At washstand.*) No soap.

VIOLET: Pardon!

GRACE: There isn't any soap.

VIOLET: There's a small cake of Cuticura in my handkerchief drawer. (*She finds it; takes soap, gives to* GRACE.) Here you are; I never leave it out, servants are so untrustworthy nowadays.

GRACE: Oh! quite, quite. Thank you so much.

> *While* GRACE *is washing rather noisily,* VIOLET *seizes the opportunity to put on her nightgown, which she does with becoming modesty, loosening all her underclothes first, then putting the nightgown over her head, and jumping until the cast-offs lie in a ring round her feet. She steps out of the ring with great refinement and proceeds to put her clothes away.*

VIOLET: I must say this nightie was a bargain for 2/11¾. I always like Liberty's.

GRACE: I never allow them!

VIOLET: You probably did when you were my age. Talking of liberties ... (*Crosses to chair left.*) What an outrageous man Mr. Harris is, isn't he?

GRACE (*drying herself*): I really never noticed.

VIOLET (*removing stockings*): My dear, the things he said to me when we were thinking of a charade. I didn't know where to look.

GRACE (*bitterly*): These mixed games always lead to unpleasantness. I remember when I was staying in the Cleveland Hydro at Swanage one Christmas ...

VIOLET: Oh! I don't mind really, you know; travelling teaches one to look after oneself. I can pass anything off with a laugh.

GRACE (*crosses to front of bed*): I remember when I was staying at the Cleveland Hydro at Swanage one Christmas, there was a man ...

VIOLET: It's so easy to manage men, you know, if only you have the knack, and being abroad so much, naturally one ...

GRACE (*irately*): There was a man with a long red beard.

VIOLET (*greasing her face, crosses to table*): Oh! I can't stand a beard.

GRACE (*putting on her nightgown in the same way as* VIOLET): And if it hadn't been for Amy, I don't know what would have happened.

VIOLET: As I was saying, Mr. Harris ... he pinched me very sharply, just at the beginning of the second syllable.

GRACE: How disgusting!

VIOLET: Naturally I ignored him for the rest of the evening, but it only shows you what men are.

GRACE: I always discourage that sort of thing; it's so common.

VIOLET: Sometimes one can't help oneself, but perhaps you don't find that?

GRACE: Any man will behave badly if he's led on.

VIOLET (*with slight rancour*): Really, I hope you're not insinuating.

GRACE: Certainly not; I was only stating a fact.

VIOLET: Well, with me, I'm afraid it's rather the reverse. The more I retire into my shell, the more the men come rushing after me.

GRACE: I promised Hubbard on his death-bed that I'd never look at another man, and I never have. (*Up at window.*)

VIOLET: Well, I must say one can do a lot without looking. (*She giggles.*)

GRACE: Really, Mrs. Banks; I don't consider that remark in the best of taste.

VIOLET: A little touch of the green-eyed monster, I'm afraid, Mrs. Hubbard.

GRACE: What was that you called me?

VIOLET: Please don't let us commence the New Year with a quarrel.

GRACE: I have no intention of quarrelling, but I must say I dislike lewdity.

VIOLET: What did you say?

GRACE (*crosses left*): Lewdity; and if you can find a better word in French, you're at liberty to translate it.

VIOLET (*outraged*): Oh!

The rest of their toilet is concluded in an offended silence and GRACE *wrestles unsuccessfully with the Venetian blind.*

(*Grandly.*) Please, please allow me ... I'm used to Venetians. We had them in our house at Boulogne when I was a girl. (*She tries to pull the string suddenly, and the whole blind falls down, almost crushing her beneath it.*)

GRACE: There now!

VIOLET: I am afraid you must have pulled the wrong string in the first place.

GRACE (*laughing hollowly, sits on bed left*): That's very funny. Me pull the wrong string! Very funny indeed. Oh dear; oh, dear!

VIOLET: Perhaps you would be so kind as to control your hysteria and assist me to draw the lace curtains.

GRACE: With pleasure.

They both unloop the lace curtains and drag them across.

VIOLET: I fear they will not meet.

GRACE: I could have told you that when I first saw them. I should think the watchword of this house is Economy. (*Crosses right, front of bed, and lights candle.*)

VIOLET: On the contrary, Mrs. Rogers is the soul of generosity, besides being a personal friend of mine.

GRACE: I beg your pardon, I'm sure.

VIOLET: Granted. (*There is a silence, then she says with forced brightness.*) And so to bed. (*Crosses to bed left, lights her candle.*)

GRACE (*lighting her candle*): Will you turn out the gas, or shall I?

VIOLET: I really don't mind! (*She turns it out and gets into bed.*)

GRACE (*looking under her bed before getting into it*): I always do this in case of cat burglars.

VIOLET: How droll of you. I'm never nervous of that sort of thing.

GRACE: Indeed!

VIOLET: I expect it comes of being so cosmopolitan. Midnight visitors hold no terrors for me.

GRACE: I should be more inclined to conceal that fact than boast of it. Good night! (*She blows out her candle.*)

VIOLET (*with great dignity*): Good night! (*She blows out her candle and there is absolute silence and pitch darkness.*

The clock strikes somewhere.

There is the sound of voices, the door opens, and MR. HARRIS *and* MR. FRENCH *enter. They cannot be seen, but by their voices it is obvious that they are a trifle intoxicated. They close the door after them.*

CHARLES (*enters door right*): Got any matches? (*Feeling way along wall.*)

STEPHEN: Yes, half a mo'. (*He is heard fumbling.*)

CHARLES: This is our room all right, isn't it?

STEPHEN: Of course! I left them downstairs.

CHARLES: There'll be some on the bed-table. (*There is the sound of a lot of groping and fumbling.*)

STEPHEN: Can't you find any?

CHARLES: Hell! No!

STEPHEN: Well, I'm hanged if I'm going down those ruddy stairs again; it was bad enough coming up. We'll undress in the dark.

CHARLES: Oh! all right!

STEPHEN: That was a jolly good one you told about the woman in the bath. (*He laughs.*)

CHARLES (*also laughing*): A chap told it to me at the office last week.

STEPHEN: Do you know the one about the newly-married couple?

CHARLES: No.

STEPHEN: Well, there was a newly-married couple ... stop me if you've heard it ...

CHARLES: Righto.

STEPHEN: And they get to the hotel ...

CHARLES: Oh! dash!

STEPHEN (*interrupting*): What's the matter now?

CHARLES: We've left our bags downstairs.

STEPHEN: Hell!

CHARLES: Go and get 'em, there's a pal.

STEPHEN: Not likely. I'm nearly undressed and stone cold.

CHARLES: So am I!

STEPHEN: I'll tell you. We'll go to bed in our shirts and have the bags up in the morning. (*Crosses to bed left.*)

CHARLES: All right!

STEPHEN: I'll take this bed. (*He approaches* VIOLET's *bed.*)
She suddenly gives a piercing shriek.

VIOLET: If you come a step nearer, I'll scream the house down.

STEPHEN: Oh! my God!

There is the sound of a scuffle from GRACE's *bed; then she speaks in a very cooing and ingratiating voice.*

GRACE: Well, young man, and what can I do for you?

CURTAIN

CLASS

written 1924

Class and the observation of its different manifestations was
the bedrock on which much of Noël's work was based.
Sometimes – as in the upstairs/downstairs Marryots and
Bridges in *Cavalcade* (1931) – the notes he struck were true
ones. At other times, although the affection was clearly felt, the
touch was less sure and the result could appear patronising.

Noël himself found it hard to come to terms with such a
verdict. After all, had he not emerged from the lower ranks?
Indeed, he had – and with utmost speed. Although he felt the
rhythms and knew the vocabulary of working-class speech, it
rapidly became a foreign language. He was *from* the lower
class but never *of* the lower class. As John Osborne was to
observe, he was his own invention.

CAST

INTRODUCER   Ernest Thesiger

SCENE I:
ALF HIGGINS   Lance Lister
ADA, *his wife*   Helen Gardom
MR. HIGGINS   Nigel Bruce
MRS. HIGGINS   Violet Gould
MAUDE   Hermione Baddeley

SCENE II:
ALFRED HIGGINS   Lance Lister
LADY ADA HIGGINS, *his wife*   Helen Gardom
SIR HERBERT HIGGINS, BART   Nigel Bruce
LADY HIGGINS   Violet Gould
A BUTLER   Ernest Lindsay
A FOOTMAN   Jean Perrie
MAUDE   Hermione Baddeley

Introductory Speech before Scene I

Ladies and gentlemen: in the democratic England of to-day there is a good deal of discussion as to whether there are actual class differences or not. That all men are equal is undoubtedly a magnanimous theory, but strip the so-called "upper classes" of their luxurious surroundings, and the usual trappings of gilded ease, and, I ask you, what happens?

Scene I

The scene is an extremely squalid room in the East End. The table is laid for high tea. There are shrimps, winkles, etc., and a very sticky pot of jam. A canary in a minute cage in the window, and a few group photographs of ALF'S *wedding on the mantelpiece. When the curtain rises* ALF *is seated in a tilted-up chair with his feet on another, reading the "Star". He is in his shirt-sleeves, and has a cap on. He is smoking a Woodbine.* ADA, *in a pink blouse, with her hair in curlers, is laying the table.*

ALF: What is Mother doing? We shall be frightfully late!

ADA: She always takes hours dressing.

ALF: I loathe getting in in the middle of the big picture.

ADA: Never mind, we can stay through the whole programme until it comes round again.

ALF (*scratching his head*): Look here, Ada, I'm a bit worried about Maude.

ADA: I don't think you need be. She's absolutely capable of looking after herself.

ALF: I'm not so sure. She's so liable to allow herself to be carried away by her emotions.

ADA: Hasn't she sent a telegram or anything?

ALF: No; she just went straight out of the house on Saturday without a word. I think Mother's getting anxious.

ADA: It's her own fault, really dear. Let's face it. She was awfully tiresome over that fried fish.

ALF: Yes, but you know what she is. I've always realised that it's necessary to humour her over trifles.

Enter MR. HIGGINS. *He is an oldish man with grey hair and a very old stained suit.*

MR. HIGGINS: This weather's ghastly. (*He hangs up his overcoat on a peg.*)

ADA: Perfectly fiendish.

MR. HIGGINS: Isn't tea ready yet?

ALF: We're waiting for Mother, as usual.

ADA: Where have you been?

MR. HIGGINS: Well, as a matter of fact I dropped into the "Green Man" and had a couple of Guinnesses with Joe Harris and some other fellows. Any news of Maude?

ALF: Not a thing.

MR. HIGGINS: It's really extremely inconsiderate of her.

Enter MRS. HIGGINS, *blowzy and overdressed in third-rate flashy clothes.*

MRS. HIGGINS: My dears, I'm frightfully sorry, my hair's been driving me mad. Is the kettle boiling yet?

ADA: The tea's been made for hours, it will be black as ink.

MRS. HIGGINS: Don't exaggerate, Ada darling. (*To* MR. HIGGINS.) Cheer up, Bertie dear, we've got shrimps as it's your birthday.

MR. HIGGINS: Oh! good!

MRS. HIGGINS: You appear to be utterly plunged in impenetrable gloom.

ALF: Father's worried about Maude.

MRS. HIGGINS: So are we all, but I've been trying not to think about it.

ADA: She'll be all right.

MRS. HIGGINS: I feel dreadful about it. Where in heaven's name can she be?

43

ALF: She's probably gone down to the Bennetts.

MRS. HIGGINS: No, I saw Mary Bennett yesterday; she hadn't heard from her either.

ADA: Oh well, we'd better have tea. Come along.

They all draw up their chairs and begin to have tea.

MR. HIGGINS (*helping himself to winkles*): Lend me a hairpin, Emily dear.

MRS. HIGGINS: You'd better have my brooch, it's much sharper. (*She unpins her brooch and hands it to him.*)

MR. HIGGINS: Thanks. I hope these are going to turn out better than the last lot you had.

He proceeds to pick out winkles, the door opens and
MAUDE *enters. She is flashily dressed, but she looks pale and rather furtive.*

MRS. HIGGINS: Maude! (*Kisses her absently.*)

MAUDE: Hullo, Mother.

ALF: Where on earth have you been?

MAUDE: Don't be tiresome and brotherly, Alfred. I can't bear it. (*She kisses* MR. HIGGINS.) Many happy returns of the day, Father. I've got a dreary little present for you. (*She gives him a small parcel.*)

MR. HIGGINS (*undoing it and disclosing a pair of coloured braces*): Thank you, Maude, you couldn't have given me anything I like better.

MAUDE (*taking off her hat and sitting down*): I'm glad you're pleased with them. I've been wracking my brains to think of something for you. Pass the shrimps, Ada.

ADA (*passing them*): Here you are, the salt's near you.

MRS. HIGGINS: Where have you been, Maude?

ALF: Leave her alone, Mother, it's much wiser.

MAUDE: I've been away.

MRS. HIGGINS: Yes, but where?

MAUDE: With the Bennetts.

MR. HIGGINS: What?

MAUDE: You knew I was going.

MRS. HIGGINS: Maude!

MAUDE (*impatiently*): Oh! what?

MRS. HIGGINS: That is a deliberate lie.

MAUDE: Now look here, Mother . . .

MRS. HIGGINS: I met Mary yesterday, she hadn't seen you for days.

MAUDE: How unfortunate. You shouldn't go out so much, Mother, it would save complications.

MR. HIGGINS: Maude, what have you been doing?

MAUDE: For heaven's sake, Father, don't you start being tiresome too.

MRS. HIGGINS (*bursting into tears*): Oh, my God! Something terrible's happened. I know it, I can feel it in my bones.

ADA (*patting* MRS. HIGGINS *shoulder*): Don't, dear; don't give way.

MR. HIGGINS (*sternly*): Maude, tell us where you've been and put an end to this suspense.

MAUDE (*rising angrily*): Very well, I will. If you all persist in being so ridiculous and browbeating me. I determined to take a decisive step a long time ago, and now I've done it. I've been away with Harry Norfolk.

MR. HIGGINS: What?

MRS. HIGGINS (*moaning*): Oh! Oh! Oh!

MAUDE: Don't go on like that, Mother. It's absurd. It's my life, and I fully intend to do what I like with it. I love Harry and he loves me, and we both love one another too much to marry. We neither of us feel that we could face the hideous little intimacies that constitute marriage. It kills all the romance and glamour, and ultimately love. How could it be otherwise? Particularly in these days of women's emancipation. When you and Mother married things were different; women were content to run houses and have babies and allow themselves to be lulled into a squalid domestic security. Nowadays women demand more. They demand passion and adventure and thrill. I'm in love for the first time in my life and I don't intend to sacrifice it for convention. I've done what I've done deliberately with my eyes open, and far from being ashamed, I'm positively elated. I mean to have complete freedom, physically and morally, and you can all exactly do what you choose about it.

Introductory Speech before Scene II

You have witnessed an orthodox upper-class family in low-class surroundings dealing with the situation which might quite conceivably be common to both. We will now endeavour to present to you the reaction of the lower-class mind in higher-class surroundings in identically the same situation.

Scene II

The scene is a beautifully furnished dining-room in Mayfair. Everything rich, luxurious and in exquisite taste. When the curtain rises ALFRED *(in dinner-jacket) is reading the "Tatler" and smoking through a long onyx cigarette-holder.* ADA *is looking out of the window. She is wearing a beautifully simple dinner-dress and pearls. She is also smoking and sipping a cocktail. She turns and comes down and helps herself to an olive.*

ALF: Where the 'ell's Ma? We shan't arf be late.

ADA: She always takes 'ours doing 'erself up.

ALF (*grumbling*): We'll get there bang in the middle of the six-reel drama.

ADA: Oh, shut up! We can sit the 'ole programme through 'til it comes round again, can't we?

ALF: I've got the wind up about Maudie.

ADA: Well, you needn't 'ave. Maudie's all right.

ALF: Oh, is she?

ADA: Ain't she sent a telegram or nothing?

ALF: No! She banged out of the 'ouse on Saturday.

ADA: It's all Ma's fault, she's such a "nagger". Look 'ow she went on over that grouse being a bit 'igh.

ALF: Oh, you know what she is; she wants a bit of getting round.

> *Enter* SIR HERBERT HIGGINS; *he is appropriately dressed in a dinner-jacket.*

SIR HERBERT: Watcher, Alf, this weather's bleeding awful.

ADA: You've said it.

SIR HERBERT: Ain't dinner ready yet?

ALF: We're waiting for Ma; she's mucking about upstairs.

ADA: What you been up to?

SIR HERBERT: I been round to the Embassy and 'ad a couple of 'ow-d'yer-dos wiv Joe. Anyone seen our Maudie?

ALF: What a hope!

SIR HERBERT: Coo! Lummie! What a cow!

> *Enter* LADY HIGGINS *in an exquisite cloak, dress and fan.*

LADY HIGGINS: My 'air's been driving me fair batty. Why ain't the food up?

ADA: It ain't no use us ringing for it 'til you've finished fixing your face. (*She rings for it.*)

LADY HIGGINS: Oh! look a bit brighter, Bert, for the love of Gawd! It's yer birthday, ain't it?

SIR HERBERT: Yus.

LADY HIGGINS: Well then, Gloomy Gus.

ALF: Pa's worried about Maudie.

LADY HIGGINS: So I should think; ungrateful little slut.

ADA: Oh, Maudie's O.K.

LADY HIGGINS: I don't know where she's got to; she ain't with May Bennett 'cos I saw 'er yesterday.

> *Two* FOOTMEN *enter.*

ADA: Oh well, let's 'ave a bite. Come on.

> *They all sit down.*

> FOOTMEN *serve the soup and go out.*

SIR HERBERT: This soup's blarsted 'ot.

LADY HIGGINS: Oh! shut yer face.

> *The door opens and* MAUDIE *enters. She is attractively dressed in travelling clothes.*

Maudie!

MAUDIE: What oh! Mum. (*She kisses her.*)

ALF: Wat 'ave you been a-doing of?

MAUDIE: Now look 'ere, Alf, you just keep your tongue between your teeth and leave me be. (*She kisses* SIR HERBERT.) 'Ere, Pa old cock, comps of the season and all that; there's something to go on with. (*She gives him a small parcel.*)

SIR HERBERT (*opening it and disclosing some wonderful links*): Blimey! Look, Ma, ain't they bonza?

MAUDIE: Oh well, as long as you're pleased. This 'at's giving me a 'eadache. (*She takes it off and sits down.*)

LADY HIGGINS: Maudie, where 'ave you been?

ALF: Oh, cheese it, Ma; leave the poor girl alone.

MAUDIE: Where d'yer think I been?

LADY HIGGINS: 'Ow the devil do I know?

MAUDIE: I been with May Bennett.

LADY HIGGINS: You dirty little liar.

MAUDIE: Now look 'ere ...

LADY HIGGINS: I saw 'er yesterday at the Grosvenor 'Ouse Bazaar.

MAUDIE: You ought to stay in more, nosy parker.

SIR HERBERT: Wat's 'appened to you?

MAUDIE: Nothing.

LADY HIGGINS: You've gone wrong; I can feel it in me bones. I'm like that. Not clairvoyant, but septic.

MAUDIE: Well, if you want it you shall 'ave it. I bin off with 'Arry.

SIR HERBERT: 'Arry. 'Arry Norfolk?

MAUDIE: Yus. Now then!

SIR HERBERT: You ... you ...

MAUDIE: Now you shut up, Pa. I know which side my bread's buttered.

LADY HIGGINS: Oh, my Gawd!

MAUDIE: 'E loves me, and I love 'im, and we ain't the marrying sort neither. There ain't nothing in marriage nowadays, any'ow. Women know a damn sight too much;

they've learnt 'ow to 'ave a bit of fun when they want it wiv'out tying theirselves up until Kingdom comes. I'm in love good and proper. You can lay your shirt on that. All right, all right. And I ain't goin' to do it in by muckin' about, see? Wat I've done I've done, and I'm proud of it, and if you don't like it you can all bloody well go to 'ell.

BLACKOUT

TRAVELLING LIGHT
or A Thief in the Night

written 1924

Cast

A Young Woman	Alice Delysia
A Young Man	Nigel Bruce
A Wagon-Lit Attendant	Ernest Thesiger

*The scene is a compartment in the Orient Express. On the left
side is the sliding door, opening into the corridor, and in
the right the window. The two corner seats have reserved
notices pinned over them. The* ATTENDANT *ushers in the*
YOUNG WOMAN *and places her bag in the rack.* ATTEND-
ANT *goes left.*

WOMAN: Is there anyone else in this carriage?

ATTENDANT: Yes, madame, a young gentleman. He is in the
restaurant.

      The train gives a sudden jerk and starts.

WOMAN: I thought we waited here longer than that.

ATTENDANT: No, madame; only quarter of an hour.

WOMAN: Look here, attendant. Are there no sleepers
vacant?

ATTENDANT: No, madame; not until we get to the frontier.

WOMAN: When will that be?

ATTENDANT: About half-past two.

WOMAN: You'd better reserve me one, then.

ATTENDANT: Very well, madame.

WOMAN: Unfortunately, I've had my handbag stolen, so I
shall not be able to pay for it until we arrive at Trieste. My
friends are meeting me there.

ATTENDANT: Very sorry, madame, but you can't have a
sleeper unless you pay in advance. That's one of the
company's rules.

WOMAN: Could you break it? Just this once.

ATTENDANT: I'm afraid not.

WOMAN: But I tell you, my friends are meeting me at
Trieste. They'll settle up with you.

ATTENDANT: I'm sorry, madame; it's out of the question.

WOMAN: But this is outrageous; surely you can trust me!

ATTENDANT: The company's orders are "not to trust
anyone".

WOMAN: I'll make it worth your while.

ATTENDANT: It's no good, madame, I can't do it.

WOMAN: Well, all I can say is, it's disgusting. I've travelled by this route hundreds of times, and now because I have the misfortune to lose my bag, I am treated as though I were a suspicious character.

ATTENDANT: Anyone who loses their bag is a suspicious character, madame; that's another of the company's rules.

WOMAN: Please don't be impertinent.

ATTENDANT: I'm sorry, madame.

WOMAN: I haven't even got any change; I shan't be able to have so much as a cup of coffee.

ATTENDANT: I wouldn't mind standing you a cup of coffee.

WOMAN: Kindly go away, and don't be familiar.

ATTENDANT: Certainly, madame. I hope you'll spend a comfortable night.

WOMAN (*angrily*): Oh!

> The ATTENDANT *withdraws; the* WOMAN *opens an attaché case. Just as she is settling herself, the* YOUNG MAN *enters.*

YOUNG MAN (*stepping over her feet*): Excuse me.

WOMAN: I'm sorry. (*She tucks her legs under the seat.*)

> The YOUNG MAN *sits down in his corner, they both observe one another covertly for a little while.*

YOUNG MAN: Do you mind if I smoke?

WOMAN: Not at all.

YOUNG MAN (*producing cigarette-case*): Perhaps you'd like one?

WOMAN: Oh, thank you so much. (*She takes one and he lights them.*) I'm in an absolute fury.

YOUNG MAN: Why?

WOMAN: There aren't any sleepers vacant.

YOUNG MAN: I know. It's frightfully annoying. The man said there might be some going at the frontier. I'm only going as far as Milan, so it wouldn't really be worth it.

WOMAN: It's all very badly arranged.

YOUNG MAN: Yes. The only thing is to make ourselves as comfortable as possible here.

WOMAN: Yes! I suppose it is!

There is silence.

YOUNG MAN (*peering out of the window*): I think it has started to rain.

WOMAN: How lovely!

YOUNG MAN: I say, don't snap at me!

WOMAN: I warned you that I was cross.

YOUNG MAN: Yes, but not with me!

WOMAN: Not yet.

YOUNG MAN: Oh!

There is another silence.

I didn't see you in the restaurant car.

WOMAN: I've only just got in.

YOUNG MAN: I loathe dining on the train, anyhow.

WOMAN: I haven't dined at all.

YOUNG MAN: Oh, I say! Why not?

WOMAN: I hadn't got any ... time.

YOUNG MAN: Look here, I've got a little food and some champagne. Will you have it?

WOMAN: Oh! really, I couldn't.

YOUNG MAN: Oh! please do. It will only be wasted if you don't.

WOMAN: It's extremely kind of you.

He gets hamper down from the rack and opens it. Then he serves her with some chicken and salad on a paper plate.

How delicious! It really is charming of you.

YOUNG MAN: I'll open the bottle.

WOMAN: Do be careful. I'm terrified of champagne corks.

YOUNG MAN: They are rather violent, aren't they. (*He opens it successfully.*)

WOMAN: Yes, they are. You must have some too.

YOUNG MAN: There's only one glass.

WOMAN: Never mind, we'll share it. (*He pours out a glassful.*)

YOUNG MAN: You first.

WOMAN: Yes! (*Drinking some and handing it back.*) Now you.

YOUNG MAN (*drinking*): Thanks. This is rather fun, isn't it?

WOMAN: You're saving my life and my temper.

YOUNG MAN: Have some more.

WOMAN: Yes. (*She has some more.*)

YOUNG MAN: Is that chicken all right?

WOMAN: Perfect.

YOUNG MAN: Good.

    There is a silence.

How's the salad?

WOMAN: Divine.

YOUNG MAN: It looks rather old.

WOMAN: I prefer it old.

YOUNG MAN: Have some more champagne.

WOMAN: All right. I hope it won't go to my head.

YOUNG MAN: I hope it will. (*He pours out some more.*)

WOMAN: That was very naughty of you.

YOUNG MAN: Here.

WOMAN: No, you first this time.

YOUNG MAN: Righto! (*He drinks some.*) Now you.

WOMAN: Thank you. I drink to your health, wealth and happiness.

YOUNG MAN (*bowing*): I possess two of those quantities at the present moment. (*Sits again.*)

WOMAN: I'm so glad. There now, I've eaten enormously.

YOUNG MAN: Allow me. (*He takes her plate and puts it back in the basket.*) There's some very sombre-looking cake and an apple.

WOMAN: No more, thank you.

YOUNG MAN: Sure?

WOMAN: Positive.

YOUNG MAN: We'll put the hamper away, then. All except the champagne.

WOMAN: You must put that away, too. I couldn't drink any more.

YOUNG MAN (*putting hamper back on rack*): Nonsense, there's a lot left.

WOMAN: I'm afraid it couldn't have been an ordinary sized bottle.

YOUNG MAN (*handing her glass*): Here.

WOMAN: No, no: really!

YOUNG MAN: Come along. Please, just a little.

WOMAN: Only a sip, then. (*She spills a few drops.*)

YOUNG MAN: Oh! that's lucky! Permit me. (*He wets his fingers in the wine and rubs some behind her ears.*)

WOMAN: Oh! you're tickling me. You must have some too. (*She does the same.*) For luck. (*Business. Gives him glass.*)

YOUNG MAN: Won't you take off your hat?

WOMAN: Shall I?

YOUNG MAN: It would be cosier.

WOMAN: Very well. (*She does so and fluffs out her hair before the glass.*) There ...

YOUNG MAN: What pretty hair!

WOMAN: Sh! Tut! Tut! You mustn't say things like that.

YOUNG MAN: Why not, if I'm sincere?

WOMAN: Are you?

YOUNG MAN: Damnably.

> There is a slight pause, while they gaze into each other's eyes.

WOMAN: Yes!

YOUNG MAN: Let's finish the champagne.

WOMAN: Very well.

YOUNG MAN (*pouring it out*): You first, this time.

WOMAN: Yes. (*She drinks.*) Now you.

> YOUNG MAN *looking into her eyes, he turns the glass round and drinks from where she has drunk. She looks down.*

Please may I have another cigarette? (*Pause . . . repeat.*)

YOUNG MAN: Oh yes, of course!

He lights fresh cigarette for her.

WOMAN: I suppose we'd better try to sleep a little.

YOUNG MAN: Yes, I suppose we had. (*Puts coat over himself.*)

WOMAN: Would you think it dreadful of me if I took off my shoes?

YOUNG MAN: Lord, no! Let me help you.

WOMAN: No, please not. (*She kicks them off.*)

YOUNG MAN: Won't you have a rug?

WOMAN: No, really, thank you!

YOUNG MAN: I insist; I have my overcoat.

She tucks her feet up and he wraps the rug round her.

WOMAN: You're being most frightfully sweet to me, and I am so, so grateful.

YOUNG MAN: If you only knew what a pleasure it was. (*Sits.*) Shall we turn out the light or keep it on?

WOMAN: Leave it on. (*Business.*) Put it out.

He turns out the light.

In the darkness the two glowing cigarette-ends appear to draw closer and closer to each other; when they meet the curtain falls. It rises again in a moment or two. A few hours have elapsed. The YOUNG MAN *is asleep and snoring. The* YOUNG WOMAN *is putting on her shoes. The* ATTENDANT *enters.*

ATTENDANT: You rang, madame?

WOMAN: Shh! He's asleep.

ATTENDANT: Very human, madame. Life's like that.

WOMAN: When do we reach the frontier?

ATTENDANT: In about ten minutes.

WOMAN (*handing him some money*): I find I shall be able to pay for that sleeper after all.

ATTENDANT (*taking it*): Life's like that, madame.

BLACKOUT

THIS YEAR OF GRACE!
originally called Charles B. Cochran's 1928 Revue

Presented by Charles B. Cochran at the London Pavilion on
22 March 1928 (316 performances)

This Year of Grace! was generally considered to be the best of
the Coward–Cochran collaborations and probably the best
revue Noël ever wrote. Critic St. John Ervine in the *Observer*
found it "the most amusing, the most brilliant, the cleverest,
the daintiest, the most exquisite, the most fanciful, the most
graceful, the happiest, the most ironical, the jolliest, the most
kaleidoscopic, the loveliest, the most magnificent, the neatest
and nicest, the most opulent, the pithiest, the quickest, the
richest, the most superb and tasteful, the most uberous, the
most versatile, the wittiest..." – before he ran out of letters
of the alphabet.

This time there were no pseudo-collaborations. Cochran
cheerfully accepted the inevitable. "The whole show was to be
mine," Coward wrote later: "music, book, lyrics and supervi-
sion of production ... I remember leaving his [Cochran's]
office much cheered."

A TUBE STATION
or The Tube

written 1928

In this case the result of Noël's form of interwoven song and sketch is a mini-musical and a sequence so ambitious in scale that it would induce cardiac arrest in subsequent producers of revues that depended on half a dozen artistes and a couple of pianos. "A Tube" calls for a cast of no less than forty! No wonder it has never been revived.

CAST

Fred, *a bookstall attendant*	Fred Groves
Urchin/Office Boy	Tommy Hayes
Bank Clerk	Sonnie Hale
Lift Man	Billy Shaw
Lady Gwendolyn Verney	Joan Clarkson
The Hon. Millicent Bloodworthy	Ann Codrington
Harry, *a booking-clerk*	Lance Lister
Cecil	William Cavanagh
Lawrence	Cecil Stafford
Charles	Douglas Byng
Mary	Jessie Matthews
1st Girl	Sheilah Graham
2nd Girl	Moya Nugent

Female Passengers: Madeline Gibson, Florita Fey, Greta Taylor, Marjorie Robertson, Betty Davis, Gladys Godby, Peter May, Marjorie Browne, Peggy Wynne, Marie Masters, Dinka Starace, Nancy Barnett, Decilia Mobray, Doreen Austin, Nancy Fielder, Isla Bevan, Nora Olive, Kathleen Coram

Male Passengers: Arthur Warren, Syd Shields, Eddie Grant, Edward Coventry, Charles Farey, Frank Fox, Richard Haydon, Fred Le Roy, Fred Herries

The scene is the booking-office of an underground railway station. There is a newspaper stand on the left and on the right on an angle up stage are the lift gates, which are closed.

THREE PEOPLE come on quite quietly—buy papers and tickets at the slot machines, then take their stand by the lift. They open their papers and read them—a dirty little URCHIN enters, gets a ticket and also takes his stand, then gradually two by two and in groups the entire company come on (with the exception of a few principals required in the ensuing scene). All buy papers and tickets and queue up waiting for the lift. Everyone is completely preoccupied and dressed in ordinary workaday clothes, and there should be no sound at all but the click of the slot machine and the rustle of newspapers. Suddenly the little URCHIN, who has been unable to afford a paper, begins to whistle through his teeth—quite softly at first. One or two people lower their papers and regard him rather impatiently for a moment—the tune he is whistling is a very definite dance rhythm—he whistles a little louder—a woman a few feet away from him, without looking up, begins to shuffle her feet unconsciously. The man with her stops her with an irritable nudge. The URCHIN continues to whistle—an elderly business man immersed in his paper begins to shuffle his feet—then the woman starts again— gradually as the boy's whistle gets louder, everyone starts moving slightly—the man at the bookstall takes up the tune and hums it carelessly, then almost imperceptibly at first, the orchestra takes up the tune—it swells louder until everybody is dancing hard. At this moment a young BANK CLERK rushes in hurriedly, buys a ticket and a paper— looks at everyone jigging about—recognises the tune and sings it.

BANK CLERK *sings one verse, one chorus.* BANK CLERK
and CHORUS *sing one chorus, and into dance as arranged.*

"WAITING IN A QUEUE"

Verse

In a rut
In a rut
In a rut
We go along.
Nothing but
Nothing but
Nothing but
The same old song.
To those who view us lightly
We must seem slightly
Absurd.
We never break the ritual
One habitual
Herd.

Refrain

Waiting in a queue
Waiting in a queue
Everybody's always waiting in a queue.
Fat and thin
They all begin
To take their stand—it's grand—queuing it.
Everywhere you go
Everywhere you go
Everybody's always standing in a row.
Short and tall
And one and all
The same as sheep—just keep—doing it.
No one says why

No one says how
No one says what is this for?
No one says no
No one says go
No one says this is a bore.
If you want to do
Anything that's new
If you're feeling happy, furious or blue
Wet or fine
You get in line
For everybody's waiting in a queue.

At the end of the number the lift comes up—the ATTENDANT *dances out and everyone dances in, the* YOUNG MAN *and the* ATTENDANT *last. The gates close and the lift disappears and the* MAN *in the bookstall stops humming as the rhythm dies away in the orchestra.*

Enter I E.R. LADY GWENDOLYN VERNEY *and* THE HON. MILLICENT BLOODWORTHY, *elaborately and expensively dressed. They look round, slightly bewildered.*

LADY GWENDOLYN: What do we do now, darling?

MILLICENT: Get our tickets, I suppose.

LADY GWENDOLYN: Yes, but where? Life's agony, isn't it?

MILLICENT: Torture, dear—but it's no use grumbling—we can't possibly use our cars with all the roads up—we must just be brave and do what the common people do.

LADY GWENDOLYN: It all seems very complicated. (*Turns and sees ticket machines.*) Look at these funny grey things!

MILLICENT: Those must be the ticket machines.

LADY GWENDOLYN: My dear, how delicious! We must put in some pennies, or something.

MILLICENT: I haven't any change.

LADY GWENDOLYN: Neither have I. We'll get it at the bookstall.

MILLICENT (*crosses to news-stand*): Have you got *Vogue*?

FRED *is in front of newspaper stand.*

FRED: 'Ave I got wot?

MILLICENT: *Vogue.*

FRED: Wot's that?

LADY GWENDOLYN: It's a paper, I'm afraid.

FRED: I got *Tit Bits*, *Answers*, an' all the dailies.

MILLICENT: Have you change for a pound?

FRED: Mostly in pennies, mum.

LADY GWENDOLYN: How divine—we can buy things with them.

FRED: I shouldn't do that, ma'am, if I was you. I should send them to the British Museum as curiosities. (*Goes to back of stall and gets change.*)

MILLICENT: Here's the pound.

FRED (*counting out change*): There y'are, lady. There's three and six in coppers, five and five's ten, and ten's a pound.

MILLICENT: Thank you a thousand times.

FRED: It's a pleasure, so 'elp me God.

LADY GWENDOLYN: Come along, darling. (*Crosses to machines.*)

MILLICENT (*putting a penny in the ticket machine*): It's really quite an adventure, isn't it?

The ticket comes out.

LADY GWENDOLYN: I'm thrilled—we must have some more—— (*She puts in several pennies.*)

MILLICENT (*also cramming pennies in*): What tremendous fun!

FRED: 'Ere, 'ere, 'ere, wot you think you're doing? (*He comes over to the machine.*)

LADY GWENDOLYN: I'm afraid it's stuck.

FRED: This ain't Wembley, you know. (*He shakes the machine.*)

MILLICENT: There now—I've got fourteen. How many have you, darling?

LADY GWENDOLYN: I've got tons.

FRED: Wot's the idea? That's what I want to know. Wot's the idea? Where d'yer want to go?

LADY GWENDOLYN: Well, we want ultimately to get to the Ritz.

FRED (*crosses to right shouting*): 'Arry, 'Arry, come 'ere!

HARRY: 'Allo!

> HARRY, *the booking-clerk, comes out of his office and comes to centre.*

What's the matter?

FRED: 'Ere's a couple of bejewelled duchesses bunging up one of the " 'ow-d'yer-do's".

HARRY (*shaking the machine*): What d'you want to come mucking about 'ere for? You ought to be at home looking after your children.

MILLICENT: We happen to be unmarried.

FRED: I shouldn't 'ave thought you'd let a little thing like that stand in yer way.

LADY GWENDOLYN: Horrible brute!

FRED: Who's 'orrible?

MILLICENT: Come away, Gwen dear, they're insulting us.

> *Goes off* 1 E.L.

LADY GWENDOLYN: There are your ridiculous tickets!

> *She throws them over both the men and goes out grandly* 1 E.L.

HARRY: Well, I'll be damned!

FRED: There you are—that's class.

HARRY: Class, phew! If my old woman made up 'er eyes like that, I'd lock 'er in the scullery!

FRED: Wot do they want to come nosing round 'ere for—bloated aristocrats.

HARRY: You know the trouble with you, Fred, is you're a bit Bolshie.

FRED: No, all this democracy makes life 'ellish uncomfortable.

HARRY: What we want in England is more and better birth control.

FRED: Oh no, we don't.

HARRY: Oh yes we do.

FRED: It's men like you as is responsible for the birth-rate falling.

HARRY: Well, if you're responsible for it rising, you ought to be ashamed of yourself. This country's over-populated.

Enter CHARLES, *a very exquisite young man. Crosses to centre, looks at them and then goes up to ticket machines.*

FRED: No, it ain't. It's all right—you've won. I'm all for birth control.

CHARLES *puts a penny in the slot machine and cannot work it.*

CHARLES: I say!—attendant—it's stuck.

Lift rises.

FRED: Give it a shake.

CHARLES *shakes it gently.*

CHARLES: I'm afraid it's still stuck.

Lift doors open. Exit two people right and left.

FRED: I said shake it—not stroke it! 'Ere! (FRED *comes over to machine.*) Where d'you want to go—anyhow?

CHARLES: Queen's Gate.

FRED *gives the machine a violent shake—gets ticket out, gives it to* CHARLES, *then pushes him into the lift.*

FRED: Take him away, Hubert—'e's breaking my 'eart.

LIFT MAN: Right!

The lift goes down.

FRED: 'Arry, that's wot the Russian Ballet's done for England.

MARY *enters* I *E.R. She is charmingly dressed and she is reading a book in which she is so engrossed that she collides with* FRED, *who has crossed to right centre.*

MARY: Oh, I *am* so sorry.

FRED: That's all right, miss.

MARY: Could you tell me the time, please?

FRED: About eleven o'clock.

MARY: Thank you, it doesn't matter if I wait here for a little, does it? (*Crosses to centre.*)

FRED: You can wait here as long as you like.

    TWO GIRLS *come on from 1 E.L., buy tickets, and wait for the lift.*

MARY: I'm expecting a friend.

FRED: Boy-friend, I'll be bound.

MARY: You're quite right.

    1ST GIRL *suddenly sees* MARY *and crosses to left of her.*

1ST GIRL: Mary!

MARY: Hallo!

1ST GIRL: What are you doing here?

MARY: I'm waiting for Jack Burton.

2ND GIRL: Jack! We've just left him——

MARY: Oh! Perhaps I mistook the time——

1ST GIRL: Didn't you have a row with him last night?

MARY: Yes—but not a serious one.

2ND GIRL: Are you sure?

1ST GIRL: You're so difficult, you know—you won't be content with men as they are—you're always trying to alter them.

MARY: Only because they never seem a bit like what they're made out to be in books.

1ST GIRL: Books! Who cares about books?

MARY: I do.

    Lift rises.

2ND GIRL (*crosses to right*): Life comes first, duckie. If I were you, I'd step out of my beautiful dreamland and face a bit of reality—it's more comforting in the long run.

MARY: You think I'm a fool, don't you?

    Lift doors open—exit two people.

2ND GIRL: Not exactly—but you're always pretending things are what they're not.

1ST GIRL: Here's the lift. Good-bye, Mary.

MARY: Good-bye.

    They enter lift and it goes down.

CLOSE TABS 1

"MARY MAKE-BELIEVE"

Verse

I have been reading in this book of mine
  About a foolish maiden's prayer,
And every gesture, word and look of mine
  Seems to be mirrored there.
She had such terribly pedantic dreams
That her romantic schemes
  Went all awry,
Her thoughts were such
She claimed too much
  And true love passed her by.

Refrain

Mary Make-Believe
  Dreamed the whole day through
    Foolish fancies,
    Love romances,
  How could they come true?
Mary Make-Believe
  Sighed a little up her sleeve,
    Nobody claimed her,
    They only named her
  Mary Make-Believe.

During this Refrain eight GIRLS *enter from* 1 *E.R. and
eight from* 1 *E.L.*

Counter melody to be sung by CHORUS

She's just a girl who's always blowing mental bubbles
  Till she's quite out of breath—quite out of breath.
She seems to have the knack of magnifying troubles
  Till they crush her to death—crush her to death.
    She's just a duffer of the ineffective kind,

She's bound to suffer from her introspective mind,
Her indecisions quite prevent her visions—coming true.
    Imagination is a form of flagellation,
    If a sensitive child—lets it run wild
It dims the firmament till all the world is permanently blue.
    She's simply bound to make a bloomer
    Until she's found her sense of humour.
        If love should touch her ever
    She'll never, never see it through.

And MARY *sings the Refrain at the same time as* CHORUS *sing counter melody.*
Dance as arranged.
As CHORUS *exit—eight right and eight left—*MARY *is in centre of stage.*
Fade out as GIRLS *exit.*

CLOSE TABS ON MARY'S LAST NOTE

IGNORANCE IS BLISS

written 1928

Changing domestic *mores* always fascinated Noël and the revue sketch provided a perfect format for pithy social comment. Here he compares and contrasts the changing attitude in the Battle of the Sexes as typified by wedding-night nerves – or lack of them. One would give a good deal to know what he would have made of the present day equivalent.

CAST

SCENE I:
MRS. BLAKE, *proprietress of
    private hotel*   Maisie Gay
HUSBAND   Sonnie Hale
WIFE   Jessie Matthews
ANNIE, *a servant*   Moya Nugent

SCENE II:
PROPRIETOR   Douglas Byng
HUSBAND   Lance Lister
WIFE   Joan Clarkson
PAGE   Tommy Hayes

Scene I

The scene is a hotel bedroom of the Nineties.

  A Young Husband *and* Wife *are ushered in by a very fat* Proprietress—*a chambermaid comes in after them with their luggage. The furniture is ugly and heavy, and on the right is a large double brass bed.*

Proprietress: Put the things down over there, Annie.
  Annie *puts bags at the end of sofa.*
Come this way, please.
  They come on and cross to front of sofa.
I think you'll be very comfy here. (*Shakes up bed.*)
  Husband: Thank you.
  Wife (*with an effort*): I'm sure we shall.
  Proprietress: Married to-day?
  Husband: Oh no!
  Wife: } (*together*) { Oh yes!
  Proprietress (*rubbing her hands*): Now, now, now, now!
You mustn't be shy. (*To the* Maid.) Don't stand there gaping,
Annie—run away.
  Annie: Yes'm.
  She crosses back of sofa and exits door centre.
  Proprietress: Do you know Worthing well?
  Crosses to window O.P. side.
  Husband: No.
  Proprietress: You can get a lovely view of the sea from
this window 'ere—here.
  Wife (*gulping*): How nice.
  Proprietress (*archly*): But I don't suppose you'll be
looking out of the window much, will you? (*Crosses to centre.*)
  Wife: Oh, Harry!
  Husband: That will be all now, thank you, Mrs. Blake.

69

PROPRIETRESS (*crosses up to door, centre*): If you want anything you've only got to ring for it, you know.

HUSBAND: Thanks—thanks very much.

PROPRIETRESS: Not at all—a pleasure—I like to see young things standing on the threshold of life, as it were.

> *She stands and looks at them, smiling. There is a long pause.*

> HUSBAND *crosses to* WIFE *and takes off coat.*

HUSBAND: Quite.

PROPRIETRESS (*conversationally, coming down stage*): I was born 'ere, you know, born and married and widowed all in Worthing.

WIFE (*nervously*): How nice.

PROPRIETRESS: It's the close season now—but it's very gay in the summer.

HUSBAND: It must be. (*Puts coat down on sofa.*)

PROPRIETRESS: Last year we had no less than twenty-seven honeymoon couples—they all 'ad this room—separately, of course.

WIFE: Oh, Harry!

HUSBAND: That will be all now, thank you, Mrs. Blake.

PROPRIETRESS: Well—ring if you want anything, you know.

HUSBAND: Yes—thank you.

PROPRIETRESS (*roguishly*): I don't suppose you'll ring much though, will you?

WIFE: Oh, Harry!

HUSBAND: Oh, good night.

PROPRIETRESS (*laughing gaily*): It's me as should be saying that to you—sir.

> *She goes out door centre.*

WIFE: Oh, Harry! (WIFE *sits on sofa.*)

> *This whole scene to be played in an agony of embarrassment.*

> HUSBAND *sits on sofa.*

HUSBAND: Well—here we are.

WIFE: Yes—here we are.

HUSBAND: Quite a nice room, isn't it?

WIFE: Delightful.

HUSBAND: It all went off very well, didn't it?

WIFE: Yes.

HUSBAND: Yes, and now—er—well—here we are.

  HUSBAND *gets up from sofa.*

WIFE: Yes—here we are.

HUSBAND: When we've unpacked we can put the bags under—the—(*He looks in agony at the bed.*) sofa.

WIFE: Yes—we can—can't we?

HUSBAND: Yes—we can, can't we. Who's going to unpack first, you or me?

WIFE: I don't know.

HUSBAND: We'll toss up—tails you do—heads I do.

WIFE: Oh, Harry! (*Gets up from sofa—crosses to* HARRY.)

HUSBAND (*throwing coin*): It's heads—that's you!

WIFE: Oh!

HUSBAND: I'll—er—go downstairs and order breakfast for the morning—while you—er—get into—er—start to unpack.

WIFE: Very well.

HUSBAND (*kissing her hurriedly*): Cheer up, dear.

WIFE: Oh, Harry!

  He goes out quickly.

  She falls on her knees by the sofa.

(*Wailing.*) Oh, Mother—oh, Mother—oh, Mother!

BLACKOUT

SCENE II

A very modern hotel bedroom.

  A HUSBAND *and* WIFE *are ushered in by the* PROPRIETOR. *A* PAGE BOY *enters with the luggage.*

PROPRIETOR: I hope you'll be comfortable here.

WIFE: Oh yes—divine. (*She thumps the bed with her fist.*) Bed feels all right.

HUSBAND: Got a stinker on you?

WIFE: Yes—here—— (*She gives him one.*)

HUSBAND (*to* PROPRIETOR): Send up two dry Martinis, will you?

> The WIFE *opens a portable gramophone and puts on a dance record, then starts to undress.*

WIFE: Here, Harry—unhook me.

HUSBAND (*doing so*): Right—Ouch!

WIFE: What is it?

HUSBAND: I always scratch myself with this damned hook!

BLACKOUT

THE LIDO BEACH

written 1928

During the 1920s it was considered *de rigeur* for anyone who was anyone to take themselves off to the Continent for "the season" – Deauville, the French Riviera and, for those of adventurous turn – the Venice Lido. There they would be forced to mingle lugubriously with all the people they couldn't stand back home.

> This narrow strip of sand
> Makes something seem to burst in us,
> Brings out the very worst in us.

In this – and its companion piece, "The English Lido" – once again we have Noël the observer of class distinctions. The stay-at-home English defend to the death their right to take their pleasures sadly . . .

> We have a very fixed idea of fun.
> The thought of anything experimental
> Or Continental
> We shun.
> We take to innovations very badly,
> We'd rather be uncomfortable than not.

One thing does appear to cross the social barriers. Enjoying oneself can be a tedious business.

CAST

THE CONTESSA	Betty Shale
LADY FENCHURCH	Joan Clarkson
LADY SALTWOOD	Ann Codrington
LADY VERLAP	Lauri Devine
LADY MILLICENT	
SIR JOHN VERLAP	Robert Algar

SIR FREDERICK SALTWOOD	Sonnie Hale
THE CONTE	Fred Groves
SIR CHARLES FENCHURCH	Lance Lister
YOUNG MAN	William Cavanagh
BARONESS KURDLE	Douglas Byng
MR. CLARK	Cecil Stafford
VIOLET	Jessie Matthews
RUTH	Sheilah Graham
JANE	Madge Aubrey
IVY	Moya Nugent

The scene is the Lido Beach. There should be a backcloth with Excelsior Hotel on it up against bright blue sky. In the foreground a row of cabanas with coloured striped awnings and coloured mattresses and cushions.

When the curtain rises the CHORUS *is discovered in a straight line across the stage, with their hands on their knees looking out front. Some are in bathing dresses and some in gaily coloured pyjamas. There is a general air of sunshine and colour and gaiety.*

OPENING CHORUS

ALL:

A narrow strip of sand,
Where Byron used to ride about,
While stately ships would glide about,
The sea on either hand.
But now the times have changed,
For civilised society
With infinite variety
Has had it rearranged.
No more the moon
On the still Lagoon
Can please the young enchanted,
They must have this,
And they must have that,
And they take it all for granted.
They hitch their star
To a cocktail bar,
Which is all they really wanted.
That narrow strip of sand
Now reeks with assininity,
Within the near vicinity
A syncopated band

That plays the Blues—all the day long—
  And all the old Venetians say
They'd like a nice torpedo
  To blow the Lido away.

CHORUS *go up stage and form several groups.*
TWO WIVES *enter top E.R. and* TWO *top E.L. and come
down to footlights.*

WIVES:

Beneath the blue skies
Of Sunny Italy
We lie on the sand
But please understand
We're terribly grand.
We firmly married
The old nobility,
But we can spend happy days here,
Take off our stays here,
Tarnish our laurels,
Loosen our morals.
Oh! you'll never know
The great relief it is
To let our feelings go.
We're *comme il faut*
You see, and so
It doesn't matter what vulgarity
We show!

TWO HUSBANDS *enter top right and* TWO *top left and
come down and take up positions on left of each* WIFE.

HUSBANDS:

Ladies of abundant means
And less abundant minds,
Although we're not romantic
We crossed the cold Atlantic
To choose a few commercial queens

Of different sorts and kinds.
Returning with a cargo
Of girlhood from Chicago,
Tho' we regret it more from day to day,
We think it only fair to you to say:
It wasn't for your beauty that we married you,
It wasn't for your culture or your wit,
It wasn't for the quality that Mrs. Glyn describes
As "It", just It.
It wasn't your position in Society
That led us on to making such a fuss——

FOUR WIVES *start going off left,* FOUR HUSBANDS *start
going off right, singing the last three lines.*

Forgive us being frank,
But your balance in the bank
Made you just the only wives for us.

At exit of HUSBANDS *and* WIVES, CHORUS *form a
straight line across stage and sing this verse:*

ALL:
This narrow strip of sand
Makes something seem to burst in us,
Brings out the very worst in us;
But kindly understand,
We've got the blues all the day long
And every year we always say
We'd like a nice torpedo
To blow the Lido away!

Half exeunt right, half left.
*At the end of the Opening Chorus there is a general
buzz of conversation. Four people playing Bridge outside
a cabana on the left are quarrelling furiously.* LADY
MILLICENT *is lying on mattress, right.*
CONTESSA: What did you play that for?

SIR CHARLES: Because it seemed to me the most suitable card to play.

CONTESSA: I've always thought you a dreary old fool, Charles!

LADY FENCHURCH: Darling Contessa—don't be so tiresome.

CONTESSA: We're playing Bridge—not Animal Grab.

A YOUNG MAN *in a bathing suit approaches the table,* 1 *E.L.*

YOUNG MAN: Are we lunching upstairs dressed or down here undressed?

CONTESSA: Mind your own business!

YOUNG MAN: It is my business. I'm paying for lunch.

LADY FENCHURCH: Upstairs then, dear—it's more expensive.

YOUNG MAN: Look—here comes a photographer.

Everybody at once screams and rushes eagerly off the stage. SIR CHARLES *stops and looks at cards and then rushes off. After a moment they return, smiling with satisfaction. The* YOUNG MAN *lies down at bottom of mattress, right.*

SIR CHARLES: Well, I double.

The BARONESS KURDLE, *an elderly woman, comes out of her cabana in a dressing-gown—she is large and extremely feminine. She is followed by* MR. CLARK *from top E.L.*

LADY MILLICENT: Who's this? I'm new to the Lido.

CONTESSA: That's the Baroness Kurdle. Just an Austrian girl.

BARONESS: Where iss my oil?

LADY MILLICENT: Your what, dear?

BARONESS: Oil—somebody have pinched him.

MR. CLARK: Pinched who?

BARONESS: My oil. It iss my hour for sunburn.

LADY MILLICENT (*holding up bottle*): Is this it?

MR. CLARK *pulls mattress down stage.*

BARONESS: Ach yes—Mr. Clark, you will please rub my back—I my front can do myself——

LADY MILLICENT: I never know, Baroness, why you go to all this trouble, anyhow.

BARONESS (*taking off her dressing-gown and displaying a slightly inadequate bathing costume*): Sunburn is very becoming—but only when it is even—one must be careful not to look like a mixed grill. (*She undoes the shoulder-straps of her bathing suit and lies face downwards on a mattress.*) Mr. Clark, you will please begin.

MR. CLARK *dutifully begins to rub her back with oil.*

LADY MILLICENT: Look—there's a photographer.

BARONESS: My wrap—my God! my wrap—my God!

Everybody at once rushes off all entrances left. The BARONESS *is the last one off the stage.*

VIOLET, JANE, RUTH *and* IVY *enter top E.R. They are all exquisitely dressed.*

VIOLET: What's that crowd over there?

JANE: Only a camera-man.

RUTH: Really, the way these people rush after publicity is disgusting—we don't go on like that.

IVY: They're amateurs, dear—and we're professionals.

They come down stage to footlights.
Business: as arranged.

QUARTETTE: "LITTLE WOMEN"

(VIOLET, JANE, RUTH *and* IVY)

ALL:

> We're little girls of certain ages
>   Fresh from London Town,
> Like an instalment plan of Drage's
>   We want so much down.
> We have discovered years ago
>   That flesh is often clay,
>   We're not a new sin,

We're on the loose in
Quite the nicest way.
We have renounced domestic cares
For ever and for aye.
We're not so vicious,
Merely ambitious.
If there must be love,
Let it be free love.

Refrain 1

We're little women
Alluring little women,
Cute but cold fish,
Just like goldfish
Looking for a bowl to swim in.
We lead ornamental
But uncreative lives,
We may be little women,
But we're not good wives.

VIOLET:

I am just an ingénue
And shall be till I'm eighty-two;
At any rude remark my spirit winces,
    I've a keen religious sense,
    But in girlish self-defence
I always have to put my faith in princes.

ALL:

Do not trust them, gentle maiden,
They will kick you in the pants!

RUTH:

I'm not a type that is frequently seen,
    I wear my hair in a narrow bang;
I have remained at the age of eighteen
    Since I left home in a charabanc.

Tho' men all pursue me
When they woo me
They construe me as innocent;
But when I hear things suggestively phrased
I'm not unduly amazed.

ALL:

It takes far more than that to wake
Sweet wonder in her eyes!

JANE:

I waste no time on things
That other girls are arch about,
I much prefer to march about alone.
I am a baby vamp,
I'd take a postage stamp,
I just believe in grabbing
Anything that's offered me.
If Mother Hubbard proferred me—a bone
I should not be upset,
Have the darned thing re-set.

ALL:

Much further than the Swannee River
She keeps her old folks at home!

IVY:

I am a girl whose soul with domesticity abounds.
I know a man of six-foot-three who's worth a million
        pounds. (*Whoops.*)
    Tho' he is like a brother
    I haven't told my mother
He's given me a lovely house and grounds!

ALL:

Be it ever so humbug
There's no place like home.

Refrain 2

We're little women,
Alluring little women,
Cute but cold fish,
Just like goldfish
Looking for a bowl to swim in.
Tho' we're very clinging
Our independence thrives.
We may be little women
But we're not good wives.

They all exeunt 1 E.L. on the last four bars.

THE ENGLISH LIDO

written 1928

Cast

ANNOUNCER	Lance Lister
MR. FREEMAN	Fred Groves
MRS. FREEMAN	Ann Codrington
ALICE	Moya Nugent
FRANKIE	Tommy Hayes
OFFICIAL	Melville Cooper
MADGE	Sheilah Graham
DORIS	Marjorie Browne
MR. HARRIS	Sonnie Hale
MRS. HARRIS	Joan Clarkson
VI	Kitty Jacobs
GEORGIE	Jack Kosky
MRS. CLARK	Madge Aubrey
PHYLLIS	Lolita Hudson
MRS. JONES	Betty Shale
DAISY KIPSHAW	Maisie Gay

HOCKEY PLAYERS, CHILDREN, CAMERA-MEN, BATHERS, *etc.*

Preliminary Speech

Announcer comes on in front of Tabs.

Announcer: Ladies and gentlemen, it has been suggested in several newspapers of late that English seaside resorts hold out fewer attractions to visitors than Continental ones. Any true patriotic Englishman naturally resents this reflection on our national gaiety, and Mr. Cochran perhaps more keenly than anyone—so he has determined to prove conclusively once and for all that no holiday resort in the world can equal in charm, gaiety and light-hearted carefree enjoyment an average watering-place on the shores of the English Channel.

Opening Chorus

All the Chorus *are discovered in a straight line across the stage.* Mr. *and* Mrs. Harris *in middle of line, and* Mr. *and* Mrs. Freeman *to the left of them.*

All:
Hooray, hooray, hooray!
The holidays!
The jolly days,
When laughter, fun and folly days
Appear.
Hooray, hooray, hooray!
The laity
With gaiety
And charming spontaneity
Must cheer.

Mr. Harris:
I've left my bowler hat and rubber collar far behind.

MRS. HARRIS:
  I wish to God you'd left that awful Panama behind.
  It looks gaga behind!

ALL:
  But never mind, because the holidays are here,
  Our tastes are very far from Oriental,
  We have a very fixed idea of fun.
  The thought of anything experimental
  Or Continental
  We shun.
  We take to innovations very badly,
  We'd rather be uncomfortable than not.
  In fighting any new suggestion madly
  We'd gladly
  Be shot!
  We much prefer to take our pleasures sadly
  Because we're really quite contented with our lot.

  *The scene is structurally the same as the Lido scene,
  except that in place of cabanas there are bathing
  machines. The sky is leaden grey and there is a violent
  wind blowing. Some of the characters wear ill-fitting
  bathing costumes with Burberrys and mackintoshes over
  them, others are dressed respectively in flannels and
  blazers and plus-fours and cloth coats and skirts and very
  rumpled summer dresses. There broods over everything
  that air of complacent dreariness which is inseparable
  from any English seaside resort.*
  When the Opening Chorus is over, a very well-developed
  WOMAN *of about thirty runs in from* 1 E.R. *to centre.*
WOMAN: I say, girls, what about a game of beach hockey?
1ST GIRL: Topping!
2ND GIRL: Righto!
3RD GIRL: Good egg!
  About nine of them go off—leaving the stage empty

except for the HARRIS FAMILY *on the right. They sit in the two end chairs. And the* FREEMAN FAMILY *on the left, and a few odd people strolling about.* MRS. FREEMAN *is vainly trying to put up a deck chair right of bathing machine. Finally she sits down. An* OLD MAN *climbs up steps of bathing machine and looks through hole in the door.* MR. FREEMAN *sits down right of bathing machine with a newspaper.*

MR. FREEMAN: 'I—come on out of it, nosie!

OLD MAN *goes top E.R.*

MRS. FREEMAN (*sits down*): That's the first time I've been 'ot for ten days. (*Is knitting.*)

MR. FREEMAN: What are you grumblin' about?

MRS. FREEMAN: I'm not grumblin', but it's my belief this place isn't as bracing as they said it was. I feel awful.

MR. FREEMAN (*wearily*): Oh, what's the matter with you?

MRS. FREEMAN: Well, I'll tell you—I've got a cold, wind under the 'eart, I feel sick, and me feet hurt!

MR. FREEMAN: What d'you think you are—a medical magazine?

MRS. FREEMAN: Well, if you 'adn't 'ad hiccoughs all night I might 'ave got a bit of sleep and felt better!

MR. FREEMAN: Where's Alice?

MRS. FREEMAN: 'Elping Frankie on with his bathing things—'e loves the water.

Shrill screams of rage come from inside bathing machine.

MR. FREEMAN: Yes, it sounds like it, don't it?

ALICE, *a girl of about sixteen, in a very voluminous bathing gown, comes out of the bathing machine leading* FRANKIE, *a little boy of ten, clad only in striped bathing drawers—he is yelling loudly. Cross to right.*

Can't you keep the child quiet?—yer ma's not feeling well.

ALICE: 'E found a beetle in 'is bucket.

MR. FREEMAN *goes over to* FRANKIE.

MR. FREEMAN: 'Ere, 'ere, 'ere, Frankie, stop it—you're

getting a big boy now—making all that fuss about a poor innocent beetle.

MRS. FREEMAN: That child's been a bundle of nerves ever since we took him to see *Chang*.

An OFFICIAL *in uniform walks on and taps* MR. FREEMAN *on the shoulder.*

OFFICIAL: Excuse me, this little lad must have a top to 'is bathing dress.

MR. FREEMAN: Why—what for?

OFFICIAL: Corporation's rules.

MRS. FREEMAN *gets up from chair and comes down stage.*

MRS. FREEMAN: Lot of nonsense—the child's under age.

OFFICIAL: Can't 'elp that, madam.

ALICE: 'E 'asn't got a top.

OFFICIAL: The Corporation's very strict about indecent exposure.

MR. FREEMAN: Well, it's coming to something if a child of ten can't enjoy a state of nature without giving a lot of old ladies ideas.

OFFICIAL: England don't 'old with states of nature.

MRS. FREEMAN: 'Ere—'e'd better 'ave my crochet sports jacket. (*Crosses to right. She gives it to* ALICE, *who drapes it round* FRANKIE.) Will that do?

OFFICIAL: Yes—sorry to 'ave troubled you.

He goes off 2 E.L.

MR. FREEMAN: Well, I'm damned!

ALICE: Come on, Frankie.

Takes him off 1 E.R.

MR. FREEMAN: That boy looks effeminate. You going to have a bathe this morning?

MRS. FREEMAN: Not unless you want me to die this afternoon.

MR. FREEMAN: I'm off to 'ave a paddle. (*Crosses to right.*)

MRS. FREEMAN: Mind you take plenty of soda with it!

MR. FREEMAN *is going off and collides with* MADGE

and DORIS *on the way. They are crossing from right to left.*

MR. FREEMAN: Pardon.

DORIS: Granted.

SHE *and* MADGE *stroll across.*

MADGE: Where was I?

DORIS: He was just holding your hand and the band was playing *The Mikado.*

MADGE: Oh, yes—well, dear—I said "Keep your hands to yourself," and he said, "Why?" and I said, "You know why," and he said, "Come off it, Miss High-and-Mighty," and I said, "Don't be saucy," and he bought me some nougat and I didn't get home till two in the morning.

They go off.

MRS. HARRIS (*reading the paper*): Fred!

MR. HARRIS (*who has been sleeping*): 'Allo!

MRS. HARRIS: That murderer's been caught.

MR. HARRIS: Which one?

MRS. HARRIS: Last Tuesday's.

MR. HARRIS: Oh!

MRS. HARRIS: You can go and see the 'ouse where it 'appened. It's quite near 'ere. Mabel went yesterday and said it was lovely—blood all over everything.

MR. HARRIS: Coo! We might take the children this afternoon.

MRS. HARRIS: All right. I'll cut some sandwiches.

Two CHILDREN—GEORGIE *and* VI—*come running in screaming from* 1 E.R. *They go to their mother.*

MR. HARRIS: What's up now?

VI: Georgie hit me with his iron spade.

GEORGIE: No, I never!

VI: Yes, he did!

GEORGIE: No, I never!

MRS. HARRIS: Come 'ere, Georgie—that's the third time you've 'it Vi in two days—I'll teach you!

*She bends him across her knee and smacks him—the
noise is deafening.*

MR. HARRIS: Can't you leave the blighter alone?

MRS. HARRIS: Don't you tell me 'ow to bring up me own
children!

MR. HARRIS: The poor little bloke didn't mean it.

VI: Yes, 'e did.

MR. HARRIS: You shut up ... (*He slaps her. She sets up a
terrible howl.*)

VI (*screaming*): Ow! ow! ow! Father 'it me!

MRS. HARRIS: You great brute, you! (*Getting up and
taking VI in her arms.*

MR. HARRIS: Brute, am I?

MRS. HARRIS: Be quiet, Vi—stop that noise!

MR. HARRIS: I can't stand this—I'm going to get
drunk——

Goes off top E.L.

MRS. HARRIS: That'll be a change——

*A harassed mother—MRS. CLARK—enters pushing a
screaming child in front of her. They get to centre.*

MRS. CLARK: I brought you 'ere to enjoy yourself, and
enjoy yourself you're going to! Now go on—paddle!

*She smacks her hard and—the CHILD goes off scream-
ing. GEORGIE and VI follow 1 E.R.*

*MRS. CLARK sits down exhausted next to MRS. FREE-
MAN right.*

I'll never come to this place again as long as I live.

MRS. FREEMAN: I don't think I shall live long enough to be
able to!

MRS. HARRIS is fanning herself with her paper.

*MRS. JONES, a weary-looking woman, comes on top
E.R. and sits down next to her.*

MRS. JONES: Good morning, Mrs. Harris.

MRS. HARRIS: Good morning.

MRS. JONES: I've just come from the 'ospital. My little
Albert fell off a rock yesterday and cut 'is 'ead open——

They all come down stage.

"MOTHER'S COMPLAINT"

ALL:
>We're all of us mothers,
>We're all of us wives,
>The whole depressing crowd of us.
>With our kind assistance
>The Motherland thrives.
>We hope the nation's proud of us,
>For one dreary fortnight
>In each dreary year
>We bring our obstreperous families here.
>We paddle and bathe while it hails and it rains,
>In spite of anæmia and varicose veins,
>Hey nonny, ho nonny, no, no, no.
>Our lodgings are frowsy,
>Expensive and damp,
>The food is indigestible.
>We sit on the beach
>Till we're tortured with cramp
>And life is quite detestable.
>The children go out with a bucket and spade
>And injure themselves on the asphalt parade.
>There's sand in the porridge and sand in the bed,
>And if this is pleasure, we'd rather be dead.
>Hey nonny, ho nonny, no, no, no!

VI, PHYLLIS *and* GEORGIE *rush on from* 1 *E.R.*

VI: Mum, Mum, Cissie Parker's seen a whale!

MRS. HARRIS: Don't you tell such lies, Violet Harris.

PHYLLIS: It's true, it's true—I saw it too—look there!

>ALICE *and* FRANKIE FREEMAN *rush on.*

ALICE: Mother—Mother—a great big whale!

MRS. FREEMAN: May God forgive you, you wicked little fibber!

> *Several other children rush on screaming, and all the* CHORUS— *"A whale, a whale!" Also grown-ups. Finally the* OFFICIAL *re-enters top E.L. and comes to centre of stage.*

OFFICIAL: 'Ere, 'ere, 'ere—what's all this noise?

MRS. HARRIS: There's a whale—my Vi's seen a whale. Look, there it is!

> *Lots more people rush on; the* OFFICIAL *produces some glasses and looks through them.*

OFFICIAL: That's not a whale—that's Daisy Kipshaw, the Channel swimmer. She gets 'ere regularly every Friday morning from Boulogne.

> *Everybody cheers.*

> *Three* MEN *come on with cameras, and finally* DAISY KIPSHAW—*a very large woman in a bathing suit—comes on from* 1 *E.L. The three* MEN *with cameras take photos of her—one as she turns to pick up her cloak which she has dropped on getting to centre of stage. As she enters all the* CHORUS *take up lines across stage on O.P. side.*

FINALE AND NUMBER FOR DAISY KIPSHAW

She comes centre.

CHORUS:

> Hail, Neptune's daughter,
> > The pride of Finsbury Park,
> > Behold a modest clerk
> Is goddess of the water.
> > Hail, pioneer girl,
> Tho' rain and wind have come,
> You've swum and swum and swum,
> > You really are a dear girl.

DAISY:

> Kind friends, I thank you one and all
>> For your delightful greetings.
> I merely heard my country's call
>> At patriotic meetings.

CHORUS:

>> Just think of that,
>> Just think of that,
>> She got her inspiration at
>>> A patriotic meeting.
>> Oh, tell us more,
>> Oh, tell us more,
>> Oh, tell us what you do it for,
>>> It must be overheating.

DAISY:

> Kind friends, I thank you all again
> And since you ask me to,
>> I will explain.

SONG: "BRITANNIA RULES THE WAVES"

DAISY:

> Like other chaste stenographers
> I simply hate photographers,
>> I also hate publicity.

CHORUS:

> She lives for sheer simplicity!

DAISY:

> For any woman more or less
> A photo in the daily press
>> Is horribly embarrassing.

CHORUS:

> It must be dreadfully harassing.

DAISY:

> The British male

May often fail,
Our faith in sport is shaken,
So English girls awaken
And save the nation's bacon!

Refrain 1

(*Sung by* DAISY *alone first*)

Up, girls, and at 'em,
   And play the game to win.
   The men must all give in
   Before the feminine.
Bowl 'em and bat 'em
   And put them on the run,
   Defeat them every one,
   Old Caspar's work is done.
We'll do our bit till our muscles crack,
We'll put a frill on the Union Jack.
If Russia has planned
To conquer us and
   America misbehaves,
Up, girls, and at 'em,
   Britannia rules the waves!

Business with CHORUS *as arranged.*

Refrain 2

DAISY *and* CHORUS:
   Up, girls, and at 'em,
      And play the game to win.
      The men must all give in
      Before the feminine.
   Bowl 'em and bat 'em,
      And put them on the run,
      Defeat them every one,
      Old Caspar's work is done.

DAISY:

    We'll do our bit till our muscles crack.

CHORUS:

    We'll put a frill on the Union Jack.

DAISY:

    If Russia has planned to conquer us and
       America misbehaves,
    Up, girls, and at 'em,
       Britannia rules the waves.

Refrain 3

(Spoken)

Up, girls, and at 'em,
    Go out and win your spurs,
    For England much prefers
    Applauding amateurs.
Man is an atom,
    So break your silly necks
    In order to annex
    Supremacy of sex.
Valiantly over the world we'll roam,
Husbands must wait till the cows come home.
The men of to-day
Who get in our way
    Are digging their early graves.
Up, girls, and at 'em,
    Britannia rules the waves.

Refrain 4

DAISY *and* CHORUS:

    Up, girls, and at 'em,
       And play the game to win.
       The men must all give in
       Before the feminine.

Bowl 'em and bat 'em
  And put them on the run,
  Defeat them every one,
  Old Caspar's work is done.
We'll do our bit till our muscles crack,
We'll put a frill on the Union Jack.

DAISY:
  Here's to the maid
  Who isn't afraid,
    Who shingles and shoots and shaves.

CHORUS:
  Up, girls, and at 'em!
    Britannia rules the waves!

Business of CHORUS BOYS *getting in her way. They lift her up. As they all drop on stage—*

BLACKOUT

THE LEGEND OF THE LILY OF THE VALLEY

written 1928

When *This Year of Grace!* moved to New York, the leads were played by Noël and Beatrice Lillie, with Noël taking over the roles played in London by Sonnie Hale.

Cochran recalled: "In the comedy bits he was excellent but, as he admitted, he could not take himself seriously in the sentimental songs as a romantic young juvenile ... [he] was particularly good in a mock French sketch with Bea Lillie, called "La Flamme" [Bea Lillie played the part of La Flamme in the 1928 New York production of "Love, Life and Laughter"] and in other character parts; but, curiously enough, he never quite succeeded in one item in which one would have expected him to be better than his London predecessor ... This was in the speech of introduction by a pale young aesthete to the ballet absurdity, *The Legend of the Lily of the Valley*. Some of the words seem so much a travesty by himself of his own style, and the character was so much an exaggerated burlesque of his own manner ... With him it became a parody of a parody and lost some of its point."

CAST

ANNOUNCER	Sonnie Hale
FLANNELETTE	Tilly Losch
BERGAMOT	Lauri Devine
MARQUIS DE POOPINAC	Douglas Byng

FAIRIES: Florita Fey, Marjorie Robertson, Gladys Godby, Marjorie Browne, Nora Olive, Madeline Gibson

FEMALE COURTIERS: Betty Davis, Marie Masters, Nancy Barnett, Nancy Fielder, Isla Bevan, Kathleen Coram

MALE COURTIERS: Arthur Warren, Charles Farey, Edward Coventry, Richard Haydon, Fred Le Roy, Fred Jeffries

FLANNELETTE: Beaded Shaftesbury Avenue evening frock, necklace of ping-pong balls—brown leather aviator's cap, cricket pads and bare feet.

BERGAMOT: American Union two-piece bathing suit, bare legs; boots with spats and an admiral's hat—bow and arrow.

FEMALE COURTIERS: Pink flannel drawers, lace camisoles, Russian boots. The framework of hoop skirts composed of gas piping—head-dress traditional of eighteenth century with dolls' furniture festooned in the hair.

MALE COURTIERS: Jaeger long-legged combinations—football boots—brass-studded leather belts, with small jewelled swords—small gold crowns on elastic.

FAIRIES: Burberry's, bowler hats, long rope wigs reaching to the floor—gossamer wings—pink satin ballet shoes.

MARQUIS DE POOPINAC: Plus-fours—Harlequin shirt with spangles, tight-fitting cap with a celluloid windmill. Bare legs with carpet slippers.

INTRODUCTORY SPEECH

Ladies and gentlemen, as a sop to those of you who are bored and satiated with usual superficialities of light musical entertainments, Mr. Cochran has asked me to announce the production of a short ballet in which beauty, austerity and intellectuality are blended together with that spirit of progressive modernity which we have learned to demand and expect from the striking performances of Diaghilev's Russian Ballet. We live in an age of Revolution in Art and perhaps the most vital and tremendous movement in this revolution is the stern reversion to bare primitive simplicity.

The ballet we are about to present is entitled "The Legend of the Lily of the Valley". The atmosphere is definitely early eighteenth century, French, smacking of gently undulating country life, and then again, smacking ever so slightly of the debauched life at Court. The actual legend is simplicity itself. Flannelette, a dainty shepherdess of the period, is guarding her flock; occasionally she dances to them, but they pay no heed—suddenly from over the hill comes striding Bergamot, a shepherd who loves her. They execute what is technically described as a Pas de Deux, which leaves Flannelette exhausted—Bergamot plays his pipe to her for a moment and then goes sadly away. Flannelette is left dreaming on the grass, during which the love theme is repeated in the orchestra for three flutes and the cophatican. Then six fairies enter and execute with considerable spirit a Pas du Tout—Flannelette starts up amazed—Suddenly the bugle call is heard. The fairies rush off and a coach drives by—stops, and disgorges the evil and depraved Marquis de Poopinac with several Court ladies, whose tinkling false laughter sounds strangely incongruous in such sylvan surroundings. This jarring note is brought out in the music with astounding effect by a muted oboe and six clavabaladalas. The Marquis, observing Flannelette, is immediately inflamed by her beauty. He flirts with her, and she, flattered by his attention, accompanies him to a neighbouring coppice, during which the courtiers dance a stately Pavanne, which is interrupted by the re-entrance of Bergamot, who is searching wildly for Flannelette—he questions each of the courtiers in mime, or dumb show, but they only laugh mockingly—suddenly a cry is heard. Flannelette comes running in with her fichu extremely ruffled, followed by the Marquis. Bergamot attacks him, and the Marquis runs him through with his sword, and the story closes to music of transcendental beauty.

OPEN BLUE WITH MUSIC

RULES OF THREE

written 1928

Poking fun at contemporary playwrights was a staple of revue. Usually the instrument employed resembled a machete. As a playwright himself, Noël used a rapier. No one knew better how easy it was to destroy something that was difficult to create in the first place.

J. M. BARRIE (1860–1937) played a key role in his personal pantheon. "I thought he was a marvellous playwright. Construction. His plays were made of steel." Having made his own tyro mistakes by starting the writing process too soon, he soon became a convert – "I will never again embark on so much as a revue sketch that is not carefully and meticulously constructed beforehand."

Another thing he admired about Barrie was his unashamed use of sentiment. "I cannot go to any play by James Barrie without crying before the curtain goes up . . . I played in *Peter Pan* for two years and there were moments that used to fix me. I used to cry, not on the stage."

He was perfectly well aware, however, that not everyone shared his affection for this aspect of Barrie's work. To many, the sentiment was sentimentality and the Scots humour mawkish – hence the sketch.

If Noël had been asked to trace his dramatic lineage as a playwright, he would certainly have mentioned FREDERICK LONSDALE (1881–1954) as an immediate and important influence. A chronicler of the foibles of high society, Lonsdale was a leading exponent of the theatrical "comedy of manners" with plays such as *On Approval*, *The Last of Mrs. Cheyney* and *Aren't We All?* Seeing a revival of *Mrs. Cheyney* in 1967, Noël noted with some concern that "Freddie Lonsdale's dialogue sounds curiously laboured and dated." If he was concerned that his own work might suffer a similar verdict from posterity, he was worrying unnecessarily.

Of the form and its eventual theatrical fate he had his butler, Crestwell, administer the *coup de grâce* in *Relative Values* (1951): "Comedies of manners swiftly become obsolete when there are no longer any manners."

French farce *à la* FEYDEAU was another of Noël's favourites; he admired the technical virtuosity involved in the staging. In 1958 he even attempted to adapt Feydeau's farce *Occupe-toi d'Amélie* into *Look After Lulu!* with mixed results. Despite his attraction for the form, he was forced to admit – "M. Feydeau is a *very* untidy playwright. He leaves characters about all over the place and disposes of them without explanation." Within the confines of a sketch, however, who notices loose ends, when one is only concerned to hang on to one's trousers?

"Rules of Three" was a sketch in which any one of the "three" could be changed to another subject. The original third was a parody of Edgar Wallace. This was replaced by "Any Civic Repertory Play" (which became "The Order of the Day"), which was replaced in turn by the French Farce. Cast details are not available but, in view of the way the other plays were staged, Douglas Byng, Ann Codrington and Robert Algar were most probably involved.

Showing neither fear nor favour, in another sketch in which he created thumbnail parodies of current popular dramas by the likes of Sean O'Casey and – again – Edgar Wallace, he included . . . "Any Noël Coward play".

"I was particularly anxious to see the effect of this on the first-night audience. The scene consisted merely of a row of people, with an author in the centre, bowing, until at a given moment the leading lady stepped forward and, with tears in her voice, said – 'Ladies and gentlemen, this is the happiest moment of my life!' whereupon she burst into sobs and the entire orchestra and any of us in the audience who happened to be in the know, booed and raspberried with the utmost fervour."

The reference was to the opening night of *Sirocco* (1927) at which the leading lady, Frances Doble, had mistaken the jeers for cheers and stepped forward to deliver her prepared curtain speech in just these words.

"The response of the first-nighters to this was interesting. There was first of all dead silence, then a titter of shocked amazement and then a full-bellied roar of laughter."

CAST

ANNOUNCER   Joan Clarkson

1. SIR JAMES BARRIE:
THE WIFE   Moya Nugent
THE LOVER   Melville Cooper
THE HUSBAND   Fred Groves

2. FREDERICK LONSDALE:
THE WIFE   Jessie Matthews
THE LOVER   Sonnie Hale
THE BUTLER   William Cavanagh
THE HUSBAND   Lance Lister

3. FRENCH FARCE:
JEANNE, *the wife*
JACQUES, *the lover*
JEAN, *the husband*
ANNETTE, *the maid*

ANNOUNCEMENT

ANNOUNCER *comes on from* 1 *E.R. to centre.*

ANNOUNCER: Ladies and gentlemen, there has been a good deal of argument in the papers lately as to the general staleness of the English Drama. There have been bitter complaints to the effect that there *are no new* ideas any more. We now intend to demonstrate to you *our* point of view on the matter, which is that new ideas are not necessary, and that it is only the *treatment* that is important. We propose to show a perfectly commonplace situation as it would be handled by three celebrated dramatists. The situation is the Eternal Triangle. A wife is surprised during a scene with her lover by the unexpected entrance of her husband.

Moves to P.S.

First of all as Sir James Barrie would write it.

Exit 1 *E.L.*

1. SIR JAMES BARRIE

The WIFE *is darning socks by the fire.*

WIFE (*pensively*): Ah me—I often wonder if all the little pink toes of all the little pink babies in the world were counted, how many there would be.

Enter left the LOVER.

LOVER: Jeannie!

WIFE (*rising, comes D.R.C.*): Why have you come?

LOVER: I heard your voice in the wood.

WIFE: You couldna' have heard any such thing, James MacTagget, and it's a great fanciful fool you are.

LOVER: Jeannie!

WIFE: Whisht, man—away with you.

LOVER: I love you, Jeannie. I've loved you since ever I was a bairn no higher than a hiccough!

WIFE: Are you forgetting that I am a wife, James?

LOVER: Nay, I'm remembering it. The wife of a man who doesna' love or understand your ways.

WIFE: Ah, but you're wrong—John's well enough—my ways are not so difficult to grasp—I'm naught but a little shrivelled nut of a woman——

LOVER: You're a pixie to me.

WIFE: Thank you, James—a pixie's a chancy thing to be.

LOVER (*passionately*): I had a mind to be a great poet once, but the fairies made mock of me and I became an insurance agent.

WIFE: A great big brown insurance agent.

LOVER: Behind each of the company's policies I hear your laugh, and a winsome, cuddlesome sort of laugh it is. It seems to say, come away, James MacTagget, and learn how not to grow up. I'll teach you. I'll teach you.

WIFE: I *could* teach you that.

LOVER: Will you?

WIFE: Listen now—do you know how many babies there are in the world?

LOVER: No.

WIFE: Then multiply the answer by seven and you'll make a rainbow.

LOVER: Jeannie—come with me. (*He crushes her to him.*)

WIFE: No, no!

LOVER: Don't send me to the workhouse of might-have-beens.

    Enter the HUSBAND *right.*

HUSBAND: Jeannie!

WIFE: Oh!

HUSBAND: What does this mean?

WIFE (*laughing*): What a solemn face—sit down while I get your tea—you'd better be going, James.

HUSBAND: Tea—I'll not taste your tea.

WIFE: Go, James.

HUSBAND: Stay.

WIFE: Go—what fools men are——

HUSBAND: Stay!

WIFE: Verra well, stay—you great quarrelsome school-boys. If I were the mother of either of you, I'd spank you and put you to bed—come, shake hands now.

LOVER: I'll not shake hands—I love Jeannie, John, and I'll make no bones about it. Good-bye.

He goes out left.

HUSBAND: Is this true?

WIFE: Yes.

HUSBAND: Why did you not go with him?

WIFE (*putting her head on* HUSBAND's *shoulder*): Because it's you I love—you with your great laugh and your great hands and the tenderness in your eye when you see a baby having its bath and the gentleness in your voice when you take me in your arms and call me Mrs. Woodlesome Whatnot.

HUSBAND (*taking her in his arms*): Mrs. Woodlesome Whatnot!

BLACKOUT
CLOSE TABS

ANNOUNCER *comes on* 1 *E.L.*

ANNOUNCER: And now as Frederick Lonsdale would treat it.

Exit 1 *E.L.*

2. FREDERICK LONSDALE

The WIFE *is discovered dancing to a gramophone. The* LOVER *enters left.*

LOVER: Duchesses don't dance as well as they used to.

WIFE: No, my dear, but much more.

LOVER: Where's Johnnie?

WIFE (*stopping the gramophone*): Still in the House of Lords, I think.

LOVER: My God, Jean, you look chic.

WIFE: It isn't difficult to look chic nowadays. One only needs line and lipstick.

LOVER: I saw the Duke of Belgravia at lunch.

WIFE: I thought he was dead.

LOVER: He is, but he won't lie down.

WIFE: Do you think it was quite decent of you to come here?

LOVER: Decency be damned! I love you.

WIFE: As a man loves a woman or as a gentleman loves a gentlewoman?

LOVER: All four.

    The BUTLER *enters with cocktails right.*

WIFE: I've got a new cocktail for you.

LOVER: What's it called?

WIFE: The Debrett Dollop!

LOVER: Do you like being a butler, Finsbury?

BUTLER: Very much, your Grace. We are the only class left with any manners.

LOVER: What about the Upper Ten?

BUTLER: They only have bedside manners.

    He goes out right.

WIFE: I don't know what the lower orders are coming to.

LOVER: You're a silly woman, Jean, with the brains of a louse.

WIFE: Dear James, you're drunk—you must have been lunching with your mother.

LOVER: Nevertheless, I love you.

WIFE (*surrendering herself to him*): Kiss me like you did last Wednesday in the Royal Enclosure at Ascot.

    He kisses her violently.

    The HUSBAND *enters right.*

HUSBAND: My dear Jean—you might have left the door open.

LOVER (*looking up*): Hullo, Johnnie.

HUSBAND: By God, Jimmie, you're an awful swine—is there any cocktail?

WIFE: Not a drain. I love Jimmie, you know.

HUSBAND: Of course I know—everybody knows. It makes a damned good story—I've been dining out on it for weeks.

LOVER: What shall we do about it?

HUSBAND: What is there to do?—I can't divorce her because I have to have a mistress for my father's old place.

WIFE: Don't discuss me so cold-bloodedly—I'm not an electric hare.

LOVER: Well, we'd better go on as we are, I suppose.

HUSBAND: All right. (*Crosses to centre.*) Here's an extra latchkey.

LOVER: Thanks—cheerio!

Exit left.

HUSBAND: Nice fellow.

WIFE: Johnnie, I'm awfully fond of you.

HUSBAND: Why?

WIFE: Because you're a very great gentleman.

HUSBAND: What is a very great gentleman?

WIFE: I don't know. I go to so few theatres.

BLACKOUT
CLOSE TABS

3. FRENCH FARCE

The scene is JEANNE'S *bedroom. This whole episode must be played at lightning speed.*

The telephone rings.

ANNETTE *runs on.*

ANNETTE (*at telephone*): 'Allo—yes, m'sieu—no, m'sieu—yes, m'sieu—no, m'sieu—certainly, m'sieu——

She rushes off.

107

JEANNE *rushes on in highly-coloured pyjamas.*

JEANNE (*at telephone*): Jacques—darling—— yes, angel. No, angel—quickly, quickly—— (*Makes kissing noise.*) Yes, yes—darling, darling—— (*She hangs up telephone.*) Annette—Annette——

ANNETTE *rushes in.*

ANNETTE: Yes, madame.

JEANNE: My peignoir, quickly.

ANNETTE: Yes, madame.

She rushes off.

JEANNE *goes to telephone.*

JEANNE (*at telephone*): Elysée 9468—yes, yes—— No no—— Hallo—— Gaston—is it you?—— Yes—— No, I don't think so—— very well—hurry—— (*She puts telephone down.*)

ANNETTE *rushes in—a bell rings.*

Quickly, Annette—quickly—it is he—answer the door. (*She puts on her peignoir.*)

ANNETTE *rushes off.*

JACQUES *rushes on.* JEANNE *flies into his arms. They kiss passionately.*

JACQUES (*between kisses*): Darling—beloved—angel—precious—saint—divinity——

ANNETTE *rushes on with a pair of pyjamas.*

ANNETTE: Here, m'sieu.

JACQUES *rushes off.*

JEANNE: You can go now, Annette.

ANNETTE: Yes, madame.

There is the sound of the front door slamming.

JEANNE: My God, my husband!

JEAN *rushes on.*

JEAN (*clasping her in his arms*): My darling wife—I have returned from Lyons three days earlier than I expected——

JEANNE: Jean, Jean—how glad I am—— (*She casts an anxious look at the door.*)

JEAN: You seem worried, my angel.

JEANNE: It is the heat—will you go and close the spare room window?

JEAN: Certainly, beloved.

He rushes off left.

JACQUES *rushes on right in pyjamas.*

JACQUES (*clasping her in his arms*): My enchantress——

JEANNE (*pushing him back*): Hide quickly, quickly——

JACQUES: Very well——

He rushes off right.

JEAN *rushes on left.*

JEAN: There is no window in the spare room.

JEANNE: My foolish darling—it was a joke—Run and fetch my handbag for me, it is on the piano.

JEAN: Imperious angel.

He rushes towards right.

JEANNE: No, no—on the piano.

JEAN: How stupid—I'd forgotten the piano was in the bathroom.

He rushes off left.

JACQUES *rushes on right.*

JACQUES (*taking her in his arms*): Wonderful—wonderful—wonderful——

JEANNE: Quick, quick, my husband——

JACQUES *leaps into bed.*

JEAN *rushes on with a pair of shoes.*

JEAN: Here are your shoes. They were in the bureau.

JEANNE: My darling.

JEAN *sees* JACQUES' *hat.*

JEAN (*furiously*): What is this?

JEANNE: It is your mother's. She came here this afternoon.

JEAN: Where is she?

JEANNE (*hysterically*): In there! (*She points right and*—JEAN *rushes off.*

JEANNE *jumps into bed with* JACQUES. ANNETTE *rushes on in pyjamas, looks round and then beckons.*

JEAN *rushes on.*

ANNETTE: It's all right—the coast's clear.
JEAN (*clasping her in his arms*): My darling!

BLACKOUT

LAW AND ORDER

written 1928

Cast

Policewoman Pellet	Douglas Byng
Match-Seller	Betty Shale
Young Girl	Moya Nugent
Young Man	Edward Coventry
Policewoman Wendle	Maisie Gay

The scene is a street in London. This is a cloth painted with park railings and a lamp-post right.

   POLICEWOMAN PELLET *enters from right—advances to centre of stage, bends and straightens herself in traditional fashion and stands left of lamp-post. An* OLD WOMAN, *selling matches, enters from left—walks across and meets* P.W. PELLET.

PELLET: Move on—you're loitering.

OLD WOMAN: I can't move any faster—I've got fallen arches. (*Spits.*)

PELLET: Don't argue, don't argue. You're loitering. Move on. (*Sniffs.*)

   The OLD WOMAN *goes off* 1 E.R.

   PELLET *sniffs and stands still—a* GIRL *enters from right, walks to the middle of the stage—stoops down to tie her shoe lace. A* YOUNG MAN *enters also from right and bumps into her.*

MAN: I beg your pardon.

GIRL: Not at all.

   The MAN *goes off left and—*P.W. WENDLE *strides on* 1 E.L.

WENDLE: Now then, now then——

GIRL: What d'you mean "Now then"?

WENDLE: None of that.

GIRL: None of what?

WENDLE: None of what you were thinking of.

GIRL: How dare you! (*Crosses to left.*)

WENDLE: I've been watching you—flouncing about.

GIRL: Don't you talk to me like that or I shall call a policeman.

   She marches off with her head in the air.

WENDLE: Impertinence!

PELLET (*sympathetically*): They're all alike. The girls of to-day—fast, overdressed, *and* saucy!

WENDLE: I don't know what London's coming to—the higher the buildings the lower the morals.

PELLET: Been in the Force long?

WENDLE: About three months—my husband went to Australia.

PELLET: On business?

WENDLE: No, on purpose.

PELLET: It's the woman who pays, and pays.

BOTH: And pays.

PELLET: Men are all alike.

WENDLE: Only some more than others. I'm not a suspicious woman, but I don't think my husband 'as been entirely faithful to me.

PELLET: Whatever makes you think that?

WENDLE: My last child doesn't resemble him in the least.

PELLET: What you must have gone through.

WENDLE: Bottles and bottles—of aspirin.

PELLET (*producing paper bag*): 'Ave a choc?

WENDLE: Not on duty.

PELLET: Come on—there's no one about.

WENDLE: Well, as long as they 'aven't nut on 'em. (*She takes one.*)

> *They both munch.*
> *There is a loud bang off stage.*

PELLET: What was that?

WENDLE: Only one of them balloon tyres burst.

PELLET: I see the Croydon Ramblers beat the Lyons' Corner House girls last Tuesday.

WENDLE: No stamina in that Lyons lot.

PELLET: Oh, I don't know—Minnie Packer's a lovely centre forward.

WENDLE: She had to leave the field.

PELLET: Why?

WENDLE: Lost 'er bust-bodice in a scrum.

PELLET: Go on!

WENDLE: Lily Burton finished the game—and you know what she is—all hips and hysteria.

PELLET: I wish I'd been there—I 'ad to do extra duty—Vera Pearn got special leave to go to the white sales.

WENDLE: Favouritism.

PELLET: I gave Inspector Rogers a piece of my mind, I can tell you.

WENDLE: She's a mean cat, that Inspector Rogers, if ever there was one.

PELLET: And common!—My dear—do you know she——
They draw closer—PELLET *whispers.*

WENDLE: She *didn't*!

PELLET: She did—right in me face.

WENDLE: What did you do?

PELLET: I saluted and swept out—but I couldn't 'elp crying a bit when I got me 'elmet off. But luckily Sergeant Leggat came in and she lent me 'er puff and we got to talking. She told me all about Jessie Lucas.

WENDLE: What about her?

PELLET: She's in 'ospital.

WENDLE: What—again!

PELLET: No. She was on duty at Victoria Station and got three ribs broken trying to see Adolphe Menjou.

WENDLE: Adolphe Menjou?

PELLET: I love Adolphe Menjou—he's so suave.

WENDLE: He's suave right enough, but I prefer Ronald Colman—he's more bellicose—don't misunderstand, I mean more up and doing. Did you see that film—John Gilbert and Greta Garbo?

PELLET: My dear! After the first kiss I quivered like an aspen.

WENDLE: They oughtn't to do it, you know—it's past a joke. After all, we're only human——
Both bend.

PELLET: Do you remember that *robe de nuit* she wore?

WENDLE: The one with the black chiffon?

PELLET: Yes, I saw the spitting image of it in Swan and Edgar's.

WENDLE: Did you get it?

PELLET (*giggling*): Well, I know it was terribly naughty of me, but I just couldn't resist it.

WENDLE: Is it cut V-shape?—too divine!——

PELLET: Well, dear, I must say I 'ad to alter it a bit——
  Shouts off right.

WENDLE: See your skin through it——

  Their conversation is here lost in a terrible commotion off stage. Shouts and screams of "Murder". A MAN *rushes across the stage clutching a knife, followed by* TWO WOMEN *screaming and another* MAN *brandishing a revolver.* PELLET *and* WENDLE *are so engrossed that they don't see them—when the four people have gone off there is suddenly a loud single scream and a shot.*

PELLET: What was that?

WENDLE: Only another one of those tyres burst.

BLACKOUT

LOVE, LIFE AND LAUGHTER

written 1924

This sketch was first seen in *Charlot's Revue* at the Prince of Wales Theatre in 1924. Herbert was played by Hugh Sinclair, Robert by Morris Harvey, Madame by Nellie Bowman, A Waiter by Leonard Henry and La Flamme was ... Maisie Gay.

It was Noël's tongue-in-cheek *hommage* to the dozens of musical comedies in which the hero finds himself on a foreign strand and mesmerised by some exotic beauty – only to return to the safe arms of the simple girl next door (who will probably turn out to be a princess in disguise).

Cast

HERBERT	Fred Groves
ROBERT	Douglas Byng
A WOMAN	Moya Nugent
MADAME CRAPOTTE	Betty Shale
A WAITER	Melville Cooper
LA FLAMME	Maisie Gay

CUSTOMERS OF "LA CHATTE VIERGE": Ann Codrington, Madge Aubrey, Sheilah Graham, William Cavanagh, Robert Algar, Cecil Stafford

Scene I

Scene: The exterior of "La Chatte Vierge", Paris.
Time: 1890.

    Two elegant Englishmen, Rupert Shufflebotham *and his friend* Herbert, *enter.*

Herbert: This is a very dangerous quarter, Rupert.

Rupert: Nevertheless, it is the place for which we have been searching—see "La Chatte Vierge".

Herbert: Ah, Rupert, sometimes I cannot help but feel that your headstrong impetuosity will one day lead you into a scrape from which you will find it difficult to extricate yourself.

Rupert: Shhh, someone approaches——

    A Woman *slouches across.*

Herbert: Have a care, Rupert, she is a creature of the night.

Rupert: Pauvre petite! These women, Herbert, painted shadows of a great city. Nocturnal butterflies living for an hour and then—pshaw—they are gone.

Herbert: You display too much interest in these unfortunates; it is, after all, merely to see the queen of them all that we are here.

Rupert: She has beckoned me from every nook and cranny of Paris, she has tortured my imagination—I must see her—come—let us enter——

    They go into the café.

Scene II

The scene is a café in Montmartre, "La Chatte Vierge".
Time: Period about 1890.

When the curtain rises several couples are dancing with slightly forced abandon. MADAME CRAPOTTE, *the proprietress, is seated at a high desk.*

After a time two elegant ENGLISHMEN *enter in the costume of the period.* RUPERT *is the more elaborately dressed of the two—he also wears Dundreary whiskers.*

MADAME: Bon soir, monsieur.

RUPERT: So this is La Chatte Vierge.

MADAME: The only one in Paris, monsieur.

RUPERT: Come, Herbert, cast aside your melancholy air and let us order some wine.

They sit down at a table.

HERBERT: You're mad, Rupert. This place has an evil reputation.

RUPERT: A fig for your scruples. Garçon, bring champagne.

WAITER: Bien, monsieur.

The WAITER *goes to the bar, gets champagne and puts it on the table.*

HERBERT: Why have you dragged me here?

RUPERT: You ask me that? You know me, Herbert. I am young, I want life. I have come to see La Flamme.

HERBERT (*anxiously*): Shhhhh ... not so loudly.

RUPERT: I have seen her so often in the distance. Notre Dame, the Louvre, Versailles, the Moulin Rouge, the Morgue.

HERBERT (*gloomily*): She is a bad, bad woman, Rupert.

RUPERT: A bad woman? What of that if she is good company.

HERBERT (*rises*): I for one will be no partner to your crazy scheme.

RUPERT (*rises, and puts his hand on* HERBERT'S *shoulder*): The thought of her sends the blood coursing through my veins like one o'clock.

HERBERT: I shall leave you.

RUPERT: It ill becomes one of the Worcestershire Framptons to show the white feather. (*Sits.*)

HERBERT: Shh ... Here she is.

Enter LA FLAMME.

Everyone stops dancing. She is attired in a glittering sequin dress, an enormous hat and long black gloves. HERBERT *takes his leave of* RUPERT *and—goes out.*

LA FLAMME *after a bold look round seats herself at the table on the opposite side of the stage from* RUPERT *and beckons* MADAME CRAPOTTE *imperiously.*

HERBERT: Hoity toity!

LA FLAMME (*to* MADAME Crapotte): Dîtes moi. Qui est cet homme dégoûtant là?

MADAME: An Englishman—very rich, with estates all over Shropshire.

LA FLAMME (*laughing merrily*): La la la la la! Nom de Gare du Nord—bring me some absinthe.

The WAITER *brings bottle of absinthe. She pours some out—smiles alluringly across at* RUPERT *and raises her glass to him. She then beckons to him and he rises and comes over to her.*

Vous êtes Anglais, my fren'?

RUPERT: Oui, oui, I am.

LA FLAMME: You speak French like a native. Sit down.

RUPERT (*sitting down*): God forgive me—but you are wonderful.

LA FLAMME: They call me La Flamme because I make men mad. What is your name?

RUPERT: Shufflebotham.

LA FLAMME: La la la la la la! But they are droll, these English—Shooflebotaam. Tu es séduisant. We will be 'ow you say?—The good fren's, hein?

RUPERT: You beautiful white devil.

LA FLAMME: Absinthe, more absinthe. (*She pours out absinthe for them both.*) A toast, my little Shooflebotaam. (*Rises.*) I drink to love—the love of a day—the love of a night—the love of an hour. Les fleurs du mal. (*Gives him glass and sits.*)

RUPERT (*in terrible French*): Mon Dieu—comme vous êtes ravisante. You intoxicate me. I want to crush you in my arms—to smother you with red hot kisses from top to toe. Teach me to love.

LA FLAMME: Have a care, bold cabbage.

DUET: LA FLAMME *and* RUPERT

Hark to the music enthralling, appalling,
It dies away, and then——

RUPERT:

Women like you, so inviting, exciting,
Play fast and loose with men.
Fate has smiled on our meeting,
Feel my pulse madly beating.

LA FLAMME:

Call for more drinks,
This is what the world thinks
Is La Vie Parisienne.

BOTH:

Love, life and laughter,
Ta - re - da - re - da comes after.

RUPERT:

Hearts are on fire
With the flame of desire.

LA FLAMME:

Lovers surrender
Regardless of gender.
Away care and sorrow,
Never worry about to-morrow.

BOTH:

We will rule passion's kingdom for a day,
For that's the Bohemian way.

RUPERT:

Teach me the bliss of profanity's kiss
As we sway beneath the moon.

LA FLAMME:

Lovers may sip
Passion's wine from my lip
To a gay romantic tune.

RUPERT:

Cupid's dart has impaled me,
All my breeding has failed me,
I want to smite you and beat you and bite you
And swoon and swoon and swoon.

BOTH:

Love, life and laughter,
To the devil with what comes after.

RUPERT:

Here is my heart, you can tear it apart,
Nothing suffices but decadent vices

BOTH:

And mirth, folly, madness,
Never giving a thought to sadness.

LA FLAMME:

If you told me to die I should obey.

BOTH:

For that's just the Bohemian way.

DANCE

THE ORDER OF THE DAY

written 1928

Originally used as an alternative third sketch in "Rules of Three" and given the title "Any Civic Repertory Play" – presumably because of its physical farcical humour. For years provincial "rep" ran on a diet of bedroom farces with titles like *See How They Run* which tried to follow the French but were left panting – if you'll pardon the pun – far behind.

Strangely, the parody seems to me to evoke something more. Because it is so compressed both in form and language, is it stretching to sense something we would learn to call Pinteresque?

The first Harold Pinter play Noël saw he hated. It was only when he went to *The Caretaker* in 1960 that the penny dropped. "On the face of it, [it] is everything I hate most in the theatre – squalor, repetition, lack of action, etc., – but somehow it seizes hold of you ... *Nothing* happens except that somehow it does. The writing is at moments brilliant and quite unlike anyone else's." He was wrong – it was like Noël Coward's.

The first time the comparison was made it was vaguely shocking but a closer examination is revealing. Both of them specialise in the meaning inherent in the gaps between the words. As the Gertrude Lawrence character says in *Shadow Play*, "Small talk, a lot of small talk with other thoughts going on behind." Pinter might have said as much – in less!

Both writers can convey either humour or menace through the ordinary. Noël's use of place names like Uckfield or the terminally flat Norfolk is echoed by Pinter's repetition of Sidcup, that Mecca the tramp, Davies, must reach to get his "things".

All of which is perhaps to put too great a weight on a one-page sketch to prove this particular thesis but it may help to explain the unerring sense of pacing, placing and structure that, time and again, builds a scene to a point where an ordinary word or everyday phrase like "This haddock's disgusting!" releases the relevant emotion in a way that an impassioned peroration never could.

To misquote Pope – "What oft was thought but ne'er expressed."

CHARACTERS

WIFE
HUSBAND

*The scene is a front cloth of a street with, on the right, three
steps leading to the front door of a neat little house.*

    The HUSBAND *and* WIFE *come out—he is wearing a
business suit, bowler hat, etc., and carrying a little bag.*

WIFE: Well, good-bye, dear.
HUSBAND: Good-bye.
WIFE: Be home in good time for dinner.
HUSBAND: I always am.
WIFE: Have you got everything?
HUSBAND: Yes—everything. Good-bye. (*He kisses her
and—walks off left.*)

    *When she has waved to him she goes into the house and
comes out again with a pail of water and a scrubbing
brush—she kneels down with her back to the audience
and proceeds to scrub the steps—the* HUSBAND *comes on
again left tapping his pockets, obviously having forgotten
something—he sees his wife—smiles—and, meaning to
surprise her, creeps gaily up behind her and gives her a
playful slap.*

WIFE (*without turning her head*): Only half a pint this
morning, Mr. Jones.

BLACKOUT

CHARLES B. COCHRAN'S
1931
REVUE

Presented by Charles B. Cochran at the London Pavilion
Theatre on 19 March 1931 (27 performances)

This revue, advertised as having "Music by Noël Coward and
others", in fact had only five Coward numbers and only one
of them could be considered as a semi-sketch – or the by now
familiar sketch-leading-into-song. The show itself failed to
catch the public mood and – unusually for a Cochran revue –
ran for only a few performances. From the debris, however,
Noël managed to rescue two items that continued to have an
afterlife of their own – the jaunty "Any Little Fish" and
"Half-Caste Woman".

HALF-CASTE WOMAN

written 1930

The song was also sung by torch-singer, Helen Morgan, perched on her trademark grand piano, in *The Ziegfeld Follies of 1931* (Ziegfeld Theatre, New York, 1 July 1931).

CAST

DAISY	Ada-May
A SEAMAN	Henry Mollinson
HIS FRIEND	Edward Coventry
CHINESE WOMAN	Betty Shale
HALF-CASTE WAITER	John Mills
FRUIT SELLER	Miles Arlen
LOLA	Sonia Watson
ZAZA	Molly Molloy

OTHER SEAMEN: Fred Leroy, William Tinkler, Anthony Pélissier

The scene is a cheap café on the waterfront of any Far Eastern port. An electric piano is grinding out some popular tune, and two or three couples are dancing. Flashy tarts, sailors, merchantmen, and one or two more or less drunken habitués in creased tropical suits. There is a Chinese woman behind the bar, and a slovenly WAITER *carrying drinks. He is a half-caste and wears a dirty white coat over black silk trousers.*

When the curtain rises DAISY *is sitting with her back to the audience with her arms round the necks of two* MERCHANTMEN *in rather grimy white duck uniforms.* DAISY *wears a scarlet or yellow evening dress, very décolletée and covered mostly with sequins. She has several bangles jangling on her arms and lots of false pearls. Her hair is black and sleek, and behind her ear she wears a flower, probably a hibiscus, or a camelia.*

There is a lot of noise and drunken laughter. Suddenly, outside in the grey dusk three blasts on a ship's siren are heard. The men disentangle themselves from DAISY, *the* WAITER *brings them the bill, which one of them pays. Four or five people go out into the street. The old* CHINESE WOMAN *rounds the rest of them up until the café is empty except for* DAISY *and the* WAITER. *He staggers off through a bead curtain doorway behind the bar, carrying a tray of glasses. The* OLD WOMAN *shuts the door and locks it. Outside on the waterfront it is getting lighter, a long way off down the street can be heard the intermittent wailing of some Eastern reed instrument.* DAISY *gets up and goes over to the bar, pours herself out a drink and leans there wearily, her face is grey and tired. Suddenly there comes a rapping at the window. The* OLD WOMAN *looks up and sees one of the* MERCHANTMEN *signing to be let in. She shakes her head.* DAISY *pushes her out of the way and unlocks the door. The* YOUNG MAN *comes in.*

MAN: I left my hat.

DAISY (*listlessly*): It's there, under the table.

MAN: Thanks. (*He picks it up.*) It's been a swell evening.

DAISY: Has it?

MAN: Haven't you enjoyed it?

DAISY: Like hell I have.

MAN: I've got to get back to the ship now.

DAISY: That's all right with me.

MAN: You were different a little while ago; don't you like me any more?

DAISY: I'm crazy about you, baby; you've just changed everything with your bright trusting blue eyes. Pardon me for yawning.

MAN: Oh, I see. (*He hesitates.*) I'm sorry—(*He turns to go.*) Good night.

DAISY: Why did you come back?

MAN (*sullenly*): To get my hat.

DAISY: That all?

MAN: Yes. Good night.

DAISY (*suddenly clutching his arm*): Here, here's something to be going on with. (*She kisses him almost fiercely on the mouth.*)

MAN: What did you do that for?

DAISY: Don't you know?

MAN: Daisy—listen—I——

DAISY (*interrupting*): Come back again some day, but don't leave it too long.

> *The ship's siren gives another loud blast.*

Go on—hurry—— (*She pushes him towards the door.*)

MAN (*taking her into his arms and kissing her tenderly*): Good-bye, old girl.

DAISY (*as he goes*): Give my love to the world.

> *She goes wearily back to the bar.*

"Half-caste Woman"

Verse

Drink a bit, laugh a bit, love a bit more,
I can supply your need.
Think a bit, chaff a bit. What's it all for?
That's my Eurasian creed.
Sailors with sentimental hearts who love and sail away,
When the Dawn is grey,
Look at me and say

Refrain

Half-caste woman,
Living a life apart,
Where did your story begin?
Half-caste woman,
Have you a secret heart
Waiting for someone to win?
Were you born of some queer magic
In your shimmering gown?
Is there something strange and tragic
Deep, deep down?
Half-caste woman,
What are your slanting eyes
Waiting and hoping to see?
Scanning the far horizon
Wondering what the end will be.

Interlude

Down along the river
The sky is a-quiver,
For Dawn is beginning to break.
Hear the sirens wailing,
Some big ship is sailing,
And losing my dreams in its wake.

Why should I remember the things that are past,
Moments so swiftly gone?
Why worry, for the Lord knows Time goes on.
Go to bed in daylight,
Try to sleep in vain.
Get up in the evening,
Work begins again.
Tinker, tailor, soldier sailor, rich man, poor man, beggar
    man, thief,
Questioning the same refrain.

Repeat Refrain

THE THIRD LITTLE SHOW

Presented by Dwight Deer Wiman at the Music Box Theatre, New York, on 1 June 1931 (136 performances)

As the name would suggest, this was the third in a series of revues staged at the Music Box. This particular production has a claim to fame for giving the opportunity for Beatrice Lillie to introduce "Mad Dogs and Englishmen" for the first time on any stage. For its English debut a year later in *Words and Music* it was integrated into a more elaborate number sung by the Reverend Inigo Banks (Romney Brent), which included another song, "Planters' Wives".

The only other Coward item in the New York revue was "Cat's Cradle".

CAT'S CRADLE

written 1928

The sketch was written for two women but in the New York production it was played by a man and a woman. When it was included in the London revue, *All Clear* (1939), it was performed as published but with Miss Lilian Mawdsley played by a man (Bobby Howes).

CHARACTERS

MISS EVA TASSEL	Beatrice Lillie
MISS LILIAN MAWDSLEY	Ernest Truex

The scene is the back view of two suburban villas. The two small gardens are separated by a low brick wall. At the back of each are french windows leading into the respective drawing-rooms—both gardens are very neat.

When the curtain rises it is about 8.30 on a summer evening. MISS MAWDSLEY *appears at her french windows carrying a saucer of milk—she is dressed rather austerely in a blouse and skirt—she wears pince-nez, and her hair is done rather high on her head.*

MISS MAWDSLEY (*calling*): Minnie—Minnie—Min, Min, Min, Min, Min—come here, you bad cat. (*She puts the saucer of milk down on the step and retires indoors.*)

> MISS TASSEL *comes out of her house—she is elaborately dressed in a violet-coloured tea-gown—her hair is fair and shingled, she is wearing gauntlet gardening gloves and carries a cigarette in a long holder in one hand and a small green watering-can in the other. She looks cautiously over the wall into* MISS MAWDSLEY'S *garden, and seeing no one there, proceeds to water her plants— humming a little tune as she does so.* MISS MAWDSLEY *reappears at the french windows and comes out into the garden.* MISS TASSEL *sees her, but pretends not to, and continues to hum nonchalantly.*

MISS MAWDSLEY: Good evening, Miss Tassel.

MISS TASSEL (*affectedly*): Oh dear—what a fright you gave me.

MISS MAWDSLEY: I'm sure I'm very sorry.

MISS TASSEL: Oh, not at all. I've been terribly nervy ever since my last operation.

MISS MAWDSLEY: It's a fine night.

MISS TASSEL: Quaite, quaite, perfect——

MISS MAWDSLEY: We shall have a full moon.

MISS TASSEL: Lovely—too lovely. Whenever I see a full moon I *do* believe in fairies—don't you?

MISS MAWDSLEY: Well, to be frank, Miss Tassel, I don't.

MISS TASSEL: Neither do I really—I just like pretending—I live in a world of my own, you know.

MISS MAWDSLEY: I suppose you 'aven't seen my Minnie anywhere, 'ave you?

MISS TASSEL: Your what, Miss Mawdsley?

MISS MAWDSLEY: My Minnie—my cat. I thought you might have noticed her in your world—she doesn't seem to be in mine.

MISS TASSEL: No—I fear—I haven't.

MISS MAWDSLEY: She's mousing, sure as fate. Minnie—Min, Min, Min, Min—I can't bear 'er to be out too late—you never know what might happen.

MISS TASSEL: Quaite.

MISS MAWDSLEY: How are your nasturtiums?

MISS TASSEL: Quaite extraordinary—they grow so absurdly quickly. I feel just like Jack and the Beanstalk. (*She laughs affectedly.*)

MISS MAWDSLEY: Something seems to have gone wrong with mine—look!

MISS TASSEL (*craning over the wall*): My deah—how dreadful! What's that black thing?

MISS MAWDSLEY (*flicking it away*): Only a bootlace.

MISS TASSEL: I thought it was a great black worm.

MISS MAWDSLEY: I can't 'elp feeling Minnie's been up to a bit of no good with my forget-me-nots—they were as right as rain yesterday, and look at 'em now.

MISS TASSEL (*peering*): Are those forget-me-nots?

MISS MAWDSLEY: What did you think they were, starfish?

MISS TASSEL: The light's so bad—it's difficult to see——

MISS MAWDSLEY: I'm afraid Minnie's been rolling about on them—she dearly loves to play, you know.

MISS TASSEL: Such a pretty cat.

MISS MAWDSLEY: Very nice markings and intelligent. Well when I say she's human I'm underrating her.

MISS TASSEL: Fancy!

MISS MAWDSLEY: Only the other day—you would 'ave laughed—oh dear, oh dear. (*She laughs.*)

MISS TASSEL: What happened?

MISS MAWDSLEY: Well, you know that young couple from number fourteen? They popped in last Sunday evening quite unexpected. Well, it was Vera's evening out and I didn't know what to do, but you know you can't be inhospitable, so I said stay to supper if you don't mind taking pot luck—I knew there was some cold mutton over from Saturday and a half a blancmange and some prunes—so we all 'ad the mutton—Vera'd left the table laid before she went—and then I said, "Excuse me a moment," and down I went to the kitchen and there on the floor under the sink was a glass dish with only one prune in it—you could 'ave knocked me down with a feather—I looked under the table and there was Minnie washing herself. "Minnie," I said—"Minnie, you bad cat, what 'ave you done with them pruins?" She never looked up, so again I said very sternly, "Minnie, what 'ave you done with them pruins?" My dear, would you believe it, she gave me one look and walked straight out of the kitchen. I 'adn't the 'eart to scold her—she makes believe they're mice, you know!

MISS TASSEL: Charming; quaite, quaite charming. As a matter of fact, Miss Mawdsley, I have for a long time been wishing to discuss a certain subject with you.

MISS MAWDSLEY: How d'you mean?

MISS TASSEL: Well, it's rather delicate. I hardly know where to begin.

MISS MAWDSLEY: If you're alluding to our slight upset of last week, Miss Tassel, as I told you at the time it was nobody's fault. Vera took off the lid of the dustbin and whatever you found in your rockery must have blown there.

MISS TASSEL: Not at all—all that is forgiven and forgotten.

This is something quite different—something much nearer my heart—it's about my Walter.

MISS MAWDSLEY: What's 'e been up to?

MISS TASSEL: He hasn't been up to anything—that's just the trouble.

MISS MAWDSLEY: In what way?

MISS TASSEL: Well, we're both women of the world, I trust.

MISS MAWDSLEY: Yes—go on.

MISS TASSEL: It's wiser to speak frankly.

MISS MAWDSLEY: By hall means.

MISS TASSEL: Well, Walter's getting a big cat now, and we feel, both my sister and I, that it's haigh time he—er—er—became—er—intimate with some other cat of his own station.

MISS MAWDSLEY: Didn't you 'ave him arranged?

MISS TASSEL: No—I'm afraid not.

MISS MAWDSLEY: You always ought to 'ave tom cats arranged, you know—it makes 'em so much more companionable.

MISS TASSEL: I never believe in tampering with nature.

MISS MAWDSLEY: Well, what can I do for you?

MISS TASSEL: Well, I thought him and your Minnie, for instance.

MISS MAWDSLEY (outraged): My Minnie!

MISS TASSEL: Well, why not?

MISS MAWDSLEY: I fear you don't understand, Minnie's not that kind of cat at all.

MISS TASSEL: How do you know?

MISS MAWDSLEY: She's led a very sheltered life.

MISS TASSEL: But surely——

MISS MAWDSLEY: I'm afraid I couldn't allow it.

MISS TASSEL: Aren't you being just the tayniest bit selfish?

MISS MAWDSLEY: In what way?

MISS TASSEL: Well, you know life's life all the world over, and you can't escape from it. You're standing in the way of Minnie's happiness.

MISS MAWDSLEY: Happiness!—Oh, Miss Tassel—'Ow can

you? If I thought Minnie 'arboured such ideas after 'er life 'ere with me I'd never forgive meself.

MISS TASSEL: Facts are facts, you know. I've seen your Minnie walking up and down with ever such a wistful look in her eye.

MISS MAWDSLEY: I don't know what to say—I don't really—I feel quite strange.

MISS TASSEL (*grandly*): Of course in the circles I move in— the facts of life are discussed quaite quaite openly—False modesty is so—er—middle class, don't you think?

MISS MAWDSLEY: False modesty's one thing, Miss Tassel, and loose thinking's another.

MISS TASSEL: I beg your pardon.

MISS MAWDSLEY: Granted as soon as asked.

MISS TASSEL: Are you insinuating——

MISS MAWDSLEY: I'm insinuating nothing, Miss Tassel— but Minnie is not as other cats—as I said before, her life has been very secluded—I merely don't care to picture her in any—er—peculiar situation.

MISS TASSEL: Well, I only hope she won't lose her fur as she gets older.

MISS MAWDSLEY: Lose 'er fur? What do you mean?

MISS TASSEL: If you had read as much as I have, Miss Mawdsley, you would realise that repression is a very bad thing.

MISS MAWDSLEY: Minnie's as 'ealthy a cat as you'd meet in a day's march.

MISS TASSEL: At present perhaps—but if in your narrow-mindedness you refuse to allow her to fulfil her natural destiny——

MISS MAWDSLEY: And what if I don't consider your Walter to be Minnie's natural destiny?

MISS TASSEL: That, Miss Mawdsley, is what the French would call un autre pair de souliers!

MISS MAWDSLEY: I've no wish to quarrel with you, Miss Tassel, but I must say you've surprised me.

MISS TASSEL (*laughing*): Surprised you! My poor Miss Mawdsley—surprised you—that's very funny.

MISS MAWDSLEY: Funny I may be—but mark my words, all these modern discussions of everything only lead to immorality—you've only got to read the papers to see that.

MISS TASSEL: That's apparently all you do read, Miss Mawdsley.

MISS MAWDSLEY (*stiffly*): Good night.

　　MISS MAWDSLEY *goes towards her house.*

MISS TASSEL: Miss Mawdsley?

MISS MAWDSLEY (*turning*): Yes?

MISS TASSEL: I fear that perhaps we have both been a trifle hasty.

MISS MAWDSLEY: That's true.

MISS TASSEL: If I said anything to offend you, I can only say I'm sorry.

MISS MAWDSLEY (*returning*): Well, of course, if you put it like that, I'm sure—I——

MISS TASSEL: I was wondering if you'd care for a cutting from my Dorothy Perkins——

MISS MAWDSLEY: You're very kind.

MISS TASSEL: I'll send it over to-morrow.

MISS MAWDSLEY (*after a slight pause*): Where is your Walter now?

MISS TASSEL: He's indoors asleep.

MISS MAWDSLEY: There's no doubt about it, 'e's a fine cat.

MISS TASSEL: It's very sweet of you to say so.

MISS MAWDSLEY: I was comparing 'im in my mind the other day with that tabby of Mrs. Pedworth's.

MISS TASSEL: Mangy brute.

MISS MAWDSLEY: Horrible cat—he's always coming sniffing round 'ere after Minnie—but fortunately she keeps 'erself to 'erself.

MISS TASSEL: Are you still definitely opposed to my little plan?

MISS MAWDSLEY: Well, I don't quite know—you see——

MISS TASSEL: You don't think that if I let Walter out to-night—and if you—er—allowed Minnie to walk in the garden by herself, that, er, what with the moon and everything——

MISS MAWDSLEY: Perhaps—it would be rather romantic in a sort of way.

MISS TASSEL: Then shall we consider that as settled.

MISS MAWDSLEY: Yes.

MISS TASSEL: About ten o'clock.

MISS MAWDSLEY: That's rather late.

> *Suddenly there is a dreadful caterwauling off stage left.* MISS MAWDSLEY *gives a cry and goes hurriedly off. She returns in a moment carrying* MINNIE, *a large tabby cat, in her arms; she walks straight into the house.*

(*Grimly over her shoulder.*) Too late!

BLACKOUT

WORDS AND MUSIC

Presented by Charles B. Cochran at the Adelphi Theatre, London, on 16 September 1932 (164 performances)

Book, lyrics and music by Noël Coward
Produced by Noël Coward

This was to be the last revue Coward and Cochran did together. The balance had now changed completely and it was Noël, fresh from the success of *Cavalcade* (1931), who could dictate terms. This he proceeded to do. Not only were the words and music all his but he had had his favourite designer, Gladys Calthrop, mock up scene and costume designs and he even provided Cochran with a running order.

Cochran's instincts about the form were by this time well developed. "The essence of revue," he once said, "is variety, rapidity, change of mood and contrast of line and colour." He also believed in the blending of talents because "homogeneity can lead to monotony". And yet here was one man doing literally everything.

Despite his misgivings, the impresario went ahead – and was proved largely right. Despite its many high spots, *Words and Music* did only moderate business at the box office. None the less, those who liked it liked it a lot. J. T. Grein in the *Sketch* wrote that Noël had rehabilitated revue as a form of dramatic art. The show, he felt, "surveys and satirises actualities with pungent humour and playful music. To the valiant sapper, which is Mr. Noël Coward, nothing is sacred, and so he goes hell-for-leather for all manner of crazes, with side-blows at the elder and wiser, who are as dense as the young generation are 'bright' in the maniacal sense of modernity. The whole merry affair was a feast of wit, wisdom and mockery, charmingly assembled in a picturesque frame."

CHILDREN'S HOUR

From a ridiculously early age Noël seems to have been concerned with the next generation pursuing him along his precocious path. Songs like "Poor Little Rich Girl" and "Dance, Little Lady" were his version of social commentary, as he depicted twenties flaming youth burning the candle at both ends. By *Words and Music* he was convinced that

> There's a Younger Generation
> Knock knock knocking at the door.

And once the door was inevitably opened, out would go its predecessors ...

> Children of the Ritz,
> Children of the Ritz,
> Vaguely debonair.
> Only half aware
> That all we've counted on is breaking into bits.

The prematurely sophisticated child of this new generation was most certainly the father (or mother) of the man or woman who was nominally raising it. Heaven knew how much worse the situation was than one imagined.

> Where we'll end up
> Nobody can tell
> So pardon the phrase
> We mean to be raising Hell!

CAST

1ST MAMMA	Ann Codrington
2ND MAMMA	Naomi Waters
LILLI	Steffi Duna
JANE	Doris Hare
BOBBY	John Mills

The scene is a nursery.

LILLI, JANE *and* BOBBY *are demurely playing with their toys, which consist of a rocking-horse, a doll's house, a clockwork train, etc. The two* MAMMAS *are watching them complacently.*

1ST MAMMA: They seem to be getting along splendidly.

2ND MAMMA: It is more than good that my Lilli should have playmates of her own age. At home in Vienna her little friends are so formal, so *comme il faut*. Here everything is more free and gay.

1ST MAMMA: I'm afraid that my two are terrible little tomboys sometimes, they play the naughtiest practical jokes, but I always say that it does children no harm to run wild occasionally.

2ND MAMMA: You English are so sensible. It is *wunderbar*.

1ST MAMMA: I think we can leave them now, don't you, so that they can really get to know one another?

2ND MAMMA: Certainly. Be good, my Lilli.

LILLI: Yes, Mamma.

1ST MAMMA: Show Lilli your doll's house, Jane, and let her play with Laura. (To 2ND MAMMA.) That's her best doll, you know. I always encourage them to be unselfish.

JANE: Yes, Mamma.

1ST MAMMA: Don't make too much noise.

BOBBY: No, Mamma.

The TWO MOTHERS *go out.*

The THREE CHILDREN *look at each other.*

JANE (*to* LILLI): Is it true about your friends in Vienna being so formal?

LILLI: Quite true. Most of them are damned little prigs.

BOBBY: Environment, I expect, it's all a question of environment.

JANE: We're better off here I think on the whole, we keep

our parents in ignorance of the facts of life until the last possible moment.

LILLI (*laughing*): You English are so sensible. It's *wunderbar*.

BOBBY: I think the moment has come for you to show Lilli your doll's house, Jane.

JANE: It's rather amusing really, we got the idea from the Shaneborough children, they had theirs done when their mother was in Carlsbad.

She opens the doll's house and displays a perfectly fitted little cocktail bar.

LILLI: Absolutely charming—(*Examining it.*)—and a little machine for making ice as well.

BOBBY: We keep all the extras such as olives and salted almonds in a little drawer in the rocking-horse's behind. (*He demonstrates this.*)

JANE: Chic, don't you think?

LILLI: Quite, quite marvellous. I shall write to Fritzi and tell her all about it.

JANE: Mix us a drink, Bobby. Who's Fritzi?

LILLI: A friend of mine in Vienna, she's a bit *passé* now, over fifteen, but she gives very gay parties.

BOBBY: Martini?

JANE: Yes, with a dash.

BOBBY *proceeds to mix a cocktail.*

LILLI: And not too sweet.

JANE: Cigarette?

LILLI: I'll smoke my own if you don't mind—your English cigarettes play hell with my throat.

She produces a small cigarette case which is hanging from a little gold chain inside her dress.

BOBBY (*over his shoulder*): It's all a question of habit.

JANE: How is child life on the whole in Central Europe?

LILLI: We've been going through rather a bad suicide phase during the last year, all these stupid sex obsessions, you know.

JANE: It's high time people stopped making such a ridiculous fuss about sex—after all, what *can* it matter?

LILLI: Too much introspection, that's the trouble really, far too much introspection.

BOBBY: Freud started it of course, all that absurd dream nonsense. (*He hands them cocktails.*) Here, try these.

LILLI (*sipping one*): Very good.

JANE: A shade too much lemon, I think.

BOBBY: The basis of most of the unrest nowadays is just simply lack of courage.

LILLI: Very true.

BOBBY: Nobody seems to have the guts to look at themselves as they really are.

JANE: Or at Life as it really is.

BOBBY: After all, we only have so many years and then phtt!

LILLI (*smiling*): Why not enjoy them?

BOBBY: Exactly.

JANE: Live every moment for what it's worth. Take every risk, every chance, live dangerously.

TRIO: "LET'S LIVE DANGEROUSLY"

Verse

Life won't fool us
Because we're out to lick it
We've got its ticket
And we'll kick it
In the pants
Fate will never catch us asleep
We'll be ready to leap
When there's the slightest chance
Life won't rule us
Determined to subdue it
We'll give the raspberry to it

Do it in the eye
We believe in following through
All we're ready to do
Or die

Refrain 1

Let's live dangerously dangerously dangerously
Let's grab every opportunity we can
Let's swill
Each pill
Destiny has in store
Absorbing life at every pore
We'll scream and yell for more
Let's live turbulently turbulently turbulently
Let's add something to the history of man
Come what may
We'll be spectacular
And go "Hey Hey"
In the vernacular
And so until we break beneath the strain
In various ways
We're going to be raising Cain.

Refrain 2

Let's live dangerously dangerously dangerously
Let's all glory in the bludgeonings of chance
Let's win
Out in
Spite of the angry crowd
And if the simile's allowed
Be bloody but unbowed
Let's live boisterously boisterously roisterously
Let's lead moralists the devil of a dance
Let's succumb
Completely to temptation

Probe and plumb
To find a new sensation
Where we'll end up
Nobody can tell
So pardon the phrase
We mean to be raising Hell!

JOURNEY'S END
A MUSICAL VERSION OF "JOURNEY'S END"
AS PRODUCED BY ERIK CHARELL

(with acknowledgements to Erik Charell and apologies to R. C. Sherriff)

Early 1930 saw Noël and his frequent travelling companion, Jeffrey Amherst in the Far East. The exotic sights and sounds clearly proved inspirational, for it was on this trip that he wrote "Mad Dogs and Englishmen" (while travelling by car through Indo-China) and the idea for his best-known play came to him in a hotel bedroom in Tokyo (". . . the moment I switched out the lights, Gertie appeared in a white Molyneux dress on a terrace in the South of France and refused to go again until four a.m. by which time *Private Lives*, title and all, had constructed itself").

All of his creative efforts, however, were not equally successful. In Singapore Amherst was laid up with dysentry and Noël was left to kill time. His "first and principal distraction" was an English touring company called The Quaints.

One of the plays in their "almost shockingly varied" repertory was *Journey's End*, R. C. Sherriff's famous anti-war play. Over the weeks of enforced idleness Noël got to know the troupe and allowed himself to be persuaded to play Stanhope for three performances. "The élite of Singapore assembled in white ducks and flowered chiffons and politely watched me take a fine part in a fine play and throw it into the alley ... Bob Sherriff's lines remained, on the whole, intact, although I spoke the majority of them with such over-emphasis that it might have been better if they hadn't." The redeeming factor, he felt, was John Mills as Raleigh, who gave "the finest performance I have ever seen given of the part".

By way of reparation Mills subsequently appeared in several Coward shows and films, including *Cavalcade* and *Words and Music*. And, as a further form of catharsis, in the revue Noël included an extended sketch-with-music version of *Journey's End* – although precisely how he felt this would make amends to Sherriff for his earlier transgression is not immediately clear.

Erik Charell – whose style Coward parodied here – was a director with the German film company, UFA (Universum-Film-Aktiengesellschaft). His Teutonic touch was not known to be of the lightest.

CAST

ANNOUNCER	Ivy St. Helier
MARIE FRANÇOISE	Rita Lyle
STANHOPE	Romney Brent
TROTTER	Kenneth Ware
RALEIGH	Steffi Duna
FROU-FROU	Joyce Barbour
HARRY HAPPY	John Mills
THE GENERAL	Gerald Nodin
THE EMPEROR	Bill Harn

PEASANTS: Moya Nugent, Phyllis Harding, Betty Hare, Effie Atherton, Eileen Moore, Eileen Clifton

TYPISTS: Doris Hare, Ann Codrington, Verena Shaxon, Nora Howard, Millie Sim, Joy Spring

STAFF OFFICERS: Leslie Roberts, Cyril Butcher, Tony Hulley, Jack Beaumont, Tom Rees, Edward Underdown, James Seacombe, Frank Evans

SENORITAS: Elizabeth Corcoran, Thea Camacho, Naomi Waters, Elizabeth Jenns, Betty Wedgewood, Dorothy Cooper

GERMAN PRISONERS: Clifford Seagrave, Cyril Wells, Peter Crawford, Jimmy Carney, Kenneth Carten, Eddie Latimer, Edward Britten, Warren Dalmayne

NUNS: Eileen Clifton, Phyllis Harding, Betty Hare, Moya Nugent

ANNOUNCEMENT

Ladies and Gentlemen
Forgive my strange appearance
Our kindly author has
With splendid perseverance
Worked without stint for your enjoyment
And in this age of un-employment
He decided on a plan
To utilise as many aliens as he can
For, like Sir Oswald Stoll
He feels an obligation
To do his level best
To help the German Nation
And if Charell would condescend
To make a spectacle of *Journey's End*
It is our author's little scheme
To show this strange "Teutonic Dream"!

The first scene is a transparent painted curtain representing a French village. From the back of the theatre and down the centre gangway comes MARIE FRANÇOISE *in national peasant costume singing a yodelling song, followed by six show-girls also in elaborate national costume carrying large baskets. They clamber up on to the stage by means of two small rostrums on either side of the proscenium and exit,* MARIE FRANÇOISE *last, still yodelling. The interior of the dug-out gradually becomes apparent through the transparent curtain, which finally rises.* STANHOPE *is discovered seated at a table upon which is a lace table-cloth, a silver bowl of fruit, a bottle of champagne and a glass, and an elaborate silver candelabra.*

STANHOPE (*in a thick Spanish accent*): Three years of this Hell. Will it never end? God! I am tired. Only wine can keep me going. God! I am tired, tired, tired! (*He drinks a glass of champagne.*)

> *Enter* TROTTER.

TROTTER: Lieutenant Raleigh, Sir.

STANHOPE: Leave me alone. We don't want any more snivelling subalterns. (*His voice rises to an hysterical scream.*) Leave me alone, I tell you! Leave me alone!

TROTTER: Lieutenant Raleigh, sir.

> TROTTER *goes out right.*

> *Enter* RALEIGH *attired in a military overcoat and a tin hat.* STANHOPE *starts to his feet.*

STANHOPE: You!

RALEIGH: None other.

STANHOPE: Why did you come! Why did you not stay in your so beautiful England where the grass is so green and there is peace, far away from this so terrible war?

RALEIGH: I came to be near you, Mein Klein Pupchen.

> *She tears off her overcoat disclosing an evening dress made of khaki sequins. She sings a dashing song, "Klein Pupchen", in course of which she steps out of the scene. The dug-out fades behind her. Two sets of trees (ground rows) are pushed on, one from each side of the stage, also two sign-posts with "Herren" on one and "Damen" on the other. A tank is pushed on from the prompt side (flat) which disgorges twelve chorus girls, also dressed in khaki sequins and wearing tin hats. The tank is pushed off again and at the end of the number* RALEIGH *and all the girls exit prompt side. As they go off a movable platform slides on O.P. side, upon which are six small narrow tables with a Diamond typewriter on each, six fantastically dressed typists with sequin eye-shades and cuffs, and, standing behind them, six staff officers. The officers dictate to music for a few seconds and then the platform slides back again, at the same moment as the trees are pushed off,*

disclosing the dug-out again. STANHOPE *is still sitting at the table.*

STANHOPE: Three years of Hell! Will it never end? God! I am tired. Only wine can keep me going. Wine and memories.

He produces a guitar from under the table, covered in American cloth with probably a few more sequins on it, and sings a Spanish serenade, during which six beautiful Senoritas appear in elaborately stylised Spanish costume with mantillas, and dance round him, clicking castanets. They exit and TROTTER *re-enters.*

TROTTER: The German prisoners, sir.

STANHOPE (*hysterically*): Leave me alone! Leave me alone, I tell you! I don't want any German prisoners. Leave me alone!

TROTTER (*inexorably*): The German prisoners, sir.

Six German prisoners enter laughing merrily, in national costume. They execute a violent "slapping" dance interspersed with loud whoops of pleasure, in course of which the dug-out fades behind them and the trees are pushed on again. This time "Hommes" and "Dames" is painted on the sign-posts. As the German boys exit prompt side, the movable platform slides on again from O.P. identically as before, and slides off again. A gondola is pushed on from the prompt side out of which step FROU-FROU *and* HARRY HAPPY. HARRY *is a typical low comedian in comic Tyrolean costume, and* FROU-FROU *is the "cute" variety of soubrette, with very large bows on her shoes and a very small hat. They sing a duet called "A Gondola on the Somme", during which six saucily dressed nuns appear in a spotlight O.P. side and sing in harmony. At the end of the number they all exit, the trees disappear, and once more* STANHOPE *is discovered sitting in the dug-out.*

STANHOPE: Three years of Hell! Will it never end? God! I am tired. Only wine can keep me going. God! I am tired, tired, tired!

TROTTER *enters.*

TROTTER: The General to see you, sir.

STANHOPE (*frantically*): Leave me alone! Leave me alone, I tell you! I don't want the General. Leave me alone!

TROTTER: The General to see you, sir.

> TROTTER *goes out right.*
>
> *The* GENERAL *enters and goes straight into a spirited number, "Love and War". He steps out of the dug-out which fades away. The movable platform slides on again from the O.P. side. The trees also reappear, this time with "Caballeros" and "Senoras" on the sign-posts.* TROTTER *and* RALEIGH *come on with a table (painted flat), also* FROU-FROU *and* HARRY *with another one. All the chorus rush down from the back of the theatre, also with small painted tables which they plant in the aisles singing madly. At the end of the number thay all disappear and once more the dug-out is disclosed.*

STANHOPE: Three years of this Hell—

> TROTTER *enters.*

TROTTER (*interrupting him*): The attack, sir!

> *The scene fades, there is a distant booming of guns. The trees come on again, this time there is Chinese writing on the sign-posts. A small boy in a surplice walks across the stage whistling. Four chorus rush across shouting "The Emperor!" "The Emperor!" The movable platform slides on, conveying, in addition to the conference,* MARIE FRANÇOISE *in still more elaborate national costume. At the same moment an illuminated dreadnought is pushed on from the prompt side, from which steps the* KAISER.

MARIE (*curtsying low*): Sire.

KAISER (*in a strong Scotch accent*): My child!

MARIE: I am unhappy, sire.

KAISER: Happiness is ever-fleeting. Journeys end in lovers meeting.

MARIE (*again curtsying*): Oh, sire.

> *She is whisked off backwards on the movable platform while the* KAISER *retires to his dreadnought. Suddenly*

from everywhere voices are heard shouting "Stanhope!"
"The attack!" "Stanhope!" "The attack!" The trees go
away, and through the transparent curtain which has
been used for the KAISER'S *scene, the big attack is seen to*
be in progress. The transparent curtain rises as the stage
begins to revolve. In the centre of the revolve is a small
hillock with a ruined village on it. Below this, the stage is
divided into four sections by illuminated barbed-wire
entanglements, over which the chorus, representing the
Germans and the British respectively, are leaping gaily
and pelting each other with coloured-paper streamers. All
the principals make a grand chain up and down the front
of the stage, shooting puffs of powder out of diamanté
rifles. From the orchestra pit and the stage boxes coloured
balloons are flung on to the stage. The orchestra plays
"Deutschland Uber Alles".

FAIRY WHISPERS

In the early 1930s "family entertainment" was a phrase that still meant something. The family and their close friends and neighbours who had previously enjoyed a sing-song around the old upright piano would now huddle around the radio set or gramophone (complete with scratchy thorn needle) and be transported by the "theatre of the mind".

The reality behind those fantasies in sound was almost certainly something best left unexplained.

Cast

JOAN	Doris Hare
MRS. HARRISON	Ann Codrington
MR. HARRISON	Gerald Nodin
MOLLY	Joy Spring
CUTHBERT	Tommy Hayes
THE NARRATOR	Joyce Barbour
BETTY	Ivy St. Helier
ROGER	John Mills
DOTSIE	Norah Howard
JANE	Elizabeth Corcoran
FAIRY QUEEN	Millie Sim

The scene is the dining-room of a suburban villa.

MR. *and* MRS. HARRISON *and* MOLLY *are seated round
the table having just finished tea.* JOAN *enters.*

JOAN: Sorry I'm late all, but I've just got a new record. Vi
gave it to me.

MRS. HARRISON: I do hope it's not all Vo do deo dos like
the last one she gave you.

JOAN: It's called "Fairy Whispers" and it's a twelve-inch.

MR. HARRISON: Twelve inches of Fairy Whispers sounds a
bit fishy to me.

JOAN: Wait until you hear it, it's sweet.

MRS. HARRISON: Well if we don't like it we can always
send it to the hospital.

MOLLY: Put it on, Joan, it ought to be lovely.

MR. HARRISON: You'd better try a new needle, we've used
that one for seven months.

JOAN (*putting the record on the gramophone*): Keep quiet
because it says it's descriptive.

MR. HARRISON: I should think Fairy Whispers would need
to be a little descriptive.

JOAN: Here we go.

*They all sit and listen to the record. At the end of it the
lights fade and the scene changes to the interior of the
gramophone studio. Four elderly women and two men are
grouped round the microphone. In the background there
is a four-piece orchestra consisting of two violins, one
cello, and a piano. None of the artists seem to care for one
another very much, but nevertheless they proceed solemnly to make the record that we have just heard.*

NARRATOR: It is midnight, and the little silver clock in the
nursery strikes "Ding dong, ding dong" ... Hush! Not
another sound but the snoring of Rover in his kennel in the
yard ... Ohoo, what's that? ... It is little Betty waking up ...

BETTY: Oh dear—oh dear—quickly, Roger, quickly—it is midsummer night and there will be fairies on the lawn.

ROGER: I'm sleepy.

BETTY: Oh Roger, you pwomised.

ROGER: All right then, but I don't believe in fairies.

BETTY: Quickly, quickly, I'll wake Dotsie and Jane.

NARRATOR: Dotsie and Jane, little sleepy heads just refuse to wake for ever and ever so long, finally, out of bed they hop helter-skelter.

DOTSIE: Fairies! Oh pease we would so like to see the fairies.

JANE: Woger! Woger! do hurry, oh Woger!

NARRATOR: Tiptoe the madcaps scamper down the wide fumed-oak staircase and out on to the dew-drenched lawn—Hush hush or Rover will awake and kick up—Oh such a din!

JANE: Oh Woger, aren't the fairies wonderful?

DOTSIE: It's all wonderful—too too wonderful!

NARRATOR: See this dainty gossamer creature approaching—a Bluebell come to life ... a veritable flower.

FAIRY: I am the Fairy Queen.

BETTY: And I am the littlest girl

FAIRY: Will you sing for us, Littlest Girl, although you are only a mortal we should enjoy it very much indeed.

BETTY: Ess I will. (*She sings.*)

FAIRY: Now we'll all dance.

Gay dance music interspersed with childish laughter.

NARRATOR: Hush! Rover is barking—quick, back to bed—Hurry—scamper—scurry—Ooo-Ooo if Nurse should awaken—but no, all is quiet again. Good-bye, fairies ...

FAIRIES: Sweet dreams, mortals.

GOOD NIGHT

MIDNIGHT MATINÉE

The constant curse of the gifted theatrical professional is the ungifted but determined amateur – particularly when their ambition is inextricably linked to a "good cause". During his career Noël encountered more than his share of them and on more than one occasion the urge to lampoon them gently was more than he could resist.

"Midnight Matinée" was the direct antecedent to *Sigh No More*'s "Pageant" and in both the unseemly scrabbling for the more prestigious historical role and the subsequent battle to preserve personal dignity, while suffering the inevitable woes that theatrical flesh is heir to, does much to illuminate the *comédie humaine*.

Despite the fun he makes of the pretensions on show, Noël was always in two minds about using this as subject matter. He was far from flippant about his own charity work – he took over the running of the Actors' Orphanage from Sir Gerald du Maurier in 1936 and only gave it up in 1956, when he moved to Bermuda.

The tenth play in the *Tonight at 8.30* sequence – *Star Chamber* – deals with a meeting of the charity committee running a home for retired actors and actresses (a subject he would deal with at length in *Waiting in the Wings* in 1960). During the meeting it becomes clear that the individual members are much more preoccupied with their own career concerns than with the supposed matters in hand. The piece was played only once and the reason Noël gave for dropping it was that he didn't believe it was funny enough. But to the members of his "family" he confided that he was concerned that it might give offence to people who – unlike his characters – gave their time selflessly to an important cause.

Once someone was up on a stage, however, and playing for an audience's approbation ... then they were fair game.

Cast

MRS. ROWNTREE, *Organiser*	Ivy St. Helier
VISCOUNTESS HOGAN (Diane de Poitiers)	Millie Sim
LADY MILLICENT HEADLEY (Cleopatra)	Rita Lyle
THE MARCHIONESS OF LEMWORTH (Nell Gwynne)	Moya Nugent
THE HON. MRS. DOUGLAS DRAYCOTT (Salome)	Joyce Barbour
MISS ESME PONTING (Marie Antoinette)	Ann Codrington
MISS SPENCE (Joan of Arc)	Norah Howard
THE LADY WESTMORSHAM (Lady Blessington)	Naomi Waters
MRS. F.N.J. WILSON (Lady Godiva)	Elizabeth Corcoran
MR. STUART INGLEBY (Announcer)	Romney Brent
LADY ELEANOUR SHERRELL (Court Lady)	Joy Spring
MISS REBECCA MOSENTHORPE (Court Lady)	Eileen Moore
LADY PATRICIA GAINTON (Little Page)	Joan O'Neil
THE HON. JULIAN FORRAGE (Little Page)	Graham Payn
GRECIAN CHORUS	Mr. Cochran's Young Ladies

Opening Chorus

We're going to do a Midnight Matinée!
We're going to do a Midnight Show!
  We're not *quite* sure
  What Charity it's for
But probably the Press will know,
We're going to have a talk on Saturday
  To make a list of friends who'll go.
The Season's such a bore
We haven't had much excitement since the War
  And so ...
  We'll do a Midnight Show.

Last year we did a "Feather Parade"
  That was a great success.
    But some got bent
      And some would break
    And a lot got sent
      To Melton by mistake.
At Easter we went mad, I'm afraid
  We really must confess
We gave a great—
  Big "Circus Ball"
But forgot the date
  So no one came at all.

We're going to do a Midnight Matinée!
We're going to do a Midnight Show!
  A sort of "Masque"
  Where everyone will ask
And nobody will *ever* know.
We're going to have a talk on Saturday
  To make a list of friends who'll go.
God knows how much we'll fetch

But we shall have all our pictures in the *Sketch*
And so—
We'll do a Midnight Show.

After the Opening Chorus, which is sung by Six Ladies
and Mrs. Rowntree, *the scene changes to a smart
drawing-room in which the committee meeting is being
held. Everyone present has a cocktail, except* Mrs.
Rowntree, *who has a pencil and paper. The* Viscountess Hogan *rises.*

Hogan: Darlings, I must fly—I've got to dress.

Mrs. Rowntree: You *can't* go yet, we haven't settled
anything!

Hogan: Diane de Poitiers—I shall be Diane de Poitiers,
it's all arranged.

Mrs. Rowntree (*miserably*): I don't even know who she
was.

Lemworth: Effie, how can you! She was Henry the
something's little piece.

Westmorsham: She died in the most dreary agonies owing
to having the wrong child at the wrong moment and having
the wrong doctor as well and everything being awful.

Hogan: Anyhow she's the one I'm going to be. Pinkie will
do me a dress, it will probably be nothing but oilcloth and
isinglass—you know how he loves being a little different, but
it's sure to look lovely in the lights. You *will* arrange about
the lights properly this time, Effie. I don't want that Mona
Lisa business all over again. Good-bye everybody. Come on,
Millie . . .

She and Lady Millicent Headley *go out.*

Mrs. Rowntree: I did so want her to be Mary Queen of
Scots.

Mrs. Wilson: The thing that worries me is, ought I to
have a real horse or not?

MRS. ROWNTREE: Don't give it another thought, Mrs. Wilson, it will be perfectly easy to get a horse.

MISS SPENCE: After all they had camels in *Chu Chin Chow*.

LEMWORTH: And a bus in *Cavalcade*.

MRS. WILSON: And I suppose I should have the hair sewn to the tights, just in certain places.

WESTMORSHAM: You might have it sewn to the horse.

MISS SPENCE: You do think it would be better to have her victorious, don't you, and not just a simple girl?

MRS. ROWNTREE: Who?

MISS SPENCE: Joan of Arc, of course.

MRS. ROWNTREE: Don't give it another thought, Miss Spence. She must undoubtedly be completely victorious.

MRS. DRAYCOTT: You will arrange for me to have a nice lot of space, won't you, Effie dear, and no obstructions—I haven't danced for years and I'm sure to be nervous.

LEMWORTH: Do you cover *much* more ground when you're nervous, darling?

MRS. DRAYCOTT (*ignoring her*): And no tin-tacks on the stage either because I shall have bare feet.

MRS. ROWNTREE: Don't give it another thought, Mrs. Draycott. Tin-tacks. (*She makes a note.*)

LEMWORTH: I think I ought to have real oranges, don't you? Those papier-mâché ones look so unappetising.

WESTMORSHAM: Certainly—it will be divine, we'll eat them all up at rehearsals.

MISS PONTING: You know I am just the teeniest little bit worried about that ship.

MRS. ROWNTREE: Which ship?

MISS PONTING: The one Marie Antoinette had in her hair, there was a lot of talk about it at the time, I believe.

LEMWORTH: Talk to Pinkie about it, darling, he'll probably give you a wreath of Aquitanias.

WESTMORSHAM: If it's too small no one will be able to see

the ship, and if it's too big no one will be able to see you, so I should leave it altogether if I were you.

MISS SPENCE (*discouraged*): Perhaps I'd better be Catherine the Great after all.

LEMWORTH: She wasn't a Bygone Enchantress, she was just an angry old girl with idle fancies.

WESTMORSHAM: Do you know that for the last ten minutes I've been absolutely at war with myself?

LEMWORTH: How very uncomfortable. Why?

WESTMORSHAM: Lady Blessington or Flora Macdonald, which shall I be?

LEMWORTH: Neither.

MRS. ROWNTREE: Not Flora Macdonald, dear Lady Westmorsham, she was really such a drab little thing, if you know what I mean, and so terribly difficult to *convey*. Unless you came on in a rowing boat I don't think anyone would know who you were, people are so dreadfully silly nowadays.

WESTMORSHAM: If I'm Lady Blessington I shall walk with a very high stick, imperiously, you know.

LEMWORTH: Why?

WESTMORSHAM: Because I wish to, Violet.

LEMWORTH: I don't believe Lady Blessington had a very high stick.

WESTMORSHAM: Darling, how could you possibly know? There's nothing in history to prove that she didn't have hundreds and hundreds of sticks and seventeen French poodles.

LEMWORTH: I have no intention of appearing in the same programme with seventeen French poodles.

WESTMORSHAM: That, darling, wouldn't matter nearly as much as you think it would.

MRS. ROWNTREE (*peaceably*): Lady Westmorsham, please . . .

MRS. WILSON: I must say I find this discussion very tedious.

MRS. DRAYCOTT: It's always the way, nobody ever gets anything done...

MRS. ROWNTREE: I don't see why you say that, Mrs. Draycott; after all I'm sure I'm doing my best...

MISS SPENCE: No one has told me yet where I am to go for my armour...

LEMWORTH: These ridiculous arguments about sticks and poodles...

Suddenly the quarrel dies away as two flashlight photographers enter. Everybody smiles amiably. LADY WESTMORSHAM *even goes so far as to lean girlishly over* LADY LEMWORTH'S *shoulder.*

BLACKOUT

TWELVE GIRLS *in Grecian costume walk on in front of Tabs 1, and arrange themselves in a group centre. They are all wearing very beautifully made masks, so the extremely witty introductory speech in verse which they recite in unison is rather lost on the audience.*

GIRLS:

> Een arrarah ola brure
> Taala caana effalure
> Tar Apollo nuraling
> Jupiter abalaching
>
> Tanger weero avaloy
> Burel ammalee to Troy
> Baara weether dolaser
> Mount Olympus bolaser.
>
> Een arrarah ola brure
> Taala caana effalure
> Tar Apollo nuraling
> Jupiter abalaching.
>
> Hola jaaga ammo purtain
> Borrodah anula curtain.

Upon finishing this descriptive prelude they all walk off a trifle untidily.

MR. STUART INGLEBY *enters from the prompt side becomingly attired in Louis Quinze court dress, glittering with rhinestones and carrying a large sailor doll. He is greeted by a little desultory applause from the orchestra and is obviously exceedingly nervous.*

MR. INGLEBY: Your Royal Highness, My Lords, Ladies and Gentlemen. I—er—take—er—er—very great pleasure—er—in the—er—privilege of—er—having been asked—er—to appear before you in aid of this ABSOLUTELY SPLENDID Charity—We all—er—as you know owe a very—er—deep debt to—er—absolutely ANYBODY who—er—has absolutely ANYTHING to—er—do with the Sea and—er—particularly in these trying times when everything seems so—so—um—INFINITELY—er—CHAOTIC, if you know what I mean—therefore this—er—particular cause, embracing as it undoubtedly does and stretching as it undoubtedly does to the—er—furthest corners of the far-flung—er—EMPIRE—I feel—and I am sure you feel too—that nothing we any of us do could ever be—er—TOO MUCH so therefore I—er—have been asked by our brilliant Organiser, MRS. ROWNTREE—

Applause.

—who over so many years has done such SPLENDID work for every conceivable charity—who indeed could forget her Feather Fantasy of last year, and her Milky Way Ball of the year before, to say nothing of her "Amants Inconnus" Raffle at the Palladium in 1929? I have been asked by Mrs. Rowntree to auction this beautiful doll, which has been personally made by the DUCHESS OF ENDLEBROOK, who as you know is almost completely an INVALID and seldom if ever leaves her very lovely house near WINDERMERE. I have already been offered twenty-five pounds by Lord Ackle—now then—who will offer me thirty? ... Thirty pounds for this exquisitely wrought sailor—er doll—Come now—surely thirty pounds is not very much to ask in such an admirable cause—

Dead silence.

—Any advance on twenty-five pounds? Look how ABSO-
LUTELY SPLENDIDLY it has been made, perfect to the last detail,
accurate even to the LANYARD! Thirty pounds, please—

Dead silence.

MRS. ROWNTREE *calls "Thirty-five pounds" from the
side of the stage.*

—Thank you, Mrs. Rowntree—I have been bid thirty-five
pounds by Mrs. Rowntree—any advance on thirty-five
pounds—?

Dead silence.

Going—going—come now, forty pounds—will no one offer
forty pounds?

Utter silence.

Going at thirty-five pounds—Going—Going—GONE.

MRS. ROWNTREE *enters from prompt side amid
applause, attired in an elaborate evening dress with a
large spray of orchids. She takes the doll from MR.
INGLEBY with a brief and angry little bow, and marches
off again.*

Now, Your Royal Highness, My Lords, Ladies and Gentlemen, we come to the Pageant of Bygone Enchantresses.

*He nods to the Musical Director, who proceeds to play
soft music. The curtains roll back, the prompt-side one
sticks a little, but this is remedied by MRS. ROWNTREE,
who has been accidentally discovered behind them. She
tugs at the curtain and finally coaxes it off all right. There
is a frame at the back centre with a few steps leading up
to it, and a terrace balustrade running along the top of the
rostrum. The background of the frame is blue sky with
fleecy clouds painted on it. The rest of the stage is masked
in with black velvet.*

> Bygone Loves and bygone Lovers
>> Live again in History's pages.
> As one turns them one discovers
>> Love's Romance across the Ages.

DIANE DE POITIERS—THE VISCOUNTESS HOGAN

The music swells and the lights go out, a spotlight picks up the prompt-side corner of the rostrum and moves slowly along the terrace, down the steps and round the stage and off O.P. side, followed hurriedly by THE VISCOUNTESS HOGAN *as Diane de Poitiers, who is unfortunately unable to catch up with it and is therefore practically indiscernible.*

Queen of every fascination
   This Enchantress lives again
Siren of the Restoration
   Mistress Gwynn of Drury Lane.

NELL GWYNN—THE MARCHIONESS OF LEMWORTH.

Nothing happens for a moment and so he says again "NELL GWY ..." *and changes rapidly to* "CLEOPATRA" *as he sees over his shoulder* LADY MILLICENT HEADLEY *being borne on in a litter. The litter is obviously a trifle heavy for the* BEARERS, *and tilted a little to one side, but* LADY MILLICENT *rises above it by assuming an expression of slightly apprehensive serenity and is conveyed down the steps and off stage in triumph, to Nell Gwynn's music.*

Queen of every fascination
   This Enchantress lives again
Siren of the Restoration
   Mistress Gwynn of Drury Lane.

NELL GWYNN—THE MARCHIONESS OF LEMWORTH.

This time it is really THE MARCHIONESS OF LEMWORTH *as Nell Gwynn. She comes dancing on girlishly, determined not to be put out by the violently Eastern Cleopatra music which is being played by the orchestra. She carries a large basket of oranges, and just as she reaches the foot of the steps, the bottom of the basket falls out and all the oranges roll about the stage. She gives a gay, if rather false little laugh, and dances merrily off the stage.*

> Eastern Stars your light grows less
> Oh Eastern Moon your beauty pales
> Before this sinister Princess
> Salome of the Seven Veils.

SALOME—THE HONOURABLE MRS. DOUGLAS DRAYCOTT.

The lights change to blue, and MRS. DRAYCOTT *enters to suitable music as Salome. She steals sinuously along the terrace, scantily dressed and carrying a large head on a charger. On reaching the foot of the steps she suddenly realises that she has never rehearsed with the head on the charger and will be unable to dance with it, so with great sang-froid she hands it to* MR. INGLEBY, *who reluctantly accepts it, and stands holding it, looking extremely uncomfortable while* MRS. DRAYCOTT *endeavours to dance effectively without treading on any of the oranges. Finally she goes off looking faintly disagreeable before her music is quite finished.* MR. INGLEBY, *supremely embarrassed by the head on the charger, looks miserably after her in the vain hope that she may come back and fetch it. Then, still holding it, he begins his next speech, stops short, and places the charger on the stage just behind him.*

> Tragic Queen of Tragic Story
> Memory that haunts us yet
> Here we see you in your glory
> Lovely Marie Antoinette.

MARIE ANTOINETTE—MISS ESME PONTING. COURT LADIES— LADY ELEANOUR SHERREL and MISS REBECCA MOSENTHORPE. PAGES—LADY PATRICIA GAINTON and THE HONOURABLE JULIAN FORRAGE.

MISS PONTING, *as Marie Antoinette, with the* COURT LADIES *and* PAGES *enter briskly together, and owing to the width of their hoop skirts become jammed on the steps and have to retreat and come down sideways. Having succeeded in manipulating the steps they go off with a great air of eighteenth-century dignity which is slightly marred by* JULIAN FORRAGE, *the smallest page, wailing miserably throughout.*

MR. INGLEBY *is about to embark upon his next announcement when he hears a strange clicking just behind him. He is obviously puzzled but doesn't look round for fear of looking awkward. The clicking is caused by* MRS. ROWNTREE, *who is endeavouring to hook the charger off the stage with a walking-stick. Finally she gives it up and comes on bravely and carries it off.*

> Battle Queen of History
>> Gallant Memory, Brave Romance
> Welcome, Welcome, Hail to Thee
>> Joan of Arc, the Maid of France!

JOAN OF ARC—MISS SPENCE.

MISS SPENCE *enters as Joan of Arc. The orchestra plays an appropriate trumpet call. She is attired in shining armour with a very long blue cloak flowing behind her. She comes to an abrupt halt at the foot of the steps and is nearly strangled owing to her cloak catching in the balustrade at the top of the steps. She stands stock-still in a brave effort not to betray that anything is wrong.* MR. INGLEBY *goes up to her and falling on one knee repeats the last two lines of his verse. "Welcome, Welcome, Hail to Thee, Joan of Arc, the Maid of France." She shoots an agonised look at him which he doesn't understand and so he goes back to his place at the side of the stage. The orchestra plays her music through again, at last* MRS. ROWNTREE *is seen crawling along the terrace on her hands and knees. She unhitches the cloak and crawls back again.* MISS SPENCE *marches off very quickly.*

> Beauty rare, and stately calm
>> England holds your memory dear
> Queen of Fashion, Queen of Charm

Lady Blessington is here.
LADY BLESSINGTON—THE LADY WESTMORSHAM.

LADY WESTMORSHAM, *as Lady Blessington, walks on
with great dignity and a very high stick. Nothing goes
amiss with her until she is just about to go off, when her
stick catches in a hole in the stage and she has to go back
for it. Apart from this her appearance is a triumphant
success.*

Lady sweet beyond compare
  Strange the legend, strange the deed
Shielded by your flowing hair
  Riding on your snow-white steed.
LADY GODIVA—MRS. F. N. J. WILSON.

Nothing happens at all. MR. INGLEBY *looks anxiously
behind him and repeats the verse again. Still nothing
happens, a lot of whispering and scuffling is heard
offstage, interspersed with the clip-clopping of horse's
hooves and an occasional neigh.* MRS. ROWNTREE *is heard
to give a little shriek and say in audible tones: "There—
look what it's done now!" Finally* MRS. WILSON *stumps
along the terrace down the steps, and off on foot, looking
very cross indeed. The music changes and all the* BYGONE
ENCHANTRESSES *come on together, some from the terrace
at the top and some from downstage. With only a very
slight muddle they take up their positions on the steps for
the Grand Tableau.* LADY BLESSINGTON, *who enters from
the terrace rather late, trips on the top step and falls
headlong, knocking Marie Antoinette's wig a little on one
side. The others do their best to conceal this mishap from
the audience by crowding round her prone figure, so that
until the end she remains completely hidden from view.
Two angels on wires slide on at the back, about six feet
above the assembled company. They bump into each
other in mid air and remain bunched together in not quite*

the attitude that had been rehearsed. The orchestra plays a very loud chord and the lights fade.

THE PARTY'S OVER NOW

The wistful song which ends the sketch became the standard ending for Noël's cabaret act –

> The thrill has gone
> To linger on
> Would spoil it anyhow
>   Let's creep away
>   From the day
> For the Party's over now.

There was, however, to be a postscript that took place at yet another party, when the Coward finger was seen to wag at two old but now distinctly sheepish friends. Betty Comden and Adolph Green were enjoying a considerable success with their new show *Bells Are Ringing* – until Noël pointed out that its hit song, "The Party's Over (It's Time To Call It a Day)" bore more than a passing resemblance to something he had written some thirty years earlier and, while he perfectly well understood imitation to be the sincerest form of flattery, he felt he could bear to go unflattered. Or rather pithier words to that effect.

Cast

A Policeman	Gerald Nodin
1st Street Cleaner	Kenneth Ware
2nd Street Cleaner	Bill Harn
A Young Man	John Mills
A Young Girl	Doris Hare
Hostess	Joyce Barbour
Leonara	Steffi Duna
Lord Skeffington	Romney Brent
Lady Skeffington	Ivy St. Helier
Guests, etc.	

At the end of the Prelude sung by the FOUR DÉBUTANTES, *the light fades out, and in the darkness two lighted windows appear, dimly at first and then, as they grow brighter, the party music is heard and the silhouettes of the dancers are thrown on to the blinds. The scene appears dimly in a blue light and it is seen to be the outside of a house, with a lamp over the front door and painted steps leading to it.*

   A POLICEMAN *walks on from the side and meets the* TWO STREET-WASHING MEN *with their barrow and hose.*

1ST STREET CLEANER: Party goin' on?

POLICEMAN: What did you think it was—a tennis tournament?

1ST STREET CLEANER: All right, all right.

2ND STREET CLEANER: You'd never think there was a Crisis, that's wot I say—you'd never think it, not for a moment you wouldn't.

POLICEMAN: No 'arm in enjoying yourself even if there is.

2ND STREET CLEANER: Funny way to enjoy yourself, staying up all night when you don't 'ave to.

1ST STREET CLEANER: Cheer up, Frank, the Season's nearly over.

2ND STREET CLEANER: And wot a Season it 'as been! My ol' woman's been fairly rushed orf 'er feet, I give you my word. Winkle Parties and Fried Fish Cabarets every night, just a ceaseless raound of social activities.

   The LAMP-LIGHTER *comes on from right and puts the lamp out above the front door of the house. The lights all fade, and in the darkness the front scene goes up, and the same house is seen again at the back, but this time it is built and the steps are solid.*

   The door of the house opens and a YOUNG GIRL *and a* YOUNG MAN *come down the steps.*

YOUNG GIRL: We can get a taxi at the corner of the Square.

YOUNG MAN: All right—darling.

He tries to kiss her.

YOUNG GIRL: No, dear, not now.

YOUNG MAN: Why not?

YOUNG GIRL: It's over.

YOUNG MAN: What's over?

YOUNG GIRL: The Party, silly, all that was part of the Party, now we're tired. It's no use going on with things when you're tired and spoiling them.

YOUNG MAN: Not just once?

YOUNG GIRL (*smiling*): If you must.

He takes her in his arms and kisses her passionately.

YOUNG GIRL (*escaping from him*): No more, my sweet— the Party's over now.

They sing: "The Party's Over Now", and after a short dance they go off.

The front door opens again and the HOSTESS *comes out on to the steps with* LEONARA.

HOSTESS: Are you sure you won't let me telephone for a taxi for you?

LEONARA: There's a rank at the corner. I can see it from here.

HOSTESS: It was so sweet of you to come and dance for us so beautifully. I'm tremendously grateful.

LEONARA: I've had a lovely time and enjoyed every minute of it, thank you so much.

HOSTESS: I'll send you your cheque in the morning.

LEONARA: I really haven't earned it.

HOSTESS: Yes, you have. Good night, my dear.

LEONARA: Good night.

The HOSTESS *goes in again and* LEONARA *comes down the steps.*

The music swells from inside the house and she begins to dance a graceful little waltz by herself. When she has gone, the door opens again and LORD *and* LADY SKEF-FINGTON *come out.*

LADY SKEFFINGTON (*disagreeably*): Why isn't the car here?

LORD SKEFFINGTON: I sent it home.

LADY SKEFFINGTON: Quite typical of you and extremely irritating.

LORD SKEFFINGTON: You've been excessively disagreeable all the evening. It would be properly consistent to keep it up all the way home.

LADY SKEFFINGTON: You know, dear, you'd spoil a good party for anyone, let alone a dreary one like that.

LORD SKEFFINGTON: I do hope you haven't been drinking, my love.

LADY SKEFFINGTON: That is one thing you can be perfectly sure of. I haven't touched a drop of Millicent's champagne for seventeen years.

LORD SKEFFINGTON: A bad principle; it might at least make you more amiable or kill you.

They sing the second half of the Refrain.

Though we hate
Abominate
Each party we're invited to
  To stay out
  And dance about
Because we've nothing else to do.
  Though every night
  We start out bright
And finish with a row
  We've been so bored
  Thank the Lord
That the Party's over now!

They go off, and out of the house comes the HOSTESS *followed by all the* GUESTS, *singing a full Refrain.*

Verse

Night is over, dawn is breaking

175

Everywhere the Town is waking
Just as we are on our way to sleep.
  Lovers meet and dance a little
  Snatching from romance a little
Souvenir of happiness to keep.
  The music of an hour ago
Was just a sort of "Let's pretend"
  The melodies that charmed us so
        At last are ended.

Refrain

The Party's over now
The dawn is drawing very nigh
The candles gutter, the starlight leaves the sky
It's time for little boys and girls
To hurry home to bed
For there's a new day waiting just ahead.
  Life is sweet
  But time is fleet
Beneath the magic of the moon
  Dancing time
  May seem sublime
But it is ended all too soon.
  The thrill has gone
  To linger on
Would spoil it anyhow
  Let's creep away
  From the day
For the Party's over now.

SET TO MUSIC

Presented by John C. Wilson at the Music Box Theatre, New York, on 18 January 1939 (129 performances)

Book, lyrics and music by Noël Coward
Produced by Noël Coward

Set To Music was in effect the American version of the 1932 *Words and Music* with added material and the incalculable advantage of having Beatrice Lillie in the cast. In the *New York Times* Brooks Atkinson wrote: "Whether Noël Coward is Beatrice Lillie's best friend or whether the honors are the other way round is an academic question at best. For the simple fact is that *Set To Music* . . . represents both of them at their best. On the spur of the moment it looks like the best show he has written. Although Miss Lillie has been synonymous with perfection in comedy for quite a long time, an old admirer may be forgiven for believing that she also is more incandescently witty now than before. For light amusement, written and acted with impeccable taste, this London revue is off the top of the pack."

WEARY OF IT ALL

Cast

LORD BITCHETTE	Ray Dennis
DAISY, *a dresser*	Gladys Henson
ELMER VON ROBESPIERRE	Robert Shackleton
HENRY BEARDSWORTH	Anthony Pélissier
MARION DAY	Beatrice Lillie

The scene is the dressing-room of MARION DAY, *a famous
cabaret star. The room is filled with flowers and furnished
luxuriously.* DAISY, *a dresser, is bustling about putting
things tidy.* LORD BITCHETTE, *a handsome, wealthy
young man is standing by the dressing-table.* ELMER VON
ROBESPIERRE, *another handsome, wealthy young man, is
seated on the sofa.* HENRY BEARDSWORTH, *a slightly more
elderly but equally wealthy man, is seated on a chair.*

BITCHETTE: Daisy.

DAISY: Yes, my lord?

BITCHETTE (*showing her a ruby necklace in a Cartier
case*): Do you think she will like this?

DAISY: I don't know, I'm sure, my lord.

BITCHETTE (*producing a diamond bracelet*): What about
this?

DAISY: I couldn't say, I'm sure, sir.

BEARDSWORTH (*producing a double pearl necklace*): Or
this?

DAISY: I can't truly say whether she'd like it or not, sir—
she's ever so moody.

> *There is a sound of frenzied cheering*—MARION *comes
> wearily into the room and sinks down at the dressing-
> table.*

MARION: Shut the door, Daisy—shut the door—I can't
bear it.

BITCHETTE: What's the matter?

MARION (*with a wistful smile*): Nothing—everything!

BITCHETTE: I've brought you this. (*He gives her the
rubies.*)

MARION: My dear—how sweet of you—Rubies are such
cruel stones, aren't they?

BITCHETTE: Perhaps you like diamonds better. (*He gives
her the bracelet.*)

MARION (*taking it*): It's beautiful, isn't it—so cold?

BEARDSWORTH: These pearls were my mother's.

MARION (*laughing hollowly*): And did they make her happy?

BEARDSWORTH: I really don't know.

MARION: Would you leave me for a moment? I'm exhausted—utterly and completely exhausted.

BITCHETTE: Of course, my dear. (*He kisses her and goes.*) We understand. (*He goes.*)

BEARDSWORTH: When will you give me my answer?

MARION: Not now—not now—I implore you—not now.

BEARDSWORTH: The house on Long Island is waiting for you and I am opening the villa in Biarritz for you——

MARION (*far away*): Has it got an old cracked mirror?

BEARDSWORTH: No—I don't think so—why?

MARION: Nothing, I only wondered.

BEARDSWORTH: I telephoned about the sable coat—they're sending it tomorrow.

MARION: I suppose you didn't think of asking them to send me an old, faded, dusty sunbonnet?

BEARDSWORTH: No—I'm afraid I didn't.

MARION: It doesn't matter.

BEARDSWORTH: If you want one—I can get it for you.

MARION (*sadly*): No—never mind—it wouldn't be the same——

BEARDSWORTH: What is the matter? What is it that is making you so unhappy?

MARION: Life. (*She takes off one of her bracelets and looks at it pensively.*)

BEARDSWORTH (*kissing her*): I understand.

> *He goes out. She is gazing at herself in the mirror. Then she begins to sing softly.*

Verse

People that I sing to
Bring a breath of Spring to

Envy me my gay career.
No one in the city
Has much time for pity,
Nobody can be sincere;
Thousands cheer me and applaud me,
Everyone stares.
If they've wounded me and bored me
Nobody cares;
Women at the tables,
Loosening their sables,
Look at me with cruel eyes,
Then a little something in me dies
And cries.

Refrain

Weary of it all,
This getting and spending,
This futile unending
Refrain,
It's driving me insane;
I'm so weary of it all.
Other voices call,
The cattle at twilight,
The birds in the sky light
Of dawn,
Yet here am I forlorn
And so weary of it all.
I miss the wild-wood
I wandered through in childhood
With a heart as light as air,
What would I give once again to be there
With my old, deaf mother!
Night begins to fall,
By memory tortured
I dream of an orchard
In Spring,

The songs I used to sing.
Now I have to swing,
I'm so weary of it all.

Patter

Wake up in the morning
'Round about noon,
A little lunch on a tray,
Shopping without stopping till my senses swoon,
Or else some dreary matinée,
Home at five,
More dead than alive,
Another day nearly gone,
Cocktails to mix,
My face and hair to fix,
The weary round goes on.
Eight or nine,
I have to go and dine
With this or that rich man about town,
Caviare and grouse
In an overheated house,
God, how it gets me down!
Home I go defeated and depressed again,
Only time for just one hour of rest again.
Bright lights,
White lights,
Waiters leering
Faces sneering,
Laughing, chaffing,
Shouting, cheering,
Weary of it all
This giving and giving,
This life that I'm living in hell.
With broken dreams to sell,
Just an empty shell,
Weary, weary, weary of it all!

It was ironic that Noël should include a sketch about spies in his last pre-war revue. By the time "Secret Service" appeared in the English Revue, *All Clear*, at the end of 1939, England was at war – and Noël was a spy himself.

The full story of his involvement in the secret war conducted by the New York-based BSC (British Security Co-ordination) only began to emerge when confidential papers of the period were de-classified in the early 1970s and Coward gave his one and only interview on the subject shortly before his death in 1973. Even then the serious was cloaked by the superficially flippant. Of his first interview with his spymaster – "I was awfully bewildered. I thought it would be more Mata Hari – and then I told myself, 'Well, hardly that. I couldn't wear a jewel in my navel, which I believe she was given to doing.'" He claimed to regret that he had never been issued with a false beard or invisible ink but he knew perfectly well that his chief contribution was to remain – Noël Coward. "My disguise was my own reputation." And for the remainder of the war, so it proved.

CAST

THE COUNTESS	Beatrice Lillie
MADAME MOULE	Gladys Henson
ZIZI	Moya Nugent
LEOPOLD ROSEN	Angus Menzies
1ST OFFICER	Richard Haydn
2ND OFFICER	Hugh French
MAURICE	Victor Cutrer
VITTORIO, *the cello player*	Kenneth Carten
FRITZ	Ray Dennis
SERGE	Sanders Draper
IVAN	Gilbert Wilson
FRENCH GIRL	

The scene is the Café International in Geneva.

There is a small bar on the right behind which
MADAME MOULE, *the proprietress, sits at a cash desk*
knitting incessantly. She is a sinister figure of vague
nationality. At a table on the left is a man with a beard.
He is CHIEF INSPECTOR LEOPOLD ROSEN *of the Ham-*
burg Secret Police and his beard is obviously false. He is
drinking coffee and holds a newspaper up to his face
whenever anyone approaches him.

At a table near to him are seated ZIZI, *a cocotte, and*
her gigolo MAURICE. *They are drinking beer and playing*
dominoes.

At another table VITTORIO, *a seedy musician, is writing*
letters. His cello case is leaning against a chair beside him.
At another table SERGE *and* IVAN, *two Russians, are*
engrossed in whispered conversation.

FRITZ, a waiter, approaches their table. He very
ostentatiously places a roll on it and goes away. IVAN,
after a furtive glance round the café, breaks open the roll,
and extracts a piece of paper from it. LEOPOLD *peers over*
the top of his paper at him.

IVAN: The plane left Warsaw at four-thirty.
SERGE: Someone has blundered. Order one kümmel.

 SERGE *goes to the bar.*

IVAN (*loudly*): One kümmel.
SERGE: One kümmel?
FRITZ: Monsieur?

 Everyone in the café gives a little start and writes
 something down.

SERGE (*at bar*): The weather is very hot today.
MADAME MOULE (*looking at him sharply*): The heat wave
cannot continue much longer. (*She writes something down.*)

 He nods.

184

LEOPOLD (*abruptly as* FRITZ *passes*): The Countess is late.

FRITZ (*with great presence of mind*): Certainly, monsieur, I will order it immediately.

ZIZI: The Countess is late. *That* means trouble.

IVAN (*to* SERGE, *crossing back to table*): Notify Number Seven, I will be at the Black Parrot at nine.

IVAN *is about to go when* LEOPOLD *stops him.*

LEOPOLD: I advise you to go warily, my friend.

IVAN (*sullenly*): Who are you?

LEOPOLD (*detaching his beard for a moment and snapping it back again*): Leopold Rosen of the Hamburg Secret Police at your service.

IVAN (*blanching*): My God!

LEOPOLD: Don't mention it.

IVAN *rushes out right.*

The door at the back swings open and the COUNTESS *enters, laughing hilariously and accompanied by two young* OFFICERS *in uniform. The* COUNTESS *is wearing a daring evening dress, long elbow gloves and a large black hat. She carries an enormous hand-bag.*

COUNTESS (*gaily*): Foolish boy, you think that to compliment a woman on her gown is the way to her heart—fie on you for such naiveté!—Come—we will have some champagne and you shall smile at me with those gleaming white teeth and we will see, hein?

As they pass LEOPOLD'S *table she drops her handkerchief and the three of them sit at a table left.* LEOPOLD *swiftly picks up the handkerchief, extracts a note from it, reads it, then comes to the* COUNTESS.

LEOPOLD: The Frau Gretchen has dropped her handkerchief, madame.

COUNTESS (*charmingly*): Ah, a thousand thanks.

LEOPOLD: The weather is very hot today.

COUNTESS: The heat wave cannot continue much longer—it is almost bound to be cooler on the TWENTY-FIFTH or the TWENTY-SIXTH!

LEOPOLD: The cherry blossom is at its best in *May*.

> *The* COUNTESS *looks blank for a moment, then makes a rapid calculation on her fingers—then smiles with relief.*

COUNTESS: Of course, yes—how stupid of me.

1ST OFFICER: I beg your pardon?

COUNTESS: Nothing—nothing—let us order the wine—Fritz!

> FRITZ *brings her a telephone.* LEOPOLD *crosses to bar.*

COUNTESS: Give me Central 7156.

> *Everyone makes a note.*

Allo—allo—— No, no, nein, nyet—— yes, oui, yah, da—certainly—sapristi. I will tell him. On no account—the number of the car? I cannot remember—my dear, just imagine I had forgotten it was little Hugo's birthday so I have ordered him *four* clockwork trains—*two* Teddy Bears—and *fifteen* boxes of chocolates. Adios.

ZIZI: 4215. That means trouble.

LEOPOLD: Wien. Wien. Singing.

> LEOPOLD *returns to his table. On the way he drops a pencil by the* COUNTESS. *She picks it up and struggles to open it. Finally one of the* OFFICERS *comes to her assistance.*

OFFICER: Allow me.

COUNTESS: I can't open the damned thing.

OFFICER (*opening it*): There.

COUNTESS (*radiantly*): A thousand thanks. (*She extracts a note and reads it, after which she places it in the bosom of her dress. Smiling.*) You men are all alike—pigs!

> MADAME *crosses to the* COUNTESS's *table.*

Ah, my little Mouchen. I had forgotten to tell you that I'm giving a little party next Friday. I shall want *five* bottles of brandy, *two* sandwiches, *one* poached egg, *twenty* dry Martinis——

ZIZI: 52120! That means Frederick has reached the frontier!

During this conversation, Fritz *has brought and poured out the champagne.*

Madame: Madame the Countess is well?

Countess: I have never felt better since I recovered from influenza on the *twelfth* and went to Zurich on the *fourteenth*!

Madame: Bien, madame.

She crosses to the man with the Cello *and whispers "1214".*

Countess (*looking provocatively at one of the* Officers *over a glass of champagne*): Now you must tell me some more about the fortifications!

1st Officer: You are the most bewitching woman I have ever met.

2nd Officer: Be careful, Herman.

Countess: Why should he be careful? Are we not the so good friends, hein?

2nd Officer: I beg your pardon?

Countess: "Hein" was what I said, "Hein" was what I meant.

1st Officer (*passionately*): You have the most beautiful shoulders in all Geneva.

Countess (*with intense meaning, looking fixedly at the* 2nd Officer): Oh no, I haven't. The most beautiful shoulders in all Geneva belong to Mademoiselle Lincka of the Café Paradise—correct me if I am wrong, my friend—Mademoiselle Lincka who is at this moment preparing to leave for Vienna accompanied by none other than Captain Siegfried Rouhmstadt——

2nd Officer (*hoarsely*): It's a lie—it's a lie!

Countess (*relentlessly*): There is still time to prevent her if you value the honour of your regiment sufficiently to go to Number Five rue Président Wilson.

2nd Officer: My God! (*He rises violently and rushes out.*)

The Countess *makes a sign with her glove to* Leopold *who nods to the* Cello Player *who writes*

something down. There is the sound of a shot outside. The
COUNTESS *suppresses a slight start and leans alluringly to*
the 1ST OFFICER.

COUNTESS: More wine?

1ST OFFICER (*gazing at her*): You are very, very lovely.

COUNTESS: You were saying—"The gun emplacements on
the north-east corner..."

1ST OFFICER: ... the north-*west* corner ... they command
the slope of the valley—the ones on the north-east cover the
road to the frontier.

COUNTESS (*laughing*): I expect their calibres are 483 plus 86
minus 700!

1ST OFFICER: Good heavens, no—they are 999 plus 4604.

COUNTESS (*sipping her wine and writing with her left hand
on the tablecloth*): I'm sure you say that to every girl you
meet!

1ST OFFICER: ... Your eyes are like the sky at morning...

COUNTESS: How foolishly romantic you are—do you
mean to tell me that you can notice the sky at morning when
you are flying along in those triple-engine 45-by-87 bombers?

1ST OFFICER: No, quadruple-engine—87-by-54——

COUNTESS (*laughing musically*): Ah, 87-by-54, what a fool
I am. How boring it must be to you to talk of these important
things to a silly feather-brained woman like me——

1ST OFFICER: To listen to your voice is like all the poetry in
the world.

Scream off. FRENCH GIRL *enters and exits. Stove
business.*

COUNTESS: You were saying?

1ST OFFICER (*oblivious*): You are the most glamorous,
enchanting creature I have ever met.

COUNTESS: More wine—more wine——

1ST OFFICER: ... Let me be your lover—just for a little—I
will not demand too much——

The COUNTESS *changes her disguise and becomes a
Russian Anarchist. The* OFFICER *continues his pleading.*

An hour with you—an hour in your arms would be the culmination of my deepest dream, my most passionate desire——

> *He bends over her and places his arms round her just as she is struggling to don a still further disguise.*

COUNTESS: Let me go—let me go——

1ST OFFICER: Never—now that I have found you I could never, never let you go—you are to me the incarnation of all that is feminine and lovely—from the first moment when we met under the trees by the side of the lake and we talked of those plans for the new munitions factory in Potsdam, I have known that you were the only woman that I ever have loved, ever could love and ever shall love—be patient with me—do not turn away—you who have so much to give—spare me a morsel of happiness——

COUNTESS: Very well—anything you say—but not here, be calm—no one must ever know—look away from me—I implore you look away from me so that I cannot see the fervour in your eyes—we must be cautious, we must be discreet, we must be wise.

> *He turns away from her. She quickly empties a phial of poison into his champagne. He turns.*

1ST OFFICER (*simply but with great passion*): I love you.

COUNTESS: We will drink to that.

1ST OFFICER: The loveliest shoulders in all Geneva——

> *He turns her away from him with his left hand and kisses her shoulder, while with his right he changes the glasses of wine.*

COUNTESS: I surrender—I am yours.

1ST OFFICER: Now we will drink.

> *They toast each other. She, having drained her glass, puts it down and watches him closely. She becomes aware that all is not as it should be. She places her hand on her heart.*

COUNTESS (*whispering*): Who are you?

1ST OFFICER: Lieutenant-Colonel Robert Armitage of the British Intelligence.

She realises to the full what has happened.

COUNTESS (*radiantly*): You must be mad—it's delicious!

BLACKOUT

SIGH NO MORE

Presented by John C. Wilson and H. M. Tennent Ltd at the Piccadilly Theatre, London, on 22 August 1945 (213 performances)

Written, composed and directed by Noël Coward

Sigh No More was to be the last revue. Apart from contributing individual numbers to shows like *The Lyric Revue* (1951) and *The Globe Revue* (1952), there were to be no more shows bearing the legend, "Book, lyrics and music by Noël Coward".

The Times critic called it "a light, easy, amusing entertainment, disconcertingly without the impress of a definite style – disconcertingly, because it has been 'written, composed and directed' by Mr. Noël Coward". And, indeed – in view of his insistence on total control in the case of *Words and Music* – it was surprising that he would permit interpolations this time around. His *Diary* notes on the production process indicate that he had trouble accommodating some of the material written by Joyce Grenfell and Richard Addinsell and much of it was finally cut.

The likelihood is that he rushed his fences by producing a complex show too soon after the war ended. He himself had just finished a gruelling series of overseas tours entertaining the troops. At the same time he had been involved in the making of several major films, including the landmark *Brief Encounter*. His plate held one item too many.

Even so, *Sigh No More* had racked up 213 respectable performances when it closed and Noël's verdict that "the title turned out to be the best part" was unnecessarily harsh.

PAGEANT

Cast

HERALD	Gail Kendal
SPIRIT OF MASQUE	Cyril Ritchard
LADY MAUD HAILSBURY	Ann Martin
MISTRESS JOAN	Joy O'Neill
MISTRESS ALICE	Renee Stocker
SIR GUY BELCHAMPS	John Hugo
CARDINAL WOLSEY	Alan Clive
VIKING (STAGE MANAGER)	Lance Hamilton
QUEEN ELIZABETH	Josephine Wray
LORD BELCHAMPS	Howard Gilbert
CHARLES II'S PAGES	Silvia Ashmole
	Gretta Grayson
LADY PRIMROSE FAIRFIELD	Joyce Grenfell
NURSE TO LADY PRIMROSE	Fedora Bernard
CHARLES II	Graham Payn
NELSON	Cliff Gordon
LORD FAIRFIELD	Frank O'Connor
LADY FAIRFIELD	Daphne Anderson
LADY HAMILTON	Marion Gordon
TOWN CRIER	Alan Clive
BRITANNIA	Madge Elliott
NEPTUNE	Tom Linden

VILLAGE GIRLS: Zoë Jack, Mavis Ray, Irlin Hall, Vivien Merchant, Jean Allison, Sheila Calder

NELSONIAN VILLAGERS: Silvia Ashmole, Gretta Grayson, Barbara Jdanova, Gwen Bateman, Joy O'Neill, Ann Sullivan, Betty Matthews, Enid Meredith, Renee Stocker

NELSONIAN SAILORS: Charles Russell, Grant Tyler, Leslie Baker, Howard Gilbert

NOBLES, ACOLYTES, GHOST OF 3RD EARL, *etc.*

A HERALD *marches on. With great pomp he takes up a stance in the centre and blows a fanfare. Much to his surprise from the end of the trumpet there comes a shower of cigarette-ends, ash and some pieces of paper. Slightly disconcerted, he retires to the side.*

Enter the SPIRIT OF MASQUE *to a musical chord. He strikes an attitude.*

SPIRIT:

> Greetings, Nobles, Gentles all,
> Centuries beyond recall
> We have spread before your gaze
> Memories of bygone days.
> We will show and pluck a flower
> Here and there from History's bower
> From our Island story—see
> Days of gay Knight Errantry.

But ho! Who cometh hence! I do avouch 'tis none other than the Lady Maud Hailsbury with her ladies. Alack, alack, her proud spirit droops with weeping and waiting.

> Now cheer thee, fairest ladye, do not weep,
> Sir Guy, thy lover, cometh ere ye sleep.

The SPIRIT OF MASQUE *jumps aside.*
Music. Enter the LADY MAUD HAILSBURY *leaning on her two waiting women. She is in sore distress.*

MISTRESS JOAN *and* MISTRESS ALICE, *the two waiting women, give each other an anxious look accompanied by a quiet perceptible nod and speak together.*

LADIES:

> Oh, cherished ladye, lift thy heart,
> Pluck from thy bosom sorrow's dart.

LADY MAUD:
Full many a weary, weary sun has set
Through winter and through spring and summer's leaf.
I cry, "Ah Swallow, dost thou see him yet?
Hast thou no tidings to assuage my grief?"

MISTRESS JOAN:
Heed not the swallows, ladye,
Time itself is on the wing.

MISTRESS ALICE:
At last—at last—I hear the blast
Of trumpets echoing.

LADY MAUD:
Say not, say, 'tis but a dream.

MISTRESS JOAN:
Nay, nay, verily he cometh.

The LADY MAUD *almost swoons but recovers herself.*
The SPIRIT OF MASQUE *steps forward.*

SPIRIT:
The waiting years, the weary years, all draweth to a close
Sir Guy de Belchamps now appears to claim his English
rose.

The music swells. There is, off stage, the sound of
horses' hooves, cheers, etc. A female voice cries "Hail Sir
Guy" shrilly several times.
Enter SIR GUY, *alone, in armour. He drops on one knee*
at LADY MAUD's *feet. She takes a flower from her bosom*
and gives it to him. After one rather abortive effort to rise
he is assisted to his feet by LADY MAUD.

SIR GUY:
At last, sweet Sweeting, all the joys we wist
Have consecrated thus our true love's tryst.

I'll to the castle to prepare thy way
With feast and wine and joyous roundelay.

Exit SIR GUY *with great "panache", unaware that*
LADY MAUD'S *sleeve has caught in his gauntlet.*
She is dragged off after him backwards followed
disconsolately by MISTRESS JOAN *and* MISTRESS ALICE.
The SPIRIT OF MASQUE *steps forward.*

SPIRIT:

And now a merry note rings out o'er valley, hill and lee,
The Morris rings, gay ribbons fly, birds sing from every
    tree,
There's dancing on the village green and English revelry.

Enter six VILLAGE GIRLS. *They all look fairly cold, one*
has a bandage round her knee, one has rimless glasses, one
looks extremely cross throughout. They do a pastoral
dance at the end of which they put down the branches
they have been waving and two of them retire momen-
tarily and return with two red chiffon scarves with which
they all painstakingly dance, finishing, not very success-
fully, with the Cross of St. George.
After the final tableau, they curtsy unevenly and exit.
The SPIRIT OF MASQUE *steps forward.*

SPIRIT:

To Fairfield's cloistered peace there came
Fully many a year ago
A Prelate whose illustrious name
In memory still doth glow.
Cry welcome to His Eminence,
Envoy to Bluff King Hal,
Hail wisdom, wit and eloquence,
King Harry's Cardinal.

The SPIRIT OF MASQUE, *after a sharp nod to the*
conductor, does a low bow. The music rises.

With great pomp and measured tread CARDINAL WOLSEY *enters with four* ACOLYTES.

He is a very tall man. As he reaches the centre of the stage he unfortunately steps on to the front of his long red robe. He takes three agonised steps forward, stops dead, and then slowly retreats again and with a superb gesture kicks the offending robe aside. This mishap, however, causes his mind to become a complete blank.

The music stops. He opens his mouth to deliver his great speech but no sound emerges. There he stands in silence.

The SPIRIT OF MASQUE *hisses "Kingdom" out of the corner of his mouth. Various other words are flung at him from off stage such as "My King"—"Glory"—"The Pope"—"Zeal"—but it is all of no avail. Finally with a gesture of utter hopelessness, he stamps hurriedly off, followed, at a canter, by the* ACOLYTES.

The SPIRIT OF MASQUE *bounds forward and claps his hands.*

SPIRIT (*with slightly overdone enthusiasm*):
     And now we turn the greatest, noblest page
     In this our turbulent, rich Island story
     Hear ye the echoes of this golden age
     Of sage and poet and of England's glory.

At this moment a Panama hat blows on to the stage, hotly pursued by the VIKING *who retrieves it and goes off.*
SPIRIT (*to* HERALD): Ho, there, boy. Make music for thy Queen cometh.

The HERALD *blows a fanfare.*

Re-enter the VILLAGE GIRLS *to music with baskets of rose leaves. Having scattered these they form a group of welcome. They and the* HERALD *and the* SPIRIT OF MASQUE *shout "Gloriana" in unison several times. The* GIRLS *curtsy and the* SPIRIT OF MASQUE *drops on to one knee.*

Enter QUEEN ELIZABETH *surrounded by six* NOBLES.

QUEEN: What stately pile is this?

1ST NOBLE: 'Tis the Manor of Belchamps, Gracious Majesty.

QUEEN (*ruminatively*): Belchamps! Art right, I wean. Methinks I heard the gulls on Thames, the London sparrows, screech out that word against my casement, or wast perhaps my drinking glass that rang when seas rode high—"Belchamps", "Belchamps"?

2ND NOBLE: 'Twas.

QUEEN: Prate thee no more, pretty boy. Fetch ye mine host. We will receive him in a manner both fitting and royal and render gracious thanks for hospitality most fairly matching to our State and Realm.

The 2ND NOBLE *exits and re-enters with* LORD BELCHAMPS, *who bears a scroll. He kneels, kisses the* QUEEN'S *hand, adjusts his glasses and opens the scroll.*

LORD BELCHAMPS:
Welcome, thrice welcome, England's great——

At this moment his glasses slip down. He lifts his right hand to re-adjust them and the scroll rolls itself up with a clatter. He unrolls it again.

Welcome, thrice welcome, England's great and multi-
    coloured star,
And thus embalm with grace and charm this place where
    now ye are.

At this moment the large pearl on QUEEN ELIZABETH'S *forehead begins to slip down. This necessitates her holding her head further and further back during the ensuing speech.*

QUEEN: I'faith, good host, thou wieldest a pretty pen. Odd's death, Belchamps, Belchamps. The name trips light enough for foreign ears but here, by halidon, the ears are English. Belchamps, Belchamps—Fairfield—Fairfield. That be the name for thee and thine henceforth. Methinks an earldom would not come amiss for one so brave and loyal. (*Aside.*) Boy—prithee, my sword.

A NOBLE *unsheathes his sword and hands it to her. By this time her head is so far back that she is unable to see. She makes a couple of passes in the air with the sword and then, instead of tapping him lightly on the shoulder, she gives him a rather sharp crack on the head. He staggers slightly but recovers with commendable dignity.*

QUEEN:

Rise, Earl of Fairfield. By this all men shall know
Our Royal favour and our love on thee we now bestow.

There is a fanfare of trumpets. LORD FAIRFIELD *kisses her hand, rises and backs away. The* QUEEN, *head still held back, sweeps across the stage with her attendants. The* 4TH NOBLE *tears off his cloak and spreads it at her feet. Being unable to see it, she misses it and walks off to regal music.*

Exit ALL.

The cloak is left on the stage.

The SPIRIT OF MASQUE *who has disappeared during the preceding scene, now re-enters swathed in a black cloak. He walks slowly to mournful music and takes up a dejected attitude.*

SPIRIT:

And now o'er England's story there lies a scarlet stain,
Birds still their song, the roses droop, the land is rent in
    twain.

This stately and serene demesne, no less than all the rest,
Gave of its blood, its hope, its Earl—the noblest and the
    best.

And since that bleak and mournful hour when e'er the
    moon doth wane,

A ghostly figure, head 'neath arm, Lord Fairfield walks
    again.

The SPIRIT OF MASQUE *retires to the side and stands in an attitude of melancholy with his head buried in his arms. There is the sound of moaning off stage. The* GHOST *of the third* EARL OF FAIRFIELD *walks on carrying his head beneath his arm. Unfortunately, the exigencies of his costume prevent him from seeing anything that is not in the direct focus of his eye-holes. He walks downstage with majestic tread and trips over Raleigh's cloak. This mishap upsets his equilibrium and causes him to drop the head that he carries under his arm. The head, being merely a painted rubber ball, bounces. With great presence of mind the* VIKING *springs on to the stage, pursues and captures it. Meanwhile the headless figure horrified by the disaster, loses control and, in an effort to get off, proceeds to charge madly about. The* VIKING, *aided by the* SPIRIT OF MASQUE, *finally pilots him off.*

The SPIRIT OF MASQUE *re-enters gaily without his black cloak.*

SPIRIT:
Oh, England's glad and England's gay,
And English hearts are free,
And English lads and lasses all,
And English lads and lasses all,
Are dancing on the lea,
Are dancing on the lea,
For Merry Charles, long live the King,
At last has crossed the sea.
With a hey and a ho and a whack folly—o
With a hey and a ho and a whack folly—o
The King has crossed the, crossed the, crossed the sea.

He retires to the side of the stage where he sinks down cross-legged and claps his hands.
Two PAGES *bring on a rustic sea.*
The music swells.

The madcap LADY PRIMROSE FAIRFIELD *bounds on, followed sedately by her* NURSE.

NURSE: A pox on thy hoydenish ways. Thou art as forward a nursling as ever cut a cape 'twixt Severn and Thames.

LADY PRIMROSE: Be not angry, Grumbleskins, my heart is light today.

NURSE: Aye—'Twould be lighter yet did ye but do your mother's bidding and wed Sir Robert as was promised at thy cradle.

LADY PRIMROSE: Oh fie on Sir Robert—he is a very bumpkin and I—and I—(*She runs impulsively and kisses her* NURSE.) Sweet nurse, sweet Grumbleskins—take note of me. These hands, this heart, these lips, were they not fashioned for gayer wooing than that of puffing and puking old Sir Robert? I am as my father's young falcons that would try their wings.

NURSE: Whither would'st thou fly, birdling?

LADY PRIMROSE: To London—to Court—to see the King.

NURSE: My bonny is but a moppet still. Dream thy dreams later, child.

LADY PRIMROSE: Moppet or no—my heart is troubled. I fain would be alone. Leave me awhile, my sampler here will keep busy these idle fingers.

NURSE (*warningly*): Take care.

LADY PRIMROSE: Away with ye—Moll-o-Nightshade!

The NURSE *goes away.*

LADY PRIMROSE *sits on the bench with her sampler and begins to sing.*

LADY PRIMROSE (*singing*):
>   I thread my needle in and out
>   Ah, so merrily,
>   Beneath my hands the rosebuds sprout
>   Yea, yea verily
>   Yea, yea verily
>   Beyond the hills, beyond the streams
>   Hey, hey, lackaday
>   The beckoning light of London gleams

Must I remain alone with dreams?
Nay, nay, lackaday me
Nay, nay, lackaday.

She falls a-dreaming. There is the sound of a hunting-horn in the distance.
The SPIRIT OF MASQUE *springs to his feet, and, cupping his hands round his mouth, whimsically echoes the sound of the horn.*

SPIRIT:
And here began the story of that madcap, madcap maid
Who, seeking love and glory, left Fairfield's bosky glade
With Lords and Gallants lightly, nay even with the King
She danced her lovely life away and paid the reckoning.

The SPIRIT OF MASQUE *sits down again.*
Enter KING CHARLES II.

KING CHARLES: Meseems I have lost the quarry; but stay, methinks these grey walls may shelter fairer game. Sweet lady—— (*He doffs his hat and bows.*)

LADY PRIMROSE (*springing to her feet and dropping a curtsy*): Sir—who art thou?

KING CHARLES (*whimsically*):
A man from the East,
A man from the West,
A bird on a weary wing,
A peasant, a rogue, a poet, a clown,
A man, or mayhap——

LADY PRIMROSE (*recognising him and going into a deep reverence*): The King!

KING CHARLES (*raising her*): Thy name, sweet fairing?

LADY PRIMROSE: The Lady Primrose Fairfield, sir, and your most humble servant.

KING CHARLES: A truce on such humility, sweet coz. Come now, dissemble—those cherry lips were made for laughter and for kisses too, I'll warrant.

LADY PRIMROSE: Then it is true, the Merry Monarch demands of his subjects only merriment?

KING CHARLES: Pertly put, lass—would'st come to court and trip a measure in the candlelight?

LADY PRIMROSE (*dropping her eyes*): Royal Sire, thou hast divined my dearest dream. Were I but a moth to burn my wings in that same candlelight and flutter sorrowfully to earth, still I would cry Aye and Aye to that.

KING CHARLES: Take thou this ring. (*He tugs at a ring and, after some difficulty manages to get it off.*) 'Twill serve as a talisman—I'll send for thee—doubt me not and hold in thy memory my Royal promise—

> The early dew falls soft on field and dell
> And so sweet Prim, farewell—farewell, farewell——

> *The* KING *doffs his hat, this time unfortunately doffing his wig with it. He replaces both hurriedly but a trifle inaccurately and—goes off.*

LADY PRIMROSE (*lapsing once more into song*):
> I thread my needle out and in
> No more verily
> No love so gay could be a sin
> Love, laugh merrily—
> Love, laugh merrily—

> *With a hoydenish gesture she flings her sampler away and dances off gaily laughing.*
> *The* SPIRIT OF MASQUE *rises to his feet.*

SPIRIT:
> And thus love blossomed, drooped, and died in tears
> The while we turn a yet more lustrous page.
> Come skip with me a-down the pregnant years
> To where, emblazoned on the sea, appears
> The spume-flung glory of our heritage.
> England's darling, England's pride,
> (Avast—belay—the green seas over)

Who is that walks by his side?
(The broadsides crash from Nile to Dover)
England's darling, England's joy,
(Haul my hearties—pull away)
To Fairfield comes on a summer day
To render thanks as a sailor may
For Fairfield oaks and a Fairfield boy.

> *Nautical music crashes out.*
> *Enter* LORD NELSON *and* LADY HAMILTON *followed by an elderly* LORD *and* LADY FAIRFIELD *and a* SERVING-MAID *with cloaks over her arm.*

NELSON (*in a strong Welsh accent*): Farewell now to a fair prospect. You have heard my news of your boy—a stout lad is he, strong in courage as the timbers of his ancient house.

LORD FAIRFIELD: My Lord Admiral, you do us too much honour.

LADY FAIRFIELD (*curtsying*): All England is in your debt. We are e'en closer bound by your courtesy.

NELSON: 'Tis nothing, madam. And now my Lady Hamilton and I must say adieu.

LORD FAIRFIELD (*to* LADY HAMILTON): It is monstrous pleasant of your ladyship to have done us this signal honour.

LADY HAMILTON: Nay, Lord Fairfield, as a seagull follows a ship, this dear Englishman to whom my heart is bound I follow o'er horizon's furthest rim.

> *At this moment there is the noise of a violent cock-fight off stage. The* VIKING *is seen rushing across at the back with a pail of water. Presently the noise subsides into a series of diminishing yelps.*

NELSON: And now we really must depart. By God's grace and a fair wind we should make Norwich by nightfall.

LORD FAIRFIELD: Ere you "Away anchor", sir, I would warn you that all the village wenches and lads are a-tiptoe to garland their country's hero.

LADY FAIRFIELD: See, here they come.

> *There is a burst of music and a crowd of* VILLAGERS

rush on cheering. They form themselves into a group which involves a certain amount of indecision. Their leader, who is the vicar disguised as a TOWN CRIER, *gives them a sign and they break into a victorious ode to* NELSON, NEPTUNE *and* BRITANNIA.

CHORAL ODE:

> Lord of the seas whose billows break
> Against our Island shores,
> And at whose voice stout hearts awake
> And each brave spirit soars,
> All hail to ye whose stubborn might
> Our Island freedom gave,
> Behold Britannia shining bright
> With Neptune as her slave!

Enter four NELSONIAN SAILORS *dragging, with considerable difficulty, a vast gilt cockle-shell. When it has reached centre-stage it comes to a halt. The* SAILORS *tug at the gilt ropes. The shell opens, disclosing* BRITANNIA *standing with helmet and shield. At her feet, in a slightly cringing attitude, is* NEPTUNE, *holding a trident.*

Owing to an error, however, their backs are turned to the audience thereby rather destroying the illusion. Realising what has happened they proceed, with commendable presence of mind, to turn slowly and, with the music still playing, contrive to strike a more or less effective attitude as——

THE CURTAIN FALLS

PLAYLETS, ADDITIONAL
SKETCHES AND EARLY PIECES

This section contains sketches and playlets that were not part of one of the revues. They cover much of Noël's career and are arranged in chronological order.

WHAT NEXT?

A Farcical Comedy in One Act
by Esmé Wynne and Noël Coward

written 1915

Noël's writing career began as a series of collaborations with his friend and fellow child actor, Esmé Wynne, who "was determined to be a writer, an ambition that filled me with competitive fervour. She wrote poems. Reams and reams of them, love songs, sonnets and villanelles; alive with elves, mermaids, leafy glades and Pan (a good deal of Pan). . . . Our Egos were battling for recognition and encouragement and we supplied one another generously with praise and mild, very mild criticism."

They also collaborated in writing plays. The first fragment the Archives reveal is part of "What Next? A Farcical Comedy in One Act", written around 1915 and a piece with a not surprisingly autobiographical slant. ("Esmé and I became inseparable ... We alternated between childishness and strange maturity. The theatre had led us far in precocity and we discussed life and death and sex and religion with sublime sophistication. We also dressed in each other's clothes and paraded the West End.") They were also engaged in early 1916 to play Amy and Charley in a touring company version of *Charley's Aunt* "at salaries of two pounds and two pounds ten a week respectively". "What Next?" tied these threads loosely together.

CHARACTERS

HEATHER WILTON
JIM HALFORD

Scene: Drawing-room of Mrs. Wilton's House. HEATHER
   WILTON *discovered alone.*

HEATHER (*running to window and then to door*): He will
be here soon now. Oh! Won't we have fun? I wish he would
be quick, I'm simply dying for him to come.
   Knock at the door heard off.
That must be him. I'll go and see.
   Exit. Sound of door opening off.
Oh, here you are at last.
   Sound of loud kiss. Re-enter HEATHER *with* JIM
   HALFORD *who looks round in a rather surprised way.*
JIM: Hist, your Ma might hear us.
HEATHER: There's no need to hist, everybody is out. Do
you suppose that I should ask you here with Mother in the
house? Why, she'd have a fit if she saw you.
JIM: Are you alluding to my personal appearance?
HEATHER: No, of course not, silly. You know quite well
how Mother detests boys. That is just where I don't quite
agree with her.
JIM: Thanks for the compliment.
HEATHER: I mean some boys.
JIM: Pig!
HEATHER: Pig yourself.
JIM: Oh, shut up!
HEATHER: All right, let's have some tea.
   *They are just about to sit down when a loud rat-a-tat
   comes at the front door.*
HEATHER: What on earth's that?
JIM: Let's go and see.
   They go off. Sound of door opening off.
HEATHER: A telegram.
   Enter both.
Who can it be from?

JIM: I should think the best way to find out would be to open it.

HEATHER: All right, clever. (*She opens it and reads.*) "Will arrive nearly as soon as this. Arabella." My goodness gracious, what on earth's to be done? Jim, do read it.

JIM (*after reading*): Whew! My aunt, I shall have to go. I have a dim recollection of Miss Arabella's nose. But oh! I say, this is disappointing, isn't it? We were going to have such fun.

HEATHER: I've got an idea.

JIM: Does it hurt?

HEATHER: Don't be an ass—but listen. What do you say if I dress you up as a girl?

JIM: Really, Heather, I'm surprised at you.

HEATHER: Oh, I don't mean that *I* should dress you, idiot. You can dress behind the screen and I'll hand the things over to you and if you want anything special done for you, I'm here!

JIM: I say, you know, I am afraid I should make a most awful ass of myself.

HEATHER: Oh, that would be no change.

JIM: There you go again with your insulting remarks.

HEATHER: Oh, Jim, do let's do it!

JIM: But why shouldn't I just be my ordinary self?

HEATHER: Why, good gracious, she would tell Mother the very first moment she saw her.

JIM: I suppose it will *have* to be then. What clothes have you got?

HEATHER: All my summer clothes are at the wash, so you will have to have a cold and wear winter ones.

JIM: Oh, heavens!

HEATHER: Let's get the screen ready.

JIM: Righto.

> They arrange screen. HEATHER goes out and returns with a drawer full of clothes.

HEATHER: I'll get two walking-sticks and we can hand the

things over with them. You had better be arranging the screen to your satisfaction while I am getting them.

Exits.

JIM (*arranging screen*): Oh, won't there be a kick-up if I'm found out. I shall have to be careful.

Re-enter HEATHER *with sticks.*

HEATHER: Ready?

JIM: Yes.

HEATHER: Well, retire then and disrobe and for heaven's sake don't knock the screen down.

Business.

JIM (*behind the screen*): Oh, bother this bally skirt. I can't get the thing done up. How women exist with these rotten things is a puzzle to me.

HEATHER: Shall I come and help you?

JIM: No, for heaven's sake, don't knock the screen down. Look out!

Knocks screen down. HEATHER *falls on the floor flat on her face, shaking with laughter.* JIM *picks up the screen.*

HEATHER: Hurry up or I shall burst.

[*Manuscript ends*]

WOMAN AND WHISKEY
originally called THE MAJOR SAYS WHEN

A Play in One Act
by "ESNOMEL" (Esmé Wynne and Noël Coward)

written 1917

The first of Noël and Esmé's plays to be produced was a "light comedy" called *Ida Collaborates*, which had to do with the unrequited love of a charwoman's daughter for a distinguished author. The piece was written under the pen name of "ESNOMEL" (a combination of Esmé and Noël) and Esmé played the lead part of Ida when it was produced at the Theatre Royal, Aldershot (20 August, 1917), and on a subsequent tour.

ESNOMEL's second effort came a year later. *Woman and Whiskey* (originally *The Major Says When*) was produced at the Wimbledon Theatre in January 1918 as a curtain raiser to the evening's featured play – *A Pair of Silk Stockings* – and was subsequently taken on tour.

CHARACTERS

MRS. VANDELEUR
MAJOR CURTIS
NORAH CHALMERS
LONER

Scene: A small lounge in a society woman's house. She is giving
a dance and during the following scene, popular dance
music may be faintly heard.

The lounge contains orthodox furniture, a couch, some
whiskey and siphons on a side table being the only
requisite articles of the setting.

Through a curtained doorway enters MAJOR CURTIS, *a*
short, middle-aged, somewhat bronzed man. He crosses
swiftly to the whiskey and stretches out his hand for it
when MRS. VANDELEUR *appears at the doorway.*

MRS. VANDELEUR: Ah! Major Curtis! So you too are bored
with this enervating whirl! How clever of you to have found
this little retreat too. I am always very careful to find such a
spot at every house I frequent. Otherwise I fear dancing
would become too strenuous a pastime for one of my age.

MAJOR CURTIS *has screened the side table and its*
contents from sight by standing with his back to it. It
must be remembered all through this dialogue that MRS.
VANDELEUR *does not notice this table, which is the reason*
for several of her inapt remarks. Had she seen it, she is
sufficient woman of the world to have left MAJOR CURTIS
with a very different opinion of her.

CURTIS: You must not speak disparagingly about our age.
Remember, if we have not the fresh allurements of youth, we
have all the wisdom of a riper age.

MRS. VANDELEUR (*recovering herself*): Yes, excessive youth
is wearing. When one has lived as long as we have, one longs
for a quiet home shared by an intelligent companion.

CURTIS (*hastily*): Yes, yes, quite so, but I believe the
homely cheerful companion idea of a woman has gone out of
fashion now.

MRS. VANDELEUR: Yes, men expect their wives to be their
mistresses as well nowadays—that is why women are—as

they are, but I'm sure at heart there are many who would be glad to go back to the old regime.

CURTIS: Do you think so? They appear to me to be as keen on the new order as the men, and smoke and drink with equal zest. (*He steals a hopeful glance at the whiskey*)

MRS. VANDELEUR: Ah, yes. How I hate to see women drink—don't you?

CURTIS (*still stealthily gazing at the whiskey*): Well—er—yes—at times it becomes unbearably irritating.

MRS. VANDELEUR (*content*): There, I felt sure you would agree with me. I loathe drink.

CURTIS (*regretfully*): Yes, I supposed you would.

MRS. VANDELEUR: I hope you don't mind a little smoking? In moderation, of course.

CURTIS: I like it.

MRS. VANDELEUR: Then give me a cigarette, will you? (CURTIS *produces case.*) Do you really like dancing—match?—or is it a duty which must be performed?

CURTIS (*lighting cigarette*): Oh, I like it because it occasionally enables me to encircle a charming waist.

MRS. VANDELEUR: How polite and sweet of you! Thanks.

> *Enter* NORAH CHALMERS, *a young maiden of some twenty winters, dressed in an expensive white frock bought at an old-established firm which could be relied upon for turning one out really home-made. She is fair and pretty.*

NORAH: Oh, Major Curtis, I've been looking for you the whole evening. Mumsie sent a message for you and I've wanted to give it to you all this time—couldn't find you anywhere. Besides—(*Coyly.*) my programme's been so full.

CURTIS: Of course, it must be. What is the message?

NORAH (*puckering her brow for a moment*): Oh—o-oh I am a silly. D'you know, I've actually forgotten. (*Giggles.*) But I've such a lot of other things to think about—mostly military. (*Giggles.*) D'you mind if I sit with you for a little while? I really do need a rest from all those silly boys.

(*Giggles.*) Why do they always want to make love to one? It is so trying when one wants to be real friends with a man, don't you think so, Mrs. Vandeleur?

MRS. VANDELEUR: Personally I believe firmly in the theory that men behave exactly as we would have them behave. And, except for blackguards, it is generally our fault if they behave badly.

NORAH: Oh, but I *hate* flirting, and men *will* do it. They're *all* alike, *aren't* they, Major Curtis?

CURTIS: Certainly not.

NORAH: Oh, well *I've* found them so.

MRS. VANDELEUR (*acidly*): That is because those you meet are all of one type.

NORAH (*hastily*): Not at all. They're all totally different.

CURTIS (*gently*): You said we were all the same just now.

NORAH: Oh, well, you know what I mean. (*Giggles.*)

MRS. VANDELEUR: It becomes difficult at times—but we mustn't be harsh. You're very young.

NORAH (*coyly*): I know—I can't help it. (*Hoping to be contradicted.*) It *is* a pity. Of course, you think I'm a little fool.

MRS. VANDELEUR *and* CURTIS (*unconvincingly*): Oh, no.

NORAH: It wouldn't matter, of course, if I were *really* pretty like Letty Lane.

CURTIS: My dear young lady, who was that great poet who said "Kind hearts—better than pretty faces." What?

MRS. VANDELEUR: "Coronets", Major. Of course, that would be a poet's point of view.

NORAH: Now you're going to talk about poetry and it's *so* stodgy.

MRS. VANDELEUR: Do you think so? What do *you* like talking about?

NORAH: Oh, fun—and theatres. I *adore* revues.

CURTIS: Apropos of theatres, don't you admire Rosa Beauleigh?—A beautiful actress—a beautiful woman.

NORAH: Oh, Major Curtis, how *can* you? I think she's *so* affected and *far* too fat to be beautiful.

MRS. VANDELEUR: I remember the first time I saw her. I was quite a . . . child, with very short skirts and very long legs. I thought she was perfectly wonderful—*then*. I suppose she must have been about thirty—yes, a charming woman.

CURTIS (*surprised*): You surprise me! Been going all that time? Well, well, how our side of the curtain is taken in! Clever actress, though!

NORAH: Oh, *I* don't think so—she's ever so affected. Do *you* think she's clever, Mrs. Vandeleur?

MRS. VANDELEUR: Any woman is clever, my dear, who can obtain pearls and furs in such quantity and quality.

CURTIS: Yes, yes, I suppose in private life she's not quite— quite——

MRS. VANDELEUR (*shrugging wisely*): Oh, probably a very interesting woman—but why speak of her? Do you know, Major Curtis—I've met you—is it four or five times?—and you have never told me anything about yourself? I'm sure you've had an exciting varied life—you've lived a lot in India, haven't you?

CURTIS: Most of my life, yes, but I'm afraid my little experiences are all unworthy of such delightful ears.

MRS. VANDELEUR: We should be most interested, really.

NORAH: Awfully.

CURTIS: Oh—er—well, in the main it is very like other men's lives in similar circumstances.

NORAH: I'm sure it isn't. I think your face looks as though you'd passed through a lot.

MAJOR CURTIS *looks at her sharply.*

MRS. VANDELEUR: That remark might be misconstrued.

NORAH: Oh dear, have I said anything dreadful?

CURTIS: Of course not. Oh well, I suppose I have seen a good bit of life in my time. I remember once in——

NORAH: Oh, do tell us.

CURTIS: Well, when I was stationed at Poona——

MRS. VANDELEUR: Poona? Did you say Poona? How very strange! Did you happen to meet a man called Wynell?—Colonel Wynell?

CURTIS: No, he was not there in my time. As I was saying—we used to go out for long night rides——

MRS. VANDELEUR: I did hope you might know him—such a sweet man. His wife was a great friend of mine—just the least bit *passé*, poor woman, but still attractive to the opposite sex.

CURTIS: Ah yes! Well, one evening, just as we were starting, my friend Vorden and I——

MRS. VANDELEUR: Vorden!—the very man. Excuse me, Major, but this is a most extraordinary coincidence. Did he tell you, I wonder? There was a fearful scandal about him and the Colonel's wife. When they were at Bombay. I never knew whether it was a riding boot, or an indiscreet hair-pin. But everybody knew about it.

CURTIS: That makes me doubt its authenticity.

MRS. VANDELEUR: How subtle of you!

NORAH: Oh, you are funny, Major Curtis.

MRS. VANDELEUR: Well, there was a terrific row and I believe it was then Vorden got transferred and—oh, but don't let me interrupt your story, Major.

CURTIS (*once more warming to his tale*): Well, one night, just as we were starting, I said we had better take our revolvers, as the natives had been rather troublesome at that time and there was no harm in taking necessary precautions. Just then a man called Rowlands came up——

NORAH: Rowlands? Had he very blue eyes and kinky wavy fair hair? Do say! 'Cos I'm sure he must be the brother of a friend of mine. He went to some part of India about four years ago.

CURTIS: India is a large place and that was twelve years ago, Miss Chalmers, when your little friend was probably just escaping from his bibs and tuckers.

NORAH (*gravely*): No, Major. Rowly must be quite twenty-four.

MRS. VANDELEUR (*with a sigh*): I was getting so interested in your story, Major. Do let him continue, Norah dear.

NORAH: I'm *so* sorry—you *must* think me rude. *Do* go on, Major.

CURTIS: Rowlands warned us that there was too much unrest abroad to make night-riding safe—However we were not to be deterred. So we took our Brownings——

NORAH: Oh, do you like him so much! I used to recite "The Pied Piper" when I was at school—but why for a night ride?

MRS. VANDELEUR (*laughing*): Oh, Norah, you are too ridiculous.

CURTIS: There are pistols as well as poets of that name, my child.

NORAH (*giggling*): O-oh, I am a silly.

CURTIS: Well, we took our Brownings and started off. Sure enough, after we had been riding an hour or two, there came a volley of lead from an adjacent rock.

NORAH (*ecstatically*): A volcano!

CURTIS: On the contrary—natives. To resume—we hastily whipped off our horses——

NORAH: How cruel of you, Major!

MRS. VANDELEUR: Please go on.

CURTIS: Then we loaded our revolvers, all ready to fire if another volley came.

MRS. VANDELEUR (*with excessive interest*): And did it?

CURTIS: Not at once. Those beggars know how to torture. I consider those few moments the most nerve-racking of my life.

NORAH (*intelligently*): You must have been upset.

CURTIS: Then once more they fired. We returned it quickly. I potted a chap at once, I remember. I can see him falling off that rock now.

He gazes with a rapt expression at a nude pedestal on

his left. The women's eyes follow his and retire quickly in
confusion.

Then, to our horror, we perceived in the distance a whole
band of horsemen. Turning to Vorden, I cried——

MRS. VANDELEUR: It certainly must be the same man.

CURTIS (*firmly*): I cried—"The game's up, old man, unless
we run for it, and it'll have to be hell for leather if we do."

NORAH: That was naughty of you. (*Giggles.*)

MRS. VANDELEUR: And what did he say?

CURTIS: "Right, by God. We'll do the swine in yet." And,
with the bullets spattering the sands around us, we shook
hands.

NORAH: Why?

CURTIS (*lamely*): Oh—I don't know—because—because—
why, one does, y'know. (*Slight pause. He looks quickly at
both listeners who attend with polite smiles.*) Anyhow, we
jumped on our horses.

NORAH: Oh, had they come back?

CURTIS: How d'you mean?

NORAH: You said you'd whipped them off just now.

CURTIS: Oh, I didn't mean whipped them off—I meant
whipped off them.

NORAH (*hazily*): Oh, I see.

CURTIS: Well, we spurred our horses and galloped away.
God! How we galloped. On, on, across that endless plain, the
thud, thud of the natives pursuing us.

NORAH: Did they thud with a tom-tom?

MRS. VANDELEUR: Norah!

CURTIS: It was the feet of their horses that we heard
thudding.

NORAH: How exciting!

CURTIS: At last in the distance we saw the lights of Poona.
With one more effort we spurred our exhausted horses, and
arrived in the nick of time.

NORAH: How thrilling! What did the natives do?

CURTIS: I really don't know, Miss Chalmers.

NORAH (*coyly*): I expect you think I'm an awful silly.

MRS. VANDELEUR: I wonder, Norah, if you'd be a dear and tell Captain Masters I shan't be dancing again this evening. I really am not capable. Old age again—eh Major!

NORAH: Oh, all right, but I want to hear more stories, Major. You'll wait here, won't you?

CURTIS (*with an eye on the whiskey*): Oh, yes—quite, quite possibly.

    Exit NORAH.

MRS. VANDELEUR: Charming pretty girl! If youth but learnt to converse and do its hair, life for a woman of my age would be completely aimless.

CURTIS: Is your refusal to dance again final?

MRS. VANDELEUR: Is this an invitation?

CURTIS: Why, no. Personally I should prefer to stay here, but I hate to think of depriving you of pleasure.

MRS. VANDELEUR: This quiet and the conversation of one intelligent man appeals to me far more than that fearful crush and dull small talk.

CURTIS (*dutifully*): It is most charming of you to take compassion on my loneliness.

MRS. VANDELEUR: Now that that dear idiotic girl has gone, we can have a real talk. I do so want to know all the real things about you. It is difficult to talk before girls. Tell me, are women *of*, or merely *in* your life?

CURTIS: Eh? Oh—er—oh, I see what you mean, I am occasionally very fond of their company.

MRS. VANDELEUR (*smiling delightedly*): Yes, but tell me all about it—your real love affair I mean. I know by your eyes that you have experienced a *grande passion.*

CURTIS: We cannot live in our age without it, dear lady. I met her at Simla—charming girl—ardent mother—lots of frills and white dresses and pretty talk. It was soon done.

MRS. VANDELEUR: I don't understand. The love affair?

CURTIS: Why no. Even when the lady became my wife——

MRS. VANDELEUR: Your wife?

CURTIS: But I'm boring you.

MRS. VANDELEUR (*hastily*): Not in the least—not in the least. But when did—when did the sad event occur, you poor dear?

CURTIS: Sad? I don't understand.

MRS. VANDELEUR: Oh, forgive me. Of course, you wouldn't like to speak of it.

CURTIS: Of what?

MRS. VANDELEUR: Your poor dear wife's death, of course.

CURTIS: Dead? My wife dead? She's as alive as most of us. I am joining her at Brighton in a week's time.

MRS. VANDELEUR: Really?—I heard—indeed, I understood you were unmarried.

CURTIS: Ah yes, probably confounding me with my younger brother—the wealthy one, you know. Most unfair, isn't it?

> MRS. VANDELEUR *rises.*

You're not going?

MRS. VANDELEUR: Indeed yes. I had forgotten Captain Masters has promised to drive me home in his adorable car. I mustn't mortally offend him.

CURTIS: You leave me a happier man than you found me.

MRS. VANDELEUR (*going*): So sweet of you!

> *Enter* NORAH.

Ah, Norah, look after the Major. My energies are returned, so I shall be able to manage one more dance after all.

NORAH: Captain Masters has retired to the supper room for consolation. Do go and comfort him, poor man.

> MRS. VANDELEUR *smiles and goes out.*

CURTIS (*looking despairingly at the whiskey. Then squaring his shoulders for another attack*): That was considerate of Mrs. Vandeleur to leave you to take care of me, but——

NORAH: Yes, she's awfully nice—sometimes. I never understand why, 'cos women of her age are always so jealous of people who still wear their own hair and teeth.

CURTIS: Isn't that the sort of speech that gives women a reputation for cattiness?

NORAH: Yes, it *is* bad of me but she *is* horribly old, isn't she?

CURTIS: About five years younger than I am, probably.

NORAH: Ah, but men are different, aren't they? I get so tired of young men. The old ones are far more interesting.

CURTIS: Are *you* tired of dancing, too?

NORAH: Not if you want to dance, but I'm quite happy talking to you.

CURTIS (*despondently*): That is very nice of you.

NORAH: Tell me, do you think people should marry young?

CURTIS: If by people you mean women, I should advise them to marry as soon as they're asked nowadays.

NORAH: But suppose they're in love with a man who doesn't know or respond?

CURTIS: If pretty, they should hope. If plain, retire to a convent, or go to the country and forget in a whirl of gaiety.

NORAH: I believe you're laughing at me, Major. And I *do* so need advice.

CURTIS: People who need advice never ask for it.

NORAH: How clever! I think I've read that somewhere.

CURTIS: Yes, it was in the London *Mail*, but it's very rude of you to say so.

NORAH: Is it? I'm so sorry. Don't tell Mumsie. She doesn't seem to realise how frank I am by nature. She calls it tactlessness. I hate tact. It always seems to belong to those women who have a lot to conceal in their lives.

CURTIS: I believe if you were ten years older, Miss Chalmers, you'd have made that sound quite clever.

NORAH: Now *you're* being rude. I wasn't meaning to be clever.

CURTIS: I know you weren't, so I forgive you.

NORAH (*impulsively*): I like you. D'you know—we're going to be friends, aren't we?

CURTIS (*looking at whiskey*): That rests entirely with you, of course.

NORAH: Then we will be—Have you a car?

CURTIS: Two—at least—one belongs to me, and the other—to my wife.

NORAH: Your wife? Oh! (*Recovering herself.*) Oh, Major, please forgive me. I'd forgotten I'd promised this dance to Harry. He foxtrots angelically.

CURTIS: Splendid idea! Of course—of course. Give him my love.

NORAH: Why, d'you know him?

CURTIS: Not in the least, but he's a good fellow—I'm sure he's a good fellow.

NORAH (*at door, giggling*): He's a lamb.

    Exit NORAH. CURTIS *breathes a sigh of relief, pours himself out a liberal drink, is adding soda when* LONER, *a man in immaculate evening dress, enters.* CURTIS *at first looks up anxiously, then smiles and drains his glass.*

LONER: Escaped the fair sex at last, Curtis? How did you manage it?

CURTIS: Oh, awful, old chap, awful. (*Again pours out whiskey.*) I'm not in a fit state to talk just now.

LONER (*smiling*): Why do you come to these crushes? Why leave the comforts of bachelor room and club for this?

CURTIS: Heaven knows! Softening of the brain and a gregarious father, I suppose. True, he left me a considerable fortune, but also the acquaintance of half the hostesses in town, though as Saki says somewhere, it seems unjust that the sins of the fathers should be visited on the children. By the way, did I hear you address me by the term "bachelor"? Please remember, when speaking to Mrs. Vandeleur and Miss Chalmers, that I'm a respectable married man with a wife— mind you, a wife—at Brighton.

LONER: My dear Curtis, was it necessary to go to this excess? Surely the Poona fabrication didn't fail you?

CURTIS: Yes, and worse, it inspired Miss Chalmers to positive gems of wit.

LONER (*sympathetically, handing cigar case*): My poor fellow!

CURTIS: Thanks. I suppose there must be women in the world to ensure sympathy among men.

CURTAIN

MILD OATS

written 1922
one-act play – unproduced

Strangely, Coward makes no mention of this piece in any of his autobiographical writings. At a time when he was just finding his dramatic voice – *The Young Idea* and *The Queen Was In the Parlour* were written in the same year – he may well have felt that it was too close for mature comfort to the Boy/Girl material he had been writing with Esmé. In addition, as a would-be writer of revue sketches – *London Calling!* was only a year away – he may have felt that *Mild Oats* lacked the dramatic "blackout" he considered essential.

None the less, it remains a wistful little piece, hinting – as much of his later writing was to do – at the feelings that lie beneath the words.

CHARACTERS

HE (Hugh Lombard)
SHE (Mary Jevon)

*When the curtain rises the stage is in darkness. There is the
    sound of voices. Enter* YOUNG MAN *followed by* YOUNG
    WOMAN. *He turns up lights, disclosing a comfortable little
    study with a sofa, arm-chairs, books, etc., and the remains
    of a fire in the grate.*

HE: Won't you sit down?

SHE: Yes—thank you. (*She comes slowly down and sits on
the sofa. She takes off her coat.*)

HE (*after a slight pause*): Do you know—the weather
really is quite chilly.

SHE (*with an effort*): Isn't it? One can feel the tang of
autumn in the air.

HE: Yes, one can.

    Another pause.

SHE (*defiantly*): I *like* London in the autumn!

HE (*with equal defiance*): So do I!

SHE: It's so—so—melancholy.

HE: Yes—yes, melancholy—that's what it is.

SHE: What's the time?

HE (*glaring at his watch*): Half-past twelve.

SHE: It's late, isn't it?

HE: Very late.

SHE: What a pretty room.

HE: Yes, isn't it?—I mean—do you think so?

SHE: Oh yes—it's so—so cosy and home-like.

HE: I'm so glad.

SHE (*rising*): Books, too. Do you read much?

HE: Now and then. I mean—you know—sometimes.

SHE (*at shelves*): Nice books—specially that one.

HE: Which one?

SHE: Here—Strindberg.

HE: Oh, Strindberg—rather depressing fellow, isn't he?

SHE: Yes, but life—real life all the time—no false sentiment and—and—hypocrisy.

HE: Oh no, rather not—as a matter of fact I haven't read him much. This flat isn't really mine, you know—only lent to me.

SHE: Oh, I see. (*She sits down again.*)

HE: I haven't been here long.

SHE: It's very central.

HE: Yes—isn't it? (*Another pause.*) Would you like something to drink?

SHE (*quickly*): Oh no, thank you. (*Correcting herself.*) That is—perhaps—(*With determination.*) Yes, I would.

HE: I'm afraid there's only whiskey and soda. (*Crosses to table.*)

SHE (*blankly*): Whiskey and soda!

HE: Yes—is that all right?

SHE: Yes—that's all right.

HE: Say when.

SHE (*hurriedly*): Not much, you know—just a little—now—there—that's enough.

HE (*handing her a colourless drink*): It's very weak.

SHE (*shutting her eyes and handing it back*): Put some more whiskey in, then.

HE (*startled by her sudden vehemence*): Oh, all right—here you are.

SHE (*taking it*): Thank you—(*She sniffs it.*) Oh dear!

HE: What is it?

SHE: Nothing——

  She sips it and shudders. He doesn't notice.

HE (*sitting next to her on sofa*): Funny my meeting you like that.

SHE (*with a nervous laugh*): Yes—wasn't it?

HE: I could have sworn I'd seen you before somewhere.

SHE: I don't think so.

HE: Silly mistake to make. Look here, I——

SHE (*edging away*): What is it?

HE: Oh, nothing.

SHE (*after a pause*): I should like you to understand that——

HE: Yes?

SHE (*looking down*): Oh, nothing.

HE (*suddenly*): It's no use; I can't——

SHE: Can't what?

HE: Can't go on any longer. (*With vehemence.*) Look here, I don't care what you think of me—you're probably laughing up your sleeve all the time—but it doesn't matter—I mean—look here, will you go now?

SHE (*with her hand to her head*): You mean?—Oh dear! (*She faints on to his shoulder.*)

HE: Good God! (*He fans her.*) This is awful—awful! Wake up for heaven's sake—Oh, this is terrible! (*He props her up with a cushion.*)

SHE (*opening her eyes*): Oh—what have I done?

HE: You fainted.

SHE (*bursting into tears*): Oh, this is awful—horrible! (*She leans on the edge of sofa and buries her head in her arms.*)

HE: I say, what's the matter? I didn't mean to be rude—honestly I didn't——

SHE (*sobbing*): I'm so ashamed—so dreadfully, dreadfully ashamed.

HE: Here, drink a little of this. (*He offers her her untasted drink.*)

SHE (*pushing it away*): Take it away, it makes me sick.

HE: All right. I say, I'm so sorry—do please stop crying.

SHE: Leave me alone—just for a minute, then I shall feel better. (*She sits up.*)

HE: I am a beast!

SHE: No you're not—that's just it—you're not, thank God. (*She rises.*) I must go at once.

HE: Where do you live?

SHE: Kensington.

HE: I'll see you home.

SHE: Oh no, please don't—it isn't necessary——

HE: I'll get you a taxi, then.

SHE: Very well—thank you.

HE: Wait here. (*He goes to door.*)

SHE: Stop.

HE (*startled*): What is it?

SHE: Please come and sit down—just for a moment. I want to tell you something——

HE: But——

SHE: Please—I really must—it may relieve this feeling of beastly degradation to tell you the truth——

HE: I wish you wouldn't look so unhappy.

SHE (*vehemently*): Unhappy! I'm desperately, bitterly ashamed—I've no words to express my utter contempt of myself——

HE: I don't understand.

SHE: I'm not what you thought I was at all.

HE (*embarrassed*): I didn't think you were after the first few minutes.

SHE: That's why you asked me to go?

HE: No, not exactly. I mean——

SHE: Oh, I am so grateful—you're a dear—I've been very, very fortunate—I—— (*She almost breaks down again.*)

HE: I say—please——

SHE (*pulling herself together*): All right—I won't cry any more—you must think I'm an abject fool—I am too—worse than that. Listen to me, I'm a perfectly ordinary girl—I live in Rutland Gate with my aunt, I go to matinees and dances and walk in the Park and help get up *tableaux vivants* for charity——

HE: But—I——

SHE: Don't look so shocked—it makes it much harder to tell you everything—I read an awful lot—all the modern writers and the papers. I've over-educated myself in all the things I shouldn't have known about at all. I've been railing against the dullness of my life—a woman's life in general—

I've read vehement feminist articles and pamphlets. I've worked myself up into a state of boiling indignation at the injustice of sex relationships—why shouldn't women have the same chances as men—lead the same lives as men—you know the sort of thing. I've been thinking myself a clever emancipated modernist—with a cool clear sense of values—and look at me—look at me—(*She giggles hysterically.*) My aunt went away to Bournemouth the day before yesterday for a week and I decided to make my experiment—to see life, real life, at close quarters—young men are allowed to go out and enjoy themselves when they're of age—why shouldn't young women have the same opportunities? Last night I went out to the theatre by myself and I started to walk home—feeling frightfully dashing—then it began to pour with rain, so I squashed into a bus and went straight to bed. To-night I was quite determined. I had dinner—by myself—at a place in Oxford Street, then I walked down into Piccadilly Circus—and down Haymarket and along the Strand, then back again to Leicester Square. I sat on a seat in the little garden place in the middle until a filthy drunk man came and sat down next to me—then I began walking again and looking at all the people—hundreds and hundreds of them—all pouring out of the theatres and crowding the pavements—it really was rather an exciting feeling—You wouldn't understand it, I know, because you're a man and you haven't always been looked after and coddled all your life—you've been encouraged to be independent—but to me it was thrilling. I was all alone—absolutely my own mistress—then I suddenly realised how tired I was, so I went into Appendrodts and had a cup of chocolate. Two awful women were at the next table with a squirmy little man, and they started to have a row over his head—it was beastly—all the things they said—but very funny; in the end they were all turned out swearing like anything! Then I went out again and everything was different—all the crowds had disappeared and there was hardly any traffic except a few taxis going very fast. I walked all down

Piccadilly—awfully quickly—because all the other women were sauntering so—I was just passing the Berkeley when an arc lamp in the middle of the road suddenly spluttered loudly—I nearly jumped out of my skin. Then I laughed at myself and began to walk more slowly—taking notice of things—the people's faces—it was strange—then—then—Oh dear! (*She closes her eyes for a moment.*) Then a man smiled at me. I thought just for a second that I knew him, so I looked round and he was standing still. Then he began to stroll after me—my heart beat horribly and I strained every nerve to try to keep cool and think what to do—calmly—but I couldn't. I lost my head and ran up a side street like a rabbit—he must have laughed. Then I leant against some railings in Curzon Street and pulled myself together—I was a coward—a weak, silly coward, so then, more in order to punish myself for my lack of courage than anything else—I made up my mind to let a man—pick me up—Oh, I know it's contemptible—don't look at me like that—but remember all this is the outcome of months—almost years—of modern literature—I wanted experience of life. Nothing could happen to me really—I'm quite capable of taking care of myself—I just wanted to see—then with the full flush of my determination still on me—I met you in Down Street. Oh dear, hasn't it been horrible! (*She sobs.*) Too utterly horrible for words——

HE: Look here, it hasn't really, you know—I won't breathe a word——

SHE: I know you won't—but—I don't feel as if I could ever shake off the shame of it——

HE: There hasn't been any shame——

SHE: I should like to go into a convent—straight away—this minute.

HE: You're taking it all much too seriously—it's funny rather—when you analyse it.

SHE: When I'm married and middle-aged I may look back upon it as being funny, but until then I shall blush down to my feet every time I think of it——

HE: I've never been out in London alone until this week—a friend of mine asked me up to stay here in this flat. Then he had to go away suddenly on business and so I was left on my own.

SHE: Is that true—really?

HE: Yes—that's why I asked you to go at first—I felt rotten.

SHE: Did you?

HE: Yes—absolutely. I thought you were laughing at me.

SHE: Laughing—Good heavens!

HE: Yes—isn't it silly the way one is always so terrified of being laughed at?—it matters so little really.

SHE: Less than anything.

HE: All my friends talk such a lot about the gay times they have in Town—you know——

SHE: Yes.

HE: I thought to myself this is a wonderful opportunity—being alone—and everything——

SHE: Just like me.

HE: Yes—exactly——

SHE: How old are you?

HE: Twenty-one.

SHE: So am I.

HE: I'm most awfully sorry if I upset you and made you feel horrid.

SHE: You've been very kind and considerate. I don't know what I should have done if it had been anyone else.

HE: Neither do I.

SHE: I wish you'd empty that whiskey away—I do hate the smell of it.

HE: I'm not crazy about it. I say—shall we make some tea?

SHE: No, I must go now—really——

HE: It would be nice—are you sure?

SHE: Yes, quite—I must.

HE: All right. (*He goes to window.*) There's probably a cab in the rank. Why, it's pouring——

SHE: Oh! Is there a cab there?

HE (*looking out sideways against the glass*): No—Damn. I'm so sorry.

SHE: I'll soon find one.

HE: No—look here—do stay a little longer until the rain stops. We could have some tea after all——

SHE: But—but——

HE: We *are* friends—aren't we? (*He holds out his hand.*)

SHE: Yes—very well—just a little longer.

    They shake hands.

HE: You'd better take off your coat again.

SHE: All right.

    He helps her off with it and puts it on chair.

HE: Now for some tea.

SHE: Where's the kettle?

HE: In the kitchen. I'll go and fill it and we can boil it in here—there's just enough fire. Will you get two cups out—they're in that cupboard, also some biscuits.

SHE: All right.

    He goes off.

    She takes cups from cupboard and puts them on table, also a biscuit tin.

HE (*off*): How many spoonfuls in the pot?

SHE (*going to door*): Two, I should think—and a half a one.

HE: Righto.

    She goes over and pokes up the fire a little. He comes in with a small tray, upon which is a tea-pot and the kettle.

I haven't put much water in so it ought to boil quickly. (*He places it on the fire.*)

SHE: Now we must possess our souls in patience. (*She sits down on sofa.*)

HE: We won't take any notice of it at all—we won't look round even if it sings.

SHE: Yes, I'm sure that's the only way.

HE: What's your name?

SHE (*hesitatingly*): Oh——

HE (*quickly*): I'm so sorry—I forgot—if you'd rather not tell me I shall quite understand—mine is Hugh Lombard.

SHE: Mine is Mary Jevon.

HE: That's a pretty name.

SHE: I used to think it was much too phlegmatic and English—but still, if you think it's pretty——

HE: Oh, rather—I like it all the better for being English.

SHE: So do I—in my heart—I've been hankering after something a little more exotic lately——

HE: Further effects of modern literature on the young.

SHE: Now don't laugh at me——

HE: Sorry.

SHE: You know what we are, don't you?

HE: No, what?

SHE: We're the victims of civilisation.

HE: Are we?

SHE: Yes we are—because we're really quite simple-minded and ordinary—deep down inside—but we've both been trying awfully hard to keep pace with the modern rate of living. If we went on much longer we'd kill all our real niceness——

HE: I say, you know you are clever.

SHE (*suddenly*): Oh, don't—don't——

HE: Don't what?

SHE: Don't pander to me—you'll undo all the good you've done!

HE: The *good* I've done—what *are* you talking about?

SHE: You've done me all the good in the world—you're thoroughly honest—and nice—and you're not really shocked at me and you like my name.

HE: I don't see where the good comes in?

SHE: You've saved me from myself—I know that sounds melodramatic—but it's true—absolutely.

HE: You've done the same for me—you made me feel awfully ashamed of myself—specially when you cried.

SHE: I am glad.

HE: So am I—why did you ask me not to pander to you?

SHE: Because I was being clever—and modern thought-ish——

HE: No you weren't—you were being sweet.

SHE: Don't be silly.

HE: But you were—awfully——

SHE (*vehemently*): Never again—never, never, never again.

HE: Never again what?

SHE: From this moment on I'm going to be myself—my real self—not my Chelsea edition——

HE: So am I—not my "young man about town" edition——

SHE: Splendid!

HE: I say—I've got an idea——

SHE: What——

HE: Look here—why shouldn't we——

SHE: The kettle's boiling.

HE: Oh—(*He gets up.*) No it isn't.

SHE: I saw some steam coming out.

HE: Only very little—it fairly spouts when it's really ready——

SHE: What were you going to say?

HE: I won't say it yet—after all——

SHE: Why not?

HE: I'm afraid of spoiling things.

SHE: Oh!

> *They sit silent for a moment.*

I wonder if it's stopped raining. (*She gets up and goes to window.*)

HE: Has it?

SHE: It's not so bad as it was—it's rather difficult to see here—one can only tell by the puddles.

HE (*joining her at window*): Aren't the pavements shining—like glass.

SHE: Yes, exactly—if you screw round the corner a bit you

can just catch a glimpse of the Park. (*She flattens her face against the pane.*)

HE: Yes, it's jolly being so near——

SHE: What part of the country do you come from?

HE: Kent—the marshes.

SHE: No!

HE: Yes, why?

SHE: I know that well—between Rye and Folkestone——

HE: Yes—Ivychurch—my home's just near Ivychurch.

SHE: How lovely—it's beautiful on the marsh with all the dykes and space and the smell of the sea——

HE: I am glad you know it—and like it——

SHE: Look, the kettle really is boiling now.

HE: Come and hold the tea-pot.

> *They crouch together by the fire—and make the tea, then they put the pot on the tray.*

Let's have it on the sofa—we can rest the tray on our knees.

SHE: All right. I'll sit down just—here—give it to me——

HE: All right—biscuits first.

> *He places tin on the floor at their feet—then he hands her tray and sits down gingerly beside her.*

SHE: Be careful.

HE: Isn't that cosy!

SHE: It isn't really drawn yet but it doesn't matter. (*She pours out.*)

HE: I don't think I've ever liked anybody so much—so quickly—before.

SHE: What nonsense!—Sugar?

HE: Yes, please—two.

SHE: I've been pretending I like lemon in my tea for months—instead of milk.

HE: I know—so Russian!

SHE (*laughing*): Exactly——

HE: I really do want to say something—important—and you keep stopping me.

SHE: I know.

HE: Why——

SHE: For the same reason you said just now—it might spoil things——

HE: It wouldn't—I don't think——

SHE: Don't let's risk it—yet.

HE (*gloomily*): All right——

> *They drink in silence for a moment.*

SHE: What do you do?

HE: How do you mean?

SHE: Work.

HE: I'm going to be a soldier.

SHE: Oh——

HE: The worst of it is—it will probably mean India——

SHE: Oh, that kind of soldier.

HE: Yes—life on verandahs with punkahs waving and clinking ices in tumblers and beautiful catty women in sequin dresses——

SHE: And spotless white breeches and polo ponies and sudden native risings and thrilling escapes—lovely!

HE: Do you think you'd like it?

SHE: Yes—anyhow at first—it sounds so—so different.

HE: I'm glad you don't hate the idea——

SHE: What's the time?

HE (*putting down his cup*): Early—look. (*He shows her his watch.*)

SHE (*putting down her cup with a bang*): I must go now—at once—really I must.

HE: Oh——

SHE: Even if it's coming down in torrents—— (*She goes to window.*)

HE: I wish you'd stay—a little longer.

SHE: No—it would be silly to linger on—I feel frightfully tired and I'm sure you are too—we should only get sleepy and bored. The rain's quite stopped—and there's actually a cab there——

HE: Damn it!

SHE: Now then!

HE: I wanted to walk with you until we found one.

SHE: You can walk with me all the way downstairs.

HE: All right.

SHE: Help me with my coat.

HE: Here.

He helps her on with her coat—then he takes her hand.
Thank you ever so much—it's been lovely.

SHE: Yes, it has——

HE: Let me say it—now.

SHE: What?

HE: Will you marry me?

SHE: Don't be silly.

HE: I'm not silly. I mean it.

SHE: We don't know one another.

HE: Yes, we do—frightfully well.

SHE: No—it's too soon.

HE: I'm beginning to love you terribly——

SHE: No you don't—not really—you can't——

HE: Why not?

SHE: I don't know.

HE: Time doesn't make the least difference—you *know* it
doesn't.

SHE: Perhaps—perhaps it doesn't——

HE: Could you ever care for me—do you think?

SHE: I don't know.

HE: Will you try?

SHE (*nods*): Don't—else I shall cry again.

HE: You are a dear!

He takes her in his arms and kisses her.

SHE (*tremulously*): Now my hat's crooked——

They go out together, his arm protectively round her.

CURTAIN

CUSTOMS HOUSE, DOVER

written 1923
unperformed

This "musical sketch" was originally intended for a revue called *Helter Skelter*, which became *London Calling!*. In the original draft the two characters were to have been called Marty and Desirée and, had the material survived until the final show, the parts would have been played by Noël and Gertie – a preview of George and Lily in *"Red Peppers"* of *Tonight at 8.30*, thirteen years later.

The song that ends the sketch – "Touring Days" – was to have an afterlife of its own. In researching the compilation revue, *Cowardy Custard* (1972), producer Alan Strachan came across a "rather ragged piece of sheet music" literally at the bottom of a trunk in Noël's London office. Noël had no memory of writing it until he saw it for himself. In an abbreviated form the song was included in the show.

The naming of the revue was more problematical. Director Wendy Toye wanted to call it *Master Pieces*. Someone suggested *The Cream of Coward*. "That," Noël said, "would be *asking for trouble*." Then, following the line of thought, he decided – *"Cowardy Custard"*. End of discussion.

CHARACTERS

JOE BUSH, *Customs official*
ENGLISHMAN
"GET-AWAY GRACE"
DETECTIVE
LULU HIGGINS

When the curtain rises the noise is deafening—the chorus in various travelling dresses are clustered round the low counter, trying to get the baggage examined quickly, and talking and shouting. Above the din can occasionally be heard the OFFICIAL'S *voice saying: "Now then, now then—anything to declare?" etc. After a moment the noise subsides a little and a few spaces are left on the counter. A young* ENGLISHMAN *strolls languidly in and planks his suitcase down in front of the* OFFICIAL.

OFFICIAL: Anything to declare—wines—spirits—cigars?

YOUNG MAN: Damn all.

OFFICIAL: What d'you mean by that?

YOUNG MAN: Damn all.

OFFICIAL: Damn all what?

YOUNG MAN: Damn all to declare.

OFFICIAL: Look 'ere, don't you try to be funny with me, see!

YOUNG MAN: Why not?

OFFICIAL (*blustering*): Never mind why not! Just open up—come on now. (*Delving in bag.*) What's this?

YOUNG MAN: Hair wash—what did you think it was, pink champagne?

OFFICIAL: You think you're very clever, don't you?

YOUNG MAN (*languidly*): Not particularly, but I think you're extremely stupid.

OFFICIAL (*leaning forward*): Do you know I'm old enough to be your father?

YOUNG MAN: Yes—and almost silly enough.

He goes off.

The OFFICIAL *scratches his head for a moment. Enter a beautifully dressed* GIRL *with a small dressing-case—she places it in front of the* OFFICIAL.

GIRL: Will you wait just a minute while I find the key?

OFFICIAL: Anything to declare—wines, spirits, cigars?

GIRL: Well, as a matter of fact there is the teeniest bottle of scent.

OFFICIAL: 'Ow big?

GIRL (*leaning towards him*): Not very big—but I'll show you when I've found the key.

OFFICIAL: It's all right, miss, there ain't no 'urry.

GIRL: Oh, but there is—it's so irritating to me to keep you waiting when you're probably so tired—oh, where can it be?

OFFICIAL: Well, I dunno—what about your 'andbag?

GIRL (*quickly*): Oh no, it wouldn't be in there—I remember now—I tied it on to a little bit of ribbon round my neck. (*She puts her hands up and produces a small piece of blue ribbon— then she gives a little cry.*) Oh!

OFFICIAL: What's up?

GIRL: It's gone.

OFFICIAL: Gone where?

GIRL: Dropped off.

OFFICIAL: P'raps it's slipped down the back.

GIRL: I wonder if you'd look for me. (*She leans towards him backwards across the counter.*)

OFFICIAL: I'll do my best.

GIRL: Put your hand there. (*She places his hand in the small of her back—he slips his arm round her waist—she breaks away with a little cry.*) Officer—that was very naughty of you!

OFFICIAL: I'm sorry, miss—I forgot meself, I——

GIRL (*bursting into tears*): Oh, this is dreadful, dreadful, what am I to do?

OFFICIAL: Oh, look 'ere, don't cry, miss—it don't matter.

GIRL: Oh, but it does—it does—I know you think I'm smuggling through all sorts of awful things—and how can I prove to you that I'm not, without my key——? (*Her voice trails off into sobs.*)

OFFICIAL: 'Ere, miss—(*He chalks her bag.*) We won't say anything about that bottle of scent—this time, see.

GIRL (*sniffing*): Oh, officer, I wouldn't get you into trouble for anything in the world.

OFFICIAL: That'll be all right, miss——

GIRL: You're very, very kind—I suppose you couldn't lend me a hanky? Mine's in the bag. (*She sobs again.*)

OFFICIAL: Now then, now then, 'ere you are—— (*He hands her an enormous handkerchief.*)

GIRL: Thank you. (*She wipes her eyes.*) Thank you very much. (*She leans her head back—he gives a quick glance round, then kisses her.*) (*Coyly.*) Oh, officer! (*She blows a kiss to him, and taking her dressing-case, runs off.*)

> A MAN *in a bowler hat and overcoat, obviously a plain-clothes detective, comes in hurriedly—he goes up to the* OFFICIAL.

DETECTIVE: Here—I want a word with you.

OFFICIAL: All right, what's up?

> *He gets over the counter and they both come down stage.*

DETECTIVE: "Get-Away Grace" left Paris last night; she's been traced as far as Calais.

OFFICIAL: "Get-Away Grace"?

DETECTIVE: She's one of the most notorious dope traders in the world—she smuggles the stuff through from Toulon and Marseilles.

OFFICIAL (*apprehensively*): What's she like?

DETECTIVE: She's quite young really, but she generally disguises herself as an older woman—she'll probably wait until the night boat, there are fewer people about. Just keep your eyes open, see—search every bag thoroughly—I'll be within call if you whistle——

OFFICIAL: But—but——

DETECTIVE (*in warning tones*): And if I were you I should be a little more spry—you've let a lot of stuff through lately—we've watched you—you're slack—stupid—lazy—see?

OFFICIAL: Oh yes, I see.

DETECTIVE: And if you don't manage to nab someone or something pretty soon you'll lose your job, see?

OFFICIAL: Oh yes, I see.

DETECTIVE (*going off*): So mark my words, and try to be a little more intelligent, see?

> *Exit.*

OFFICIAL: Oh, go to 'ell.

> *He goes dismally back to the counter, a loud engine whistle is heard, there comes an answering shriek from the boat. Enter* LULU HIGGINS. *She is a flashy, overdressed woman of about forty, her hair is tousled and her hat over one eye, she has long buttoned boots all unbuttoned—she has obviously been exceedingly seasick. A porter follows her wheeling a professional hamper on a trolley, it has "Higgins" painted on it in black letters.*

LULU (*shrieking*): 'Old it back! 'Old it back! Oh, young man, 'old it back.

OFFICIAL (*stopping her*): Steady on now—'old what back?

LULU: The train, of course. Oh, God, I've been so ill—lying on that boat in a state of coma.

OFFICIAL: Well, you've reached your full stop now all right. (*He clutches her arm.*)

LULU: Let me go—let me go!

> *There is another engine whistle off.*

OFFICIAL: Anything to declare?

LULU: Nothing, I swear I 'aven't—Oh, let me go!

OFFICIAL: What's in that 'amper?

LULU: Only me props——

OFFICIAL: Props. I don't think—open it up——

LULU: Let me go, you great hulking brute.

> *Another loud whistle, then a sound of a train starting.*

OFFICIAL: Too late.

LULU (*bursting into tears*): There now, it's gone—and it's all your fault—Oh, if only the Baron were here——

OFFICIAL: Never mind the Baron—open up.

LULU: It's only me props and me night things.

OFFICIAL: Why isn't it registered, it ain't 'and baggage?

LULU: 'Cos I wouldn't trust anything I valued on these railways alone—lot of nasty lying thieves and rogues.

OFFICIAL: Rogues, are we—rogues!

LULU: Yes, rogues and vagabonds—and if only the Baron were here he'd let you 'ave it!

OFFICIAL: Where's your key?

LULU (*giving it to him*): 'Ere. Fat lot you'll find.

OFFICIAL: I know what I'll find all right.

LULU: Well then, all I can say is that you ought to be ashamed of yourself.

> OFFICIAL *flings open the lid of the basket, various articles fall out.*

OFFICIAL: 'Ere we go.

LULU (*enraged*): Oh, it's scandalous—that's what it is, to think of all the sacred objects of a woman's toilet being mauled about by a great uncouth brute.

OFFICIAL: 'Ere, 'old on, 'old on, less of that.

LULU: Oh, I wish I could say in English what the Baron thinks in French.

OFFICIAL (*holding up a paper package*): What's this?

LULU (*trying to snatch it*): Give it to me!

OFFICIAL (*pulling it about*): Ah! I've caught yer this time.

LULU: Leave it alone.

> *They both pull the paper off and a bundle of underclothes falls to the ground. The* OFFICIAL *picks them up but* LULU *grapples with him.*

Give them to me, I'll teach you to mess about with my free-and-easies! (*She snatches them from him.*)

OFFICIAL: It isn't any treat to me.

LULU: Oh yes it is, you're revelling in it, that's what you're doing—revelling in it—I can see it in your eye.

> *He continues to rout about among her things.*

It's no use raking about with that, you won't find any hidden treasure in my hot-water bottle.

> *He holds up a bottle.*

OFFICIAL: What's this?

LULU (*airily*): Just some very expensive French stuff to make your face lovely.

OFFICIAL (*putting it back*): You'd better keep that.

LULU (*bitterly*): Oh, if only the Baron were here.

OFFICIAL: Now look here, I know you've got that dope somewhere—you'd much better own up.

LULU: Who d'you think you're talking to, young man?

OFFICIAL: "Get-Away Grace"!

LULU: "Get-Away Grace" me foot! My name's Lulu Higgins.

OFFICIAL: Lulu Higgins!

LULU (*gathering up some of the scattered clothing and putting them back in the hamper*): Yes, what's the matter with it?

OFFICIAL (*dazed*): Lulu Higgins?

LULU: Yes—why—what's the matter——?

OFFICIAL: Lulu—it's Joe—don't you remember—Joe Bush?

LULU: Well, I'm——

OFFICIAL: You—of all——

LULU: Good heavens!

OFFICIAL: After all these years.

LULU: Old Joe Bush.

  They fall into one another's arms.

OFFICIAL: But, Lulu, you're a big star now—it's wonderful!

LULU: And look at you—all got up in gold braid and everything.

OFFICIAL: Been playing over there?

LULU: Yes—Folies Bergères they call it—and the things they wanted me to do—really, those French! I know we're all made more or less alike, but there's no need to flaunt it.

OFFICIAL: What sort of stuff d'you do?

LULU: I'm a "Diseuse", dear.

OFFICIAL: What's that?

LULU: God knows, but it's very lucrative.

  They both close the hamper and sit side by side on the lid.

OFFICIAL: Who's that Baron you've been talking about so much, your husband?

LULU (*giggling*): Oh, don't be such a fool!

OFFICIAL (*sadly*): Oh, Lulu, have you broken that vow we made in the old days?

LULU: What vow?

OFFICIAL: We both swore we'd never do anything we'd be ashamed of.

LULU: Well, *I* don't—it's the Baron.

OFFICIAL: What's he like?

LULU: Not bad.

OFFICIAL: You know, you've changed, Lulu—you're more worldly than you used to be.

LULU: Well, you'd be worldly if you'd been Queen in the *Ballet of Love* for eighteen weeks.

OFFICIAL: What were you in before that?

LULU: Doing a turn of me own on the halls—very trying work—and so cosmopolitan—d'you know at one place I topped the bill with a troupe of performing animals?

OFFICIAL: Very lowering to your prestige, that sort of thing.

LULU: I don't know about me prestige, dear, but the way those monkeys used to go on in between the shows!

OFFICIAL: Do you remember when you were bitten by that bull terrier coming out of the theatre at Huddersfield?

LULU: How we laughed!

OFFICIAL: And d'you remember what you found in your bed at Oldham?

LULU: That wasn't at Oldham!

OFFICIAL: And when you upset cocoa down your dressy blouse!

LULU (*sighing*): It seems quite like old times sitting on this old prop basket.

OFFICIAL: 'Ow many years is it since we first met—it was at Leeds, wasn't it?

LULU: Yes, Wilson Barret opened on the Monday at the Grand with *The Sign of the Cross* and we were in *Hey Diddle Diddle* at the Empire.

DUET: "TOURING DAYS"

OFFICIAL: Lulu.

LULU: Joe.

OFFICIAL: It's many years ago
  Since we took the British drama by the throat.

LULU: How time flies!

OFFICIAL: You've increased in weight and size.

LULU: I feel thinner since I left the beastly boat.

OFFICIAL: I can remember
Late in November
  Opening in Ashton-under-Lyne.

LULU: Your suit was sweet
With a patch in the seat
  For the sake of Auld Lang Syne.

BOTH: Touring days, touring days,
  What ages it seems to be

OFFICIAL: Since the landlady at Norwich
Served a mouse up in the porridge
  And a beetle in the morning tea.

BOTH: Touring days, touring days,
  Far back into the past we gaze.

OFFICIAL: They battered in your luggage once at Miller's Dale,

LULU: I had to wrap my washing in the *Daily Mail*,

OFFICIAL: The platform looked exactly like a jumble sale,

BOTH: Those wonderful touring days!

BOTH: Touring days, touring days,

LULU: I frequently call to mind
What you said to Mrs. Bluett
When you broke her silver cruet
  And she made you leave your watch behind.

BOTH: Touring days, alluring days,
Far back into the past we gaze,

OFFICIAL: The landlady was always drunk at Aberdeen,
She used to keep her money in the soup tureen,
LULU: One night you swallowed half a crown and
turned pea-green,
BOTH: Those wonderful touring days.

BOTH: Touring days, touring days,
What glorious lives we led,
OFFICIAL: Was it *Caste* or *Julius Cæsar*
When you blew up with the geyser
And I dragged you from the bath half dead?
BOTH: Touring days, touring days,
Far back into the past we gaze.
OFFICIAL: Do you remember playing in *The Shulamite*?
Your understudy greased your rubber heels for
spite,
LULU: I fell and broke me contract on the Friday
night,
BOTH: Those wonderful touring days.

WEATHERWISE

A Comedy in Two Scenes

written 1923

Presented by the Noël Coward Company as an after-piece to *Home Chat* at the Festival Theatre, Malvern, on 8 September 1932. Produced by Noël Coward. (3 performances and a subsequent tour)

Another piece Noël neglects to discuss. 1923, when it was written, was a particularly busy period. In addition to *London Calling!* it was the year of *Fallen Angels* and *The Vortex*.

Weatherwise has all the trappings of a revue sketch that took on a life of its own and outgrew the format. Although the characters are pure social and theatrical stereotypes, we do begin to get to know them and several of them would emerge, more fully realised, a year or so later in *Hay Fever*.

Unlike *Mild Oats*, however, *Weatherwise* most definitely has a blackout line that plays today.

CAST

LADY WARPLE		Marjorie Harwood
MONICA		Agatha Carroll
CYNTHIA	*her daughters*	Joyce Wodeman
VIOLET		Marjorie Taylor
THE REV. HAROLD BASSET, *Monica's husband*		Keith Shepherd
REGGIE WHISTLER		James Mason
A MAID		Janet Burnell
DR. TWICKENHAM, *a psychoanalyst*		Farries Moss

The action takes place in the Library of Warple Manor in the County of Leicestershire.
One week elapses between Scenes I and II.

SCENE I

When curtain rises, it is late afternoon, after tea. LADY WARPLE *is knitting by the fire—she is a dignified and slightly austere-looking old lady.* REGGIE WHISTLER, CYNTHIA *and* VIOLET *are seated about smoking.*

CYNTHIA: And, my dear—they went up and touched him and the body was still warm!

VIOLET: What a perfectly horrible story—it gives me the creeps—ugh! (*She shudders.*)

REGGIE: You don't seriously believe in it though, do you?

CYNTHIA: Of course I do.

VIOLET: Don't you scoff, Reggie, there are more things in heaven and earth than are dreamt of in man's something or other.

REGGIE: I'm not scoffing, but I must say I think this pyschic business has been rather overdone lately.

VIOLET: It's sometimes very useful, Gloria Frimpton found out all about her first husband through a fortune-teller.

REGGIE: Only because he happened to be living with the fortune-teller at the time.

CYNTHIA: Not living *quite*—just visiting occasionally, but still it only shows——

LADY WARPLE: I fear, Violet dear, that you have not placed before Reggie's doubting mind a really convincing example of the marvels of Psychic Research. You have both witnessed, in my presence, the most amazing demonstrations—I cannot imagine why you have not quoted them to prove your point. Take for instance our wonderful conversation with your dear Auntie Clara only last Thursday. We actually heard her voice, did we not?

CYNTHIA: Yes, Reggie, we did honestly.

REGGIE: I don't see how; if she's nothing but a spirit I doubt if she even has a larynx.

VIOLET: I don't believe one speaks with one's larynx, anyhow.

REGGIE: Auntie Clara *always* did, it was one of her greatest charms.

LADY WARPLE: Even though you are an old friend of the family, Reggie, it is hardly nice of you to be facetious on such a subject.

REGGIE: But are you quite certain that you weren't all thinking of her so hard that the sound of her voice was a sort of subconscious suggestion?

LADY WARPLE: Quite certain. But if you're determined not to believe in a thing, of course you won't. Nothing can ever be proved without Faith.

CYNTHIA: You're being very tiresome, Reggie.

REGGIE: Not at all, I want to be convinced frightfully badly.

VIOLET: Nonsense, you laugh at everything.

LADY WARPLE: I read a dreadful story in the *Psychic Herald* the other day, about a woman who refused to believe—and one evening when they were doing a little table-turning after dinner—she went off into a trance.

REGGIE: I frequently go off into a trance after dinner.

CYNTHIA: Don't interrupt, Reggie.

LADY WARPLE: I repeat, she went off into a trance, and when she came to, she was found to be possessed by an evil spirit.

VIOLET: Mother—you never told us that.

CYNTHIA: What did it make her do?

LADY WARPLE: I couldn't possibly repeat it out loud—bend forward.

> CYNTHIA *leans forward and* LADY WARPLE *whispers in her ear.*

CYNTHIA: How appalling!

VIOLET: You must tell me, Cynthia.

> VIOLET *bends forward and* CYNTHIA *whispers in her ear.*
I suppose they had to dismiss the butler in sheer self-defence.

LADY WARPLE: Yes, but with a handsome compensation.

VIOLET: Naturally.

LADY WARPLE: To my mind there's something absolutely terrifying in the thought of being possessed—unconsciously possessed—by an alien spirit.

CYNTHIA: Didn't she know anything about it?

LADY WARPLE: Not until afterwards when they told her, then she went mad and imagined she was Charlotte Corday—It was all very awkward as they had a Cabinet Minister staying in the house at the time and she kept trying to get into his bathroom.

VIOLET: Poor dear, how awful!

LADY WARPLE: Eventually she had to be sent away, that sort of thing is so likely to be misconstrued—especially in Leicestershire.

REGGIE: That theory does account for a lot though. Sophie Flotch was behaving in a most peculiar way in the Ritz last week, I think her possessive spirit must be an emu, or something equally unbecoming.

CYNTHIA: Oh Mother, do let's do the Ouija board for a little while, I feel wonderfully eerie inside—we might get thrilling results.

REGGIE: What is a Ouija board?

VIOLET: My dear, don't you know? They're marvellous things.

CYNTHIA: Like Planchette, you must have seen them.

REGGIE: How many can do it at the same time?

VIOLET: Only two, but one has to sit by the side and write down the answers.

LADY WARPLE: It would be absurd to attempt it with Reggie in the room.

REGGIE: No it won't—I'm absolutely serious—do get it, Violet.

VIOLET: All right, pull the blinds down—it's here I think.

She goes over to desk and searches. REGGIE *proceeds to pull the blinds down.*

REGGIE: Surely if it's pitch dark we shan't be able to see anything at all.

CYNTHIA: It's not going to be pitch dark, there'll be fire-light—very ghostly and effective—draw up the chairs closer, Reggie.

VIOLET: Here it is—anyone got a pencil?

REGGIE: Yes.

> *They assemble round a small table by the fire—*CYNTHIA *takes* REGGIE's *pencil and balances a Bridge marker on her knee.*

CYNTHIA: You and Violet had better begin, Mother—it always starts more quickly for you than anyone else.

LADY WARPLE: I don't feel well enough to-day, dear—I'll just sit here and listen.

VIOLET: Come along then, Reggie, rest your hands quite lightly on it, and for heaven's sake don't sneer, because it's frightfully unlucky. Can you see to write, Cynthia?

CYNTHIA: Yes, but I'm not going to write all the time, I want to work the thing too.

REGGIE: We'll take it in turns.

LADY WARPLE: If it starts to say rude things like it did to Fanny Belton, you'd better stop immediately.

VIOLET: Don't press so hard.

REGGIE: I'm not.

VIOLET: What shall we ask it?

CYNTHIA: You'd better find out if it's there first.

VIOLET: All right. (*Whispering mysteriously.*) Is anyone there?

> *There is a slight pause, then the board begins to move.*

REGGIE (*looking carefully*): It says "No".

CYNTHIA: That's absurd.

VIOLET: You pushed it, Reggie.

REGGIE: I did not push it.

CYNTHIA: Ask it again.

VIOLET: You, this time, Reggie.

REGGIE (*obediently*): Is anyone there?

The board moves again.

CYNTHIA (*looking*): No.

REGGIE: This is ridiculous—there must be someone there to say "No".

VIOLET (*with superiority*): It often behaves like this at first—one must have patience.

REGGIE: Never mind if it's there or not, let's ask it a question.

VIOLET (*to the board*): Are you an Elemental?

The board moves.

CYNTHIA (*looking*): No!

REGGIE: The thing's stuck.

VIOLET (*perseveringly*): Who are you?

The board moves.

CYNTHIA (*spelling out*): QUEEN VICTORIA.

REGGIE: My hat!

VIOLET: Shut up, Reggie—(*To board.*) Have you a message for us?

The board moves.

You pushed it then, Reggie, I saw you.

REGGIE: I did *not* push it.

CYNTHIA: If you go on quarrelling over it, you can't expect it to answer.

REGGIE: She was probably pushing it herself and trying to put the blame on me.

VIOLET (*hotly*): Reggie, how *can* you tell such lies.

CYNTHIA: Oh, for goodness sake ask it what its message is.

VIOLET (*to board*): Have you got a message for us?

The board moves.

CYNTHIA (*looking*): Yes.

REGGIE (*to board*): What is it?

The board moves.

CYNTHIA (*spelling out*): WE ARE NOT AMUSED. It's Queen Victoria all right.

REGGIE: That's because we quarrelled—I suppose we'd better apologise—(*To board.*) We're awfully sorry.

VIOLET (*to board*): Have you any other message for us?

The board moves.

CYNTHIA (*looking*): Yes.

REGGIE (*intensely*): What is it?

The board moves.

CYNTHIA (*spelling out*): BOW—BOW.

VIOLET: Reggie was pushing—I felt him all the time.

REGGIE: I wasn't—I swear I wasn't—Queen Victoria really meant Bow-wow.

VIOLET: Look out—it's moving again——

The board moves quickly.

CYNTHIA (*spelling out*): WHAT—DREADFUL—WEATHER—WHAT—DREADFUL—WEATHER—OH—DEAR—OH—DEAR—BOW—BOW.

Enter MONICA, *Lady Warple's eldest daughter, with her husband, the Rev.* HAROLD BASSET. *They turn up lights.*

MONICA: What are you all doing in the dark?—We've been for a splendid tramp, right through the village and round.

VIOLET: Oh, Monica—you've ruined our séance.

REV. BASSET (*confidingly to* CYNTHIA): Yes, right through the village and round, we went—most delightful—such a holiday for me after my parish work in Shadwell.

MONICA: Not that absurd thing again, Violet—really you are ridiculous—it would have done you all more good to be out in the fresh air—we've had a ripping walk.

REGGIE: Right through the village and round?

MONICA: Yes.

REGGIE: I thought so.

MONICA (*quietly to* CYNTHIA): You know perfectly well I asked you not to encourage Mother in all this spiritualistic nonsense, she takes it seriously and it's very bad for her.

REV. BASSET: If it had been intended that we should communicate with the other world, it would have been made easy for us.

REGGIE: Nothing could be easier than sitting here with a Ouija and talking to Queen Victoria.

CYNTHIA: Look at Mother, what's the matter with her?

VIOLET: She's asleep.

MONICA: That will mean a headache all the evening. (*She goes over to* LADY WARPLE.) Wake up, Mother.

LADY WARPLE *remains quite still.*
Wake up, Mother!

VIOLET: Something's happened—she's not asleep—look at her eyes, they're open. (*She rushes to* LADY WARPLE *and shakes her.*) Mother—Mother—wake up!

MONICA: Feel her heart, quick.

VIOLET *does so.*

VIOLET: It's beating all right.

MONICA: Fetch some brandy, Harold, at once.

The REV. HAROLD *departs hurriedly into the dining-room.*

CYNTHIA: Brandy's no use—don't you see—she's in a trance!

MONICA: A trance?

CYNTHIA: Yes, and it's our fault for conjuring up evil spirits. Oh, what are we to do, what are we to do?

REGGIE (*with a certain amount of relish*): Burn feathers under her nose—that always brings people to——

He seizes a large brocade cushion and having set light to it, brandishes it about over LADY WARPLE.

MONICA: Reggie, that was one of the best brocade cushions.

REGGIE (*waving it about*): Of course, brocade smoke is much more pungent than the ordinary kind.

Re-enter the REV. HAROLD *with brandy and a glass.*

REV. BASSET (*excitedly*): Here you are—here's the brandy.

MONICA (*taking complete command of the situation*): Give it to me.

MONICA *tries to make* LADY WARPLE *swallow some brandy.*

CYNTHIA (*suddenly*): My God!

MONICA: What is it?

VIOLET: What's the matter?

CYNTHIA: Violet—Reggie—don't you remember—a trance—the woman who thought she was Charlotte Corday——

VIOLET: You mean Mother might be—Oh dear, oh dear!

MONICA: What on earth are you talking about?

CYNTHIA (*breathlessly*): There was a woman who went off into a trance and they told her afterwards and she thought she was Charlotte Corday, and she tried to get into the bathroom with a Cabinet Minister and——

REGGIE: Well, we needn't worry about that yet—the nearest Cabinet Minister is twelve miles away at Warborough.

MONICA: Are you all stark staring mad—what do you mean?

VIOLET: I'll explain. You see, when people go off into trances there's always the fear that when they come to they may be possessed by some alien spirit. Mother read about a woman in the *Psychic Herald* who—— (*She whispers in* MONICA'*s ear.*)

MONICA: Great heavens! But how could she do it in the time?

REV. BASSET: I'm sure that a dutiful Christian woman like your mother could never be possessed by anything unpleasant—the disembodied spirit of some noble heroine perhaps—working for the good of mankind——

REGGIE: Well, let's all hope it doesn't turn out to be Joan of Arc; think how embarrassing it would be if she persistently rode to hounds in shining armour.

MONICA: Look—look—she's coming to——

CYNTHIA: Don't tell her she's been in a trance *whatever* happens.

LADY WARPLE (*drowsily*): What a dreadful smell of burning.

MONICA: Here, Mother dear—sip some of this.

LADY WARPLE: How can you, Monica, you know perfectly well I hate brandy; what are you all looking so frightened for?

MONICA: Well, Mother—you see—you've just fainted and we——

LADY WARPLE (*crossly*): Fainted! What nonsense—I've

never fainted in my life—good gracious! One of my best cushions—who did this? (*She holds it up furiously.*)

REGGIE: I did—I think it saved your life.

LADY WARPLE: Have you all taken leave of your senses? Where's my dinner?—I want my dinner.

CYNTHIA: It isn't quite time for it yet, Mother dear.

REGGIE (*softly to* VIOLET): It's all right, she's only been possessed by a hearty appetite.

LADY WARPLE: I want my dinner.

VIOLET: We're all going up to dress in a moment.

LADY WARPLE: I must go out soon.

CYNTHIA: Go out? Why—where?

LADY WARPLE: Don't all jump at me like that every time I say anything; surely there's nothing extraordinary in wanting to go out?

REV. BASSET: It would have been quite understandable this afternoon—but now it's simply pouring—really you never know where you are with the English climate——

LADY WARPLE (*growls softly*): Grrrr! Grrr!

REV. BASSET: I beg your pardon.

MONICA: What did you say, Mother?

LADY WARPLE (*ferociously*): Grrrr—Grrrr—Grrrrrrr!!!

CYNTHIA: Good heavens—what's she doing?

LADY WARPLE *suddenly takes a flying leap from her chair and growling and barking furiously proceeds to career round the room on all fours—everybody shrieks.* MONICA *makes an effort to stop her but is severely bitten for her pains.* CYNTHIA *and* VIOLET *jump on to the sofa and* REGGIE *takes refuge on the club fender.* MONICA, *weeping with pain and fright, clambers with her husband on to the writing-desk.* LADY WARPLE *with yaps and growls of delight seizes the remains of the cushion in her teeth and worries it round the room, occasionally sneezing playfully and tossing the feathers in the air.*

REGGIE (*from the fender—soothingly*): Down, sir; down, sir, down!

LADY WARPLE *crouches on the rug more or less quietly and continues to tear the cushion with less ferocity but great concentration.*

CYNTHIA (*from the sofa*): It's a dog—a dog—Mother's been possessed by a dog.

REGGIE: Yes—and I *think* it must be a bull terrier.

MONICA (*furiously*): Surely this is no time to discuss the breed.

REGGIE: It's always better to be accurate—then we shall know what to say to the authorities.

VIOLET (*in tears*): Authorities—authorities—you mean—? Oh, this is horrible—horrible.

REGGIE: It's not the slightest use getting hysterical—we must keep quite calm and think things out—she'll probably get dangerous again when she's finished that cushion; perhaps we'd better ring for a bone or something——

MONICA: Don't you dare—we must get her up to bed without the servants knowing. (*Ingratiatingly to* LADY WARPLE.) Here then—here then—good dog—good ole doggie——

LADY WARPLE *snarls and shows her teeth.* REGGIE *jumps down fearlessly from the fender, pats* LADY WARPLE'S *head, and then pats the seat of her armchair insinuatingly. With a little snort she ambles across and jumps up into it, then with all the family breathlessly watching she straightens out her legs and settles herself into an ordinary human position with her eyes closed.*

REGGIE (*in a hoarse whisper to everybody*): For heaven's sake don't mention the weather—that's what does the trick.

VIOLET: That's what the Ouija meant when it said, "What weather—bow-wow!"

REGGIE: Exactly.

CYNTHIA: Oh, this is too frightful for words—poor, poor Mother.

VIOLET: I wish it had been Charlotte Corday now, or even Lucrezia Borgia—they were quiet!

REGGIE: Shhhh!!!

LADY WARPLE *slowly opens her eyes and looks round absently.*

LADY WARPLE: Has anyone seen my knitting?

QUICK CURTAIN

SCENE II

One week later.

When curtain rises, MONICA, CYNTHIA, VIOLET, *the* REV. HAROLD, *and* REGGIE WHISTLER *are all standing near the door back centre—in rather strained, listening attitudes.*

REGGIE: Unless she breaks out and does something violent he'll think we've been lying.

VIOLET: Perhaps he hasn't mentioned the weather yet.

MONICA: Didn't you tell him to?

VIOLET: No, somehow I felt that it sounded so silly.

MONICA: My dear Violet, it's sheer stupidity to try to hide anything from a doctor, specially a psychoanalyst—he must know every symptom if he is to cure her.

CYNTHIA: So far he's done nothing but question her about her childhood—I can't think why.

REV. BASSET: I believe it is in order to discover the roots of her complexities—I've heard the subject discussed—very interesting indeed.

REGGIE: He seemed awfully upset when she answered the hoop question.

CYNTHIA: I didn't hear that—what did she say?

REGGIE: Well, apparently she was a year later than the average child in bowling her first hoop—which made her correspondingly backward with her doll's perambulator.

VIOLET: Did he attach any awful significance to that?

REGGIE: He shook his head gravely and asked her if she'd ever broken a slate at school.

MONICA: Yes, I heard him—I'm sure it's all rubbish.

REGGIE: Not at all—I believe in it all implicitly—of course it's bound to take time—going through every small incident of her childhood—these psychoanalysts are marvellous—they always find something in the end.

CYNTHIA: She was possessed last Tuesday by that beastly dog, and nothing will convince me to the contrary, whatever he says, it was all our fault—she'll be wanting to go out sooner or later, and think what will happen if anyone comes up and says, "What a fine day it is" or something—she'll fly at them and bite them.

REV. BASSET: Have you tried prayer?

CYNTHIA: Yes, and without the slightest effect.

VIOLET: What are we to do if he can't cure her?

REGGIE: Well, it depends if she gets better or worse—I should refrain from chaining her up in the yard for as long as possible.

MONICA: Shhh! Here comes the doctor!

> *Enter* DOCTOR EVERARD TWICKENHAM, *the eminent psychoanalyst—he has spectacles and a rather supercilious expression.*

MONICA: Well?

DOCTOR: There is no cause for alarm.

REV. BASSET: God be praised.

DOCTOR (*breathing on his glasses and polishing them*): For a while I delved unsuccessfully in the slightly complicated psychology of her childhood—then suddenly I hit—quite by accident—upon the root of the evil.

VIOLET: What was it?

DOCTOR (*complacently*): Your mother's nurse—I gather from her descriptions rather a gaunt woman—upon her fourth birthday, snatched from her hand a small woolly dog on a stand—recently given her by her Auntie Jessie—and in a moment of anger struck her sharply on the head with it. This thoughtless act in due course formed a complex in the child's mind, the active results of which you have all witnessed.

REGGIE: They were certainly active.

MONICA: Are you sure that was the cause, Doctor Twickenham?

DOCTOR: Quite convinced of it, my dear Mrs. Basset.

VIOLET: I have a sort of confession to make, Doctor.

DOCTOR: Well, well, well, what is it?

VIOLET: I told you the story of the Ouija board and Queen Victoria and everything, but I omitted one fact——

DOCTOR: Yes?

VIOLET: You haven't seen Mother during one of her attacks, have you?

DOCTOR: Unfortunately not—but it is of no vital consequence.

VIOLET: Well, I never told you the actual cause of her outbreaks.

DOCTOR (*testily*): Surely I mentioned that I've discovered the cause for myself.

VIOLET: But you haven't—I mean—you never discussed the weather with her at all, did you?

DOCTOR: No, but all this is beside the point.

VIOLET: It *isn't* beside the point—because the weather is what makes her bark.

DOCTOR (*smiling pityingly*): My dear Miss Warple—please forgive me—but really—it's too absurd.

REGGIE: It's the truth, Doctor.

DOCTOR (*severely*): Perhaps you will allow me to know best, young man. I have made a thorough examination and I'm perfectly satisfied that—providing you carry out my instructions—your charming hostess will be her normal self by this evening. It is all extremely simple, I have worked it out psychologically. The only thing required to cure her completely is a sudden shock, and what is more, a shock possessing some relation to her present mental condition.

MONICA: How do you mean, Doctor?

DOCTOR (*consulting his watch*): It is now nearly four-thirty—in a few moments tea will be brought in, will it not?

CYNTHIA: Yes.

DOCTOR: Excellent—that is by far the best time.

REGGIE: The best time for what?

DOCTOR: Control your impatience, young man, and attend carefully. Miss Warple, your mother—being unaware of the peculiar malady from which she is suffering—will come down to tea as usual—I too will be present and we will all talk and laugh in an ordinary manner. Suddenly I will blow my nose loudly like this—(*He does so.*)—then, having claimed your undivided attention, I shall say "Bow-wow" softly. At this signal you will instantly proceed to emulate the manners and habits of dogs, making as much noise as you can. The unexpected sound of everybody barking and growling will undoubtedly restore the old lady's mind to its normal condition, and the canine complex will—by sheer force of concentrated suggestion—be completely exorcised.

CYNTHIA: Is that the only way?

DOCTOR: Absolutely.

MONICA: I suppose it wouldn't do if we got Rover in and hid him under Mother's chair?

VIOLET: Rover's bark is beautifully piercing.

DOCTOR: That would not be sufficient—concerted effort is essential.

MONICA (*unhappily*): Very well—you'd better ring for tea at once, Reggie, and we'll get it over.

VIOLET: I'll go and fetch Mother.

She goes out.

REGGIE *rings bell.*

MONICA: Forgive our apparent lack of enthusiasm over your suggestion, Doctor—but we have all been in an exceedingly nervy state during the last week—what with trying to keep everybody off the subject of the weather, and trying to hide the truth from the servants—it's all been very, very uncomfortable.

CYNTHIA: Only this morning Mother had an outbreak all by herself and disappeared—I think she must have been reading the forecast in the *Daily Mail*.

DOCTOR: Where did she go to?

CYNTHIA: We discovered her on one of the upper landings tearing the cook's bedroom slippers to pieces.

MONICA: That sort of thing is so dreadfully difficult to explain; of course we told cook it was Rover, but she looked awfully suspicious. She'll probably give notice soon.

REV. BASSET: And on Sunday evening we found out that—— (*He whispers to the* DOCTOR.)

DOCTOR: What on earth did you do?

REV. BASSET: We said it was Rover!

> *Enter* MAID *with tea-things, which she arranges round fire, and exits.*

REGGIE: You won't say "Bow-wow" until I've had at least three hot cakes, will you, Doctor?

MONICA: Don't be so selfish, Reggie—you know we want to cure Mother as soon as possible.

CYNTHIA: How long are we to go on being dogs?

DOCTOR: Until I shout "Bow-wow" a second time, then you must all run out of the room, and leave me alone with your mother.

MONICA: I do hope the Dermotts won't call—we should never hear the last of it.

> *Enter* LADY WARPLE *leaning on* VIOLET's *arm.*

LADY WARPLE: Ah, Doctor, I'm so glad you're staying—so far everyone refuses to tell me what is the matter with me—perhaps tea will make you a little less reticent on the subject; I know it can't be anything really serious because I feel so extraordinary well.

MONICA: It's nothing to worry about in the least, Mother dear—come and sit down.

> LADY WARPLE *is installed in her usual chair*—MONICA *proceeds to pour out the tea, while* REGGIE *hands round the cakes.*

LADY WARPLE: Hand me my knitting, will you, Violet dear—it's on the window seat.

VIOLET (*gives her knitting*): Here it is—you've nearly finished it.

LADY WARPLE: It's been a terrible nuisance—I get so tired of these depressing sales of work.

DOCTOR: Have you always been a parish worker?

LADY WARPLE: Now he's going to ask me some more embarrassing questions—I never know what to answer.

REGGIE (*with tea-cup*): Here's your tea, Doctor.

DOCTOR: Thank you so much.

LADY WARPLE: As if I could possibly remember "Burglar Bill".

CYNTHIA: Burglar Bill?

LADY WARPLE: Yes, I recited it at my school concert when I was six.

DOCTOR: Never mind, we jogged your memory a bit, didn't we?

LADY WARPLE: Only to the extent of saying "Wat's oo doing, Mr. Wobber." I'm sure that couldn't have conveyed anything to you.

DOCTOR (*jovially*): Ah well—I'll explain my methods at more length another time.

CYNTHIA (*softly, in answer to a whispered question from* VIOLET): No, I shall just whine—that's all.

LADY WARPLE: What did you say, Cynthia dear?

CYNTHIA (*airily*): Nothing, Mother—nothing particular——

REGGIE (*to the* DOCTOR *in a hoarse voice*): You can go ahead now, I've eaten four.

LADY WARPLE: I wish you'd all stop whispering to one another—it's exceedingly irritating.

REGGIE: I'm sorry.

LADY WARPLE: When I was eight and a half I can remember quite distinctly being sharply slapped for whispering.

DOCTOR: Ah!

LADY WARPLE (*reminiscently*): I was in the schoolroom at the time—Elizabeth Spoopin had come to tea with me—fancy—her daughter had twins only last week, how time flies——

The DOCTOR *with a look at everyone blows his nose loudly.*

LADY WARPLE (*jumping*): My dear man, what a start you gave me.

DOCTOR (*austerely*): Bow-wow!

LADY WARPLE (*astonished*): I *beg* your pardon.

With a howl, CYNTHIA *jumps on to the sofa, where she begins to scratch excitedly, whining loudly all the time.* MONICA *and* THE REV. HAROLD *leap on to the hearthrug on all fours—yapping hideously, where they proceed to worry mythical bones.* REGGIE *with a loud bark chases* VIOLET *round the room on all fours, then he catches the hanging edge of the tablecloth in his teeth and pulls everything to the ground—then he and* VIOLET *nuzzle the cakes along the carpet with their noses. The concerted noise is deafening. The* DOCTOR *stands in the background with a watch in his hand.* LADY WARPLE *looks startled for a moment and then bursts out laughing.*

(*Weakly.*) Absurd creatures—how ridiculous you are!

She proceeds with her knitting, laughing fondly. The family make renewed efforts to rouse her but with no success; at last the DOCTOR *steps forward.*

DOCTOR (*loudly*): Bow-wow!—(*Nobody hears him at first, so he has to bellow at the top of his voice.*) Bow-wow!!

The family all make a dive for the door—still yapping and barking and growling—leaving the DOCTOR *and* LADY WARPLE *alone.*

LADY WARPLE: Have you ever known anything so ludicrous—really I'm surprised at Harold—the children have always loved practical jokes and booby traps, but he never seemed to have enough spirit for that sort of thing until to-day.

DOCTOR: Lady Warple—I want you—if you don't mind—to look straight into my eyes.

LADY WARPLE (*putting down her knitting*): Must I?

DOCTOR: If you please.

LADY WARPLE (*staring into his eyes*): Is that right?

DOCTOR: Thank you—yes—I am now perfectly satisfied you are now completely and absolutely cured.

LADY WARPLE: I'm so glad, and I'm sure you've been awfully clever, but would you be so kind as to tell me what has been the matter with me?

DOCTOR: Just a slight nerve complex, that's all. You must go on being comparatively quiet and take as much fresh air as possible without over-tiring yourself—luckily the cold snap is over and the weather has become delightfully mild again——

Before he has time to defend himself, LADY WARPLE *with a fearful growl makes a spring at his throat—in a moment she gets him on to the ground and worries him like a rat—snarling ferociously. He gives one loud cry which brings all the others rushing into the room.* MONICA *with a shriek pulls* LADY WARPLE *off him, and* REGGIE *bends down and feels his heart. Then he gets up.*

REGGIE (*shaking his head sadly*): He's quite quite dead! Now we shall have to destroy Rover!

CURTAIN

SHOP-GIRLS

written 1928
unproduced

Characters

Lady Violet Angerville
The Hon. Muriel Petworth
Princess Panatelli
Lady Cicely Merle-Whidden
J. W. Vanderhoven
Vera, Duchess of Pangbourne

The scene is the showroom of VERA, DUCHESS OF PANG-
BOURNE'S *furniture shop in Shepherd's Market. There are a
few pieces of priced furniture, some knick-knacks and
lengths of coloured brocades, chintzes and linoleums.*

When the curtain rises it is about noon and MURIEL,
LADY VIOLET *and* LADY CICELY *are mixing cocktails on a
badly-pickled occasional table, from which is hanging a
large price ticket.*

MURIEL (*shaking the shaker*): Phyllis was there, of course,
looking terribly dazed.

VIOLET (*languidly*): She always does.

CICELY: One can't blame her, darling, she's had five children
in three years.

VIOLET: And her husband died on Armistice Day.

MURIEL: So muddling. Oh!

*The top comes off the shaker and everyone gets rather
wet.*

CICELY: Really, Muriel, why can't you be more careful. It's
gone all over that brand new Jacobean table.

MURIEL: Such a pity it was pickled already.

They all laugh.

Enter VERA, DUCHESS OF PANGBOURNE—*she is grey-
haired and vague and hung with pearls*

VERA: Where's Blusie?

CICELY: He's at a sale trying to get a dresser for Lady
Pinwright.

VERA: I thought she'd left the stage.

CICELY: Don't be silly, darling; not that sort of dresser.

VERA (*glancing out of the window*): Give me a cocktail
quickly, dear, there's a customer coming.

VIOLET (*devoutly*): Please God let it be an American.

CICELY (*anxiously to* MURIEL, *who is using a lipstick*): How's
my hair, darling?

MURIEL: Just an old Kentish haystack, dear.

CICELY: Don't be so horrid. (*She rushes to mirror and scrutinises herself.*) I look divine——

> J.W. VANDERHOVEN *enters. He is an insignificant-looking American.* VERA *advances toward him.*

VERA: How do you do?

VANDERHOVEN (*slightly surprised*): Pleased to meet you.

VERA: I'm sure we've met somewhere before—were you at that frightful party at Lady Dover's on Tuesday?

VANDERHOVEN: No, I got in on the *Leviathan* yesterday——

VERA: How marvellous! that's the one with those three divine red funnels, isn't it?

VANDERHOVEN: I should like to see some old tables if you have any——

VERA: We've got masses—Cicely, where's number 42?

CICELY: In the storehouse—one of its poor darling legs came off.

VERA: And Number 37?

CICELY: That's in the storehouse too, unless Blusie took it.

VERA: Where are the keys of the storehouse?

VIOLET: You had them last, dear.

VERA: No, I didn't, I remember distinctly giving them to Muriel.

MURIEL: What a terrible lie, Vera; you know perfectly well I only came back from Paris yesterday.

VERA: I gave them to you before you went to Paris.

VIOLET: We'll have to wire to Chanel, that's all.

VERA (*turning to* J.W.): There's this table, of course. It's rather fun, don't you think?

VANDERHOVEN: I'm afraid it's not quite big enough——

VERA: Of course, it all depends what you want it for, but personally I always think small tables are far more amusing than big ones.

> *The telephone rings and* CICELY *answers it.*

CICELY: Hallo—— yes—— no, dear. I'd rather die. I've seen

it five times already—I can't bear her, she always does cartwheels—— All right—I'll ask her. (*To* VERA.) Are you going to Freda's to-night late?

VERA (*to* J.W.): We've got a heavenly old Queen Anne writing-table—(*To* CICELY.) No, dear, I haven't forgiven her for her last party yet—(*She takes* J.W. *over to a writing-table.*) You must say that's fun!

VANDERHOVEN: I'm afraid I don't want a writing-table.

CICELY (*at telephone*): Yes, darling—she'd adore to come— about 11.30? All right—— Byes——

PRINCESS PANATELLI, *tall and wispy and very distracted, enters.*

PRINCESS: Vera, what *has* happened to that little mother-of-pearl hair-tidy?

VERA: It was on top of Number 32 last Monday.

PRINCESS: It isn't there now—— (*She goes off aimlessly.*)

VERA: If you're furnishing a house you *must* look at our wallpapers—Cicely—wallpapers.

CICELY *staggers over with a large book of modern wallpapers and plumps it down.*

VERA: They are perfectly entrancing—they've only just arrived from Berlin—there (*She points to a pattern.*), look at those absurd little roses. They almost make one forgive the Germans for the war, don't they?

VANDERHOVEN: I don't really need any wallpapers—you see—I have a great deal of old oak.

VERA: Pickled?

VANDERHOVEN (*offended*): I beg your pardon.

VERA: Is it pickled?

VANDERHOVEN: No—no—I'm afraid it's not.

VERA: Well, you must let us pickle it for you immediately——

The telephone rings.

Old oak now, let me see—I have the most divine little prie-dieu which would be grand fun for the dining-room——

CICELY (*at telephone*): Yes—she's here—— Vera! Cogie wants you—— (*She hands her the telephone.*)

VERA: Excuse me for a moment—hello, Cogie darling, what a surprise! I thought you were in the Isle of Wight—— No!—I couldn't be more pleased—of course—it's not true! She was all right on Friday, but drinking heavily—poor dear—very well—yes, darling—no, I won't say a word—about 7.15—— Byes—Violet, do you know that on Sunday morning Marion drove straight up the steps of the Victoria Memorial?

VIOLET: *Lèse majesté*, darling.

VERA (*to* J.W.): Do you know Marion Wendle?

VANDERHOVEN: No, I'm afraid I don't.

VERA: Well, if you did I don't suppose you'd recognise her now—what were we saying?

VANDERHOVEN: I think if you don't mind I'll come back another day when you're less busy.

VERA: Nonsense, we're not in the *least* busy—where is your house?

VANDERHOVEN: South Audley Street.

VERA: Just near the Croughboroughs? Do you know the Croughboroughs?

VANDERHOVEN: No, I'm afraid I——

VERA: But you *must*. They *are* such fun. Mustn't he know the Croughboroughs, Violet?

VIOLET: Of course he must——

> *Re-enter* PRINCESS PANATELLI

PRINCESS: I'm so terribly worried about that little mother-of-pearl hair-tidy.

> *She wanders off.*

VANDERHOVEN: I think, if you don't mind——

VERA: Are you quite sure you don't want this little table?

VANDERHOVEN (*seeing a way of escape*): Yes—yes—I'll have that—how much is it?

VERA: Seventy pounds.

VANDERHOVEN (*looking at the price-ticket*): It says fifteen on this.

VERA (*quickly*): That's the number—we have everything numbered, you know. It's so much more businesslike.

VIOLET (*kissing* VERA): I must fly, darling. I've got to go and see the young man.

She goes out.

VANDERHOVEN (*suddenly seeing a very impressionistic painting*): What's this?

VERA: That's a Pustontin.

VANDERHOVEN: A what?

VERA: Pustontin—he's a modern of the moderns, you know.

VANDERHOVEN: What's it supposed to be?

VERA: No one knows—that's what's such agony—it's fourth dimensional, of course—abstract painting. I think he does it with his feet—he designs a lot for us, but, of course, he's wildly expensive.

Re-enter PRINCESS PANATELLI.

PRINCESS: Vera, I'm dreadfully upset.

VERA: What *is* the matter?

PRINCESS: I don't care what you say—someone must have taken it.

VERA: What?

PRINCESS (*wailing*): That darling little mother-of-pearl hair-tidy!

VERA: Let's see, who's been in—now——

PRINCESS: Olga came yesterday afternoon——

VERA: Well, it's our own fault, we owe her twenty pounds commission.

The PRINCESS *wanders off.*

VANDERHOVEN: Well, good morning.

VERA: I can't dream of allowing you to go until you see our brocades—lovely brocades—they're too marvellous for words—all hand-done.

CICELY *brings some lengths of brocade, which* VERA *spreads out.*

There! Isn't that entrancing? What colours! Are you having any colour in your drawing-room?

VANDERHOVEN: I haven't decided yet really.

VERA: Well, let's decide now—it will be grand fun—what about that lovely bright dustman green with curtains of this?

VANDERHOVEN: I'd really prefer something simpler, I think.

VERA: Well, if you want simplicity, why not have the whole thing sand colour with just one or two cushions of this?

VANDERHOVEN: Would that be expensive in cushions?

VERA: No, no, not at all. Dirt cheap.

VANDERHOVEN: How much, roughly?

VERA: Oh, about ten pounds each.

VANDERHOVEN: I see. (*He puts out his hand to take the price-ticket, and is just looking at it when she snatches it from him.*) What's that?

VERA (*slightly flurried*): That's nothing, just the designer's name.

VANDERHOVEN: Designer?

VERA: Yes—one of our greatest decorative artists, Bourne and Hollingsworth!

BLACKOUT

SOME OTHER PRIVATE LIVES
or PARODY OF "PRIVATE LIVES"

Playlet, One Act

written 1930

First presented at a Gala Matinee in aid of Denville Hall at the London Hippodrome on 8 December 1930, produced by Noël Coward. Later presented by the Noël Coward Company at the Festival Theatre, Malvern, on 1 September 1932. In the version performed at the Hippodrome Elsie (referred to here as "Daisy") and Alf appeared. They were played by Adrianne Allen and Laurence Olivier.

CAST

FRED   Noël Coward
FLOSSIE   Gertrude Lawrence

The following is a burlesque of the second act of "Private Lives".

The circumstances are the same as those in the play, except that the characters are drawn from the poorer and less cultured sections of society.

The scene is a furnished sitting-room in a lower-middle-class lodging house; a deal table, on which are bread, cheese, pickles, bottled beer, etc., is centre; immediately below it is a broken-down sofa; the door is centre back.

When the curtain rises FRED *and* FLOSS *are sitting at either side of the table facing each other.*

FRED: Thank 'eaven we stopped 'ome to-night.

FLOSS: And last night.

FRED: And the night before.

FLOSS: That's right. Comfy, ain't it?

FRED: I reckon we didn't arf ought to feel a bit mingy.

FLOSS: Oh, we do once in every so often.

FRED: Garn, who does?

FLOSS: I do.

FRED: You do?

FLOSS: Yus, I do.

FRED: Ow! Wot d'you reckon about Alf and Dais? D'you reckon they got together, or d'you think they're moulding about seperate?

FLOSS: 'Ow the 'ell do I know?

FRED: They'll come poppin' in 'ere soon, I shouldn't wonder.

FLOSS: 'Old yer noise, yer making me nervy.

FRED: Orlright, orlright.

FLOSS: 'Ere, I say, are we going to get married again?

FRED: 'Ow d'you feel about it, girl, eh?

FLOSS: Ow, I dunno.

FRED: Well, this week's bin a bit of orlright, we've 'ardly used Solomon Isaacs at all.

FLOSS: Ow, Solomon Isaacs gets me toungue in a knot; wot say we shorten it, eh?

FRED: Wot to?

FLOSS: Sollocks.

FRED: You said it, Sollocks.

FLOSS: You don't 'arf look a treat; wot say I give yer a smacker?

FRED: Garn, Soppy!

  FLOSS *crosses behind table to* FRED—*they kiss.*

FLOSS: Thanks, Cock.

FRED: Par de too, par de too! Do you 'appen to be booked up for this dance, Lady Hagatha?

FLOSS: Well, I was, but the feller was suddenly took queer.

FRED: 'Ard cheese! Well, let's you and me 'ave a turn and chance it.

  Gramophone—they dance.

Floor's a bit of orlright, eh?

FLOSS: Mustn't grumble. 'Ere, ain't that the Grand Duchess Olga over there pickin' 'er nose?

FRED: Ow, yes, 'er old man got corpsed last Toosday comin' 'ome from the gasworks.

FLOSS: Wot the 'ell was 'e doin' at the gasworks?

FRED: Ow, blowing 'isself out.

  He turns off gramophone.

'Ere, girl, what's your trouble?

FLOSS: Ow, nothin', leave me be. (*Sits on sofa.*)

FRED: Come on, spit it out, spit it out.

FLOSS: I was thinkin' of young Daisy.

FRED: Oh, Dais.

FLOSS: I bet she's properly breaking 'er 'eart.

FRED: Ow, shut yer face; we've 'ad all this out before. We knew the moment we saw one another again it was no use goin' on. (*Joins* FLOSS *on sofa.*)

FLOSS: 'Ere; supposin' we 'adn't 'appened to 'ave met again? Would you 'ave been orlright with Dais?

FRED: I daresay.

FLOSS: Ow, Fred.

FRED: Well, wot of it? You'd 'ave rubbed along orlright with Alf.

FLOSS: Poor old Alf: 'e was gone on me and that's a fact.

FRED: Ain't you lucky?

FLOSS: 'E used to look at me sort of 'opeless and I'd sort of look back; and, oh, I dunno——

FRED: That must 'ave been prime.

FLOSS: 'E used to look after me so lovely—like as if I was something rare and precious.

FRED: Oh, dear, oh dear——

FLOSS: Don't talk so rude.

FRED: Go on, go on; tell us about 'is legs and 'is ears and 'is eyes and 'is lovely curly 'air; go on, tell us.

FLOSS: Mind out yer don't cut yourself, Mr. Sharp.

FRED: That's right; get ratty.

FLOSS: Who's ratty?

FRED: Ow, shut up.

FLOSS: Shut up yourself.

FRED: Well, I'm sick to death of 'earing you keep yappin' about Alf, Alf, Alf, Alf, Alf, Alf——

FLOSS: Sulky great brute!

FRED: 'Ere Floss—Sollocks—Sollocks.

> *Singing interlude.*
> *Return to sofa.*

FRED: You don't 'arf get me goin', old girl.

FLOSS: Don't be soft.

FRED: Swing yer dial round a bit, ducks.

FLOSS: 'Ow's that?

FRED: Lubly!

FLOSS: You are a cad, and no error.

FRED: We was fair batty, rowin' and muckin' things up the way we did.

FLOSS: That's right.

FRED: D'you remember that row we 'ad at the Elephant?

FLOSS: Not 'arf!

FRED: Goo, weren't we fat'eads?

FLOSS: Yus, but we ain't no more, are we?

FRED: Yer know, the real trouble that time was Ted Rawlins.

FLOSS: Yer know 'e was nothin' in my young life.

FRED: 'Ow the 'ell was I to know? 'E gave yer presents, didn't 'e?

FLOSS: Presents! A couple of bus rides and a bit of white fox.

FRED: Yus, and a mangy-lookin' thing it was, too.

FLOSS: You're a liar; it was a lovely piece and I wear it often.

FRED: Ow, yer do, do you?

FLOSS: Yus, I do, and who's to stop me?

    Long pause. He goes to table.

FRED: Want another Guinness?

FLOSS: I do not.

FRED: Ho, indeed! Well, I do.

FLOSS: Go on, soak, soak, soak, yer sozzling great fool.

FRED: It 'ud take more'n three Guinnesses to sozzle yours truly.

FLOSS: It didn't last Saturday.

FRED: Wot about last Saturday?

FLOSS: Oh, shut up shop, you give me a 'eadache.

FRED (*pouring out another Guinness*): I suppose Ted Rawlins was Temperance?

FLOSS: Well, anyhow, 'e didn't 'iccup on the froth like you do.

FRED: You're funny, you are, ain't yer? Just funny, eh?

    FLOSS *turns on gramophone.*

FLOSS: Ow, go an' boil yer face.

FRED: Shut up that noise. You're not the only lodger.

FLOSS: Yes, I am. The 'Arris's 'ave gone to the pictures.

FRED: And wot about Mrs. Clark? No ears, I suppose?

FLOSS: Well, if she 'as, she's either awake or dead by this time, yer great fog 'orn!

FRED: Turn off that instrument.

FLOSS: I shall not.

FRED: I will, then——

Business—fight over gramophone.

FLOSS: You've mucked up the record now.

FRED: And a damned good job, too.

FLOSS: Dirty bully!

FRED: Blimey, Floss—Sollocks, Sollocks!

FLOSS: Sollocks yerself.

Etc. etc. etc.—Stand-up fight, ending in undignified struggle on floor.

CURTAIN

For a Complete Catalogue of Methuen Drama titles
write to:

Methuen Drama
215 Vauxhall Bridge Road
London SW1V 1EJ